THE SILENT CRY

BY

JOHN MACPHEE

EDITED BY ASHLEY SHAW

To Brian

John B Mac
to the bitter bloody
end !

92/95

MANCHESTER
EMPIRE PUBLICATIONS

EMPIRE PUBLICATIONS LTD
45 Elsinore Road, Old Trafford, Manchester. M16 OWG

ISBN   1-901-746-08-9

Typeset by
Michael Hubbard and Ashley Shaw
Cover by Glenn Fleming
Printed in Great Britain
by MFP Design & Print
Longford Trading Estate
Thomas Street
Stretford
Manchester M32 0JT

CONTENTS

Acknowledgements iv

Foreword v

The Legend of Vukovar 2

The War and John MacPhee 6

1 - A Journey Into War 11

2 - The Road From Jajce and Beyond... 35

3 - The Silent Cry 60

4 - The Divided City 90

5 - A Personal Loss 119

6 - Street Fighting 137

7 - The Tide Turns 167

8 - The Final Cut............................. 191

9 - A War Without End 204

Appendix 215

ACKNOWLEDGEMENTS

For Armane and Axon, my two sons and also Joanne.

Thanks to Peter Ireland, who immediately captured the essence of my words and thought them worthwhile to publish. To Ashley Shaw who more than anyone believed in the need for the public to read of the particular reality of war as emerged in Bosnia and Croatia. He persevered when I, so many times, wished to call it a day. It was hard work editing my many and varied thoughts but he did it. To Kate Schofield, Mike Hubbard, and Dave Ireland who were always helpful in pushing the project forward.

This work is a testament to every life lost in the Bosnian and Croatian War. I salute them, whatever their nationality.

FOREWORD

In 'The Silent Cry' I have tried to probe my innermost feelings regarding my part in the Bosnian War, in particular the manner in which the terrible deaths and my personal involvement in the fight for freedom affected me. Despite the four-year gap between my last action in Bosnia and the present day the images and memories haunt me still.

Soldiers play a special role in war as they are trained to kill and obey without question. My intention here has been to allow the non-combatant to understand the mind of a soldier, a trained killer. Like anyone, however, soldiers are human. They are prone to emotion: dread, fear, anger and sometimes they act in accordance with the latter and exact a personal revenge when those they love are tortured and murdered.

War is a terrifying, chilling business – much of the time killing is undertaken in a cold, professional manner. But sometimes emotions come to the surface all to easily when your land, livelihood and the lives of your family and friends are at stake. During the conflict UN and UNHCR officials seemed to ignore these basic emotions. They would mouth their personal, highly paid views, whereas I lived or died on a £3 a week wage during my first months as a HVO soldier.

The officials sent to protect the civilians in Bosnia didn't seem to understand the war. In particular a lot of them failed to understand the basis of the conflict and the emotion and desperation of those directly involved in it. At the end of the day they did not count the dead and dying among their friends and relatives, they did not bury their lover and her child as I did.

The death of those closest to me left me isolated. My only means of escape was to kill. Perhaps this book may hold some key as to the fascination of war but in all honesty I have written the whole thing from an anti-war stance. I met many brave and dauntless characters during the course of the conflict: soldiers and civilians, Croats, Serbs and Muslims and it is not my intent here to shock or scare the reader with graphic detail of death and destruction, as a result I have held back from some of the seedier details.

Where I have not held back however is in my quest to show the reality of war. The manner in which I have written my account of the conflict is consequently at odds with many British soldier books you may have read. I am not tied to the UK government by a need to keep 'Official Secrets' and the reality of the situation is given immediacy by my honest assessment of the forces in Bosnia during the war. These include the Western Powers' humanitarian arms in the guise of the UN and Nato.

Consequently it has been my intention to challenge the Western media's view of the conflict. I have tried to write from the standpoint of someone who has seen the images behind the TV cameras, spoken to the survivors and bereaved without an interpreter, suffered the indignity of shell-attack and mortar fire and witnessed the helplessness of the forces sent to keep the peace.

As a result I hope this book will awaken people to the brutal reality of conflict before it takes place, rather than after 7,000 people have died as they did in Srebrenica under the guise of UN protection. It wasn't ordinary people who started the Bosnian War. In this case it was the failed diplomacy of international politicians that made all-out conflict inevitable. I believe all this could have been avoided with strong leadership from the West.

Some of the stories written here may appear melo-dramatic. But in all cases remember that truth is often stranger than fiction – I have done everything within my power to remember the people who I fought alongside and met during my three years in the Balkans. If I have omitted anyone then I can only apologise and blame the aftereffects of the war on my memory and state of mind.

John MacPhee,
January 2000.

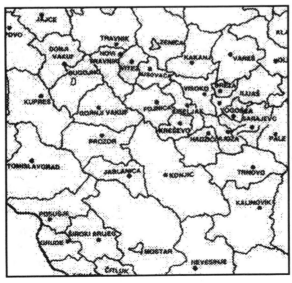

ABOVE:
Map of Bosnia-Herzegovina reproduced courtesy of the Library of the University of Texas.
www.lib.utexas.edu
Copyright CIA 1994

LEFT:
John MacPhee's principal areas of patrol.

1

THE LEGEND OF VUKOVAR

I was languishing in a prison cell in Manchester's Strangeways prison in October 1991 when the soldiers and civilians of Vukovar finally surrendered to the Federal Yugoslav Army. They had been starved out. Food, ammunition and medical supplies long since cut off from the East Slavonian town on the border with Serbia. I soon developed a sympathy for such a beleaguered people.

Day after day the TV news showed pictures of suffering beyond belief. This in turn pushed me toward a decision that it was time to move out of England and away from my criminal past. Croatia, I reasoned, could be a clean slate for me, a chance to prove that I was better than the sum total of my criminal life, its bitter cycle of prison and re-offending.

The following description of the town comes from conversations with many of my Croat comrades who fought in Vukovar until the last days. By this time, the TV cameras had moved out of Vukovar and waited for news; if they had hung around long enough this is what the rest of the world would have witnessed...

On the day the town fell Yugoslav soldiers marched through the streets of the town ordering the locals to bring salad as they were about to slaughter every last man, woman and child in Vukovar. Croats were marched through the streets as the Serb forces continued to loot, kill and rape. The hospital, which had been the main focus of attention for both sides during the 3 month siege, was finally overrun and its occupants (both wounded and staff) dragged away - most of them never to be seen again. Until an invasion became inevitable the hastily assembled Croat army fought bravely and it was with great anguish that Croat commanders left their people behind. It was inevitable and necessary - to re-group and re-arm, to live to fight for Croatia another day.

Since 1945 there had been only one armed force in Yugoslavia - the Serb dominated JNA (Yugoslav Federal Army). None of the states that made up Yugoslavia were allowed their own force and many of the men fighting in defence of Vukovar were raw recruits, a mixture of old men

2

who could remember the Second World War and youngsters barely out of school. Others were part of HOS, Croatian paramilitaries not directly commanded by the army. For this force, and indeed for the newly declared Republic of Croatia as a whole, the bombardment of Vukovar was a baptism of fire.

This siege set the rules of the Bosnian War to follow - to be captured was a certain way to face torture and a long, suffering death. The Serb enemy were ruthless; paramilitaries were given licence to clear whole villages inventing a new term - ethnic cleansing. Consequently for three months or more the citizens, volunteers and patriots of Croatia held out against the irresistible force. For the Croats to have knocked out so many Serb tanks and soldiers was regarded as a crime by the invading forces and they sought their terrible revenge once they forced their way through.

The UN (offering an early indication of their later inaction in Bosnia) attempted to broker a peace agreement but to little avail. It was all far too late for the citizens of Vukovar as the Serbian onslaught engulfed the town - the dead and dying found amid a ruined, blitzed town reminiscent of Stalingrad in the Second World War. In the final weeks of the siege, an old farm track that wound through a cornfield was the only way to get in and out of the town. And, as the net closed in, the artillery barrages intensified, pulverising buildings and people.

The streets of the town were defended by soldiers who dodged from ruined building to ruined building. They slowly starved to death as they carried ammunition and water to their few remaining comrades. Fighting their last for their country, their town, their way of life - their grip weakening with every pull of the trigger, every breath and stride as they sought out sustenance in a desert of destruction.

Communications had all but gone, Croat wounded were dragged into cellars and finished off. The few survivors were paraded on Belgrade television in an attempt to degrade those who had fought bravely against Serb tyranny. The streets, littered with broken slate, glass and wooden beams, played host to small fires that smouldered until rain came to put them out. The soldiers fought for their lives as blood poured from their bodies before finally passing away.

The morgue at Vukovar hospital was full to overflowing and, as winter approached, the ground hardened making burying the dead an ordeal which required an energy the living could no longer muster. Severed limbs lay here and there in the streets - black, blue and rotting as the rats came to devour the human remains.

The line between the living and the dead became blurred. Bomb shelters housed some of the living but their faces were gaunt, their minds shot from three months of siege, shelling and starvation - people of all walks of life were united by hunger as their guts ached with ulcers - there was little hope of food or medical assistance. Babies died in their mother's arms deprived of life's basic requirements - milk and bread. Hiding in the bunkers for day after day children were starved of sunlight - to take a peek out of the bunker was to invite a sniper's bullet or shrapnel - the only familiar smell to most civilians was the rotting of living flesh as gangrene claimed victim after victim.

As the shelling intensified (up to 7,000 shells falling every 24 hours), Vukovar played host to the first of many War Crimes perpetrated during the disintegration of Yugoslavia. Even Serb civilians didn't escape torment as they cowered in cellars and bunkers - many of them had tried to help their Croat neighbours fight the invading army. But it was they who suffered the most once the town was overrun with JNA and Serb paramilitaries, many of their neighbours pointing them out before they were dragged away never to be seen again.

All these stories came pouring out later as I made friends with some of those who had fought at Vukovar. Many of the defenders of Vukovar were part of HOS (Croatian Defence Force) and were originally from Herzegovina (Southwest Bosnia), the place where I joined the HVO (Bosnian Croatian army). The survivors told me their tragic stories as the armoured might of Serbia finally broke through into the streets of the town - smashing the last remnants of defence and humanity with each tank; machine-gunning all who crossed their path, decimating everything within sight. Everyone and everything became a target as the increasingly drunken invaders made a sport of cruelty and barbarism; a bitter hors d'oeuvres to the Bosnian War to follow.

Following their successful invasion of Vukovar, Serb attentions turned to Bosnia. Because of the Serb actions in Croatia, Germany became the first Western power to recognise Croatia and Slovenia on December 23rd 1991. Moreover by January 1992 the European Community had followed suit, much to the annoyance of the Serbian government, Great Britain and the United States, who all regarded the conflict as an internal matter. In response, the Bosnian Serbs, led by Radovan Karadzic, announced an Autonomous Serbian Republic in Bosnia-Herzegovina and within a week the newly declared Bosnian government had held and won a referendum (which Bosnian-Serbs boycotted) on independence.

In May 1992, Bosnia, Croatia and Slovenia are recognised by the UN and the Yugoslav Army move into Bosnia to 'maintain order'. By May they are engaged in a war with Croat forces in Mostar, Kupres and Jajce in Western Bosnia while the Muslims muster an army in an attempt to hold onto the Bosnian capital Sarajevo. In response, the Yugoslav army shell Dubrovnik on the Dalmatian coast and by July 1992 Bosnian-Croatian leader Mate Boban declares the Independent Bosnian-Croatian State of Herceg-Bosna with an army, the newly formed HVO (Bosnian-Croatian defence force), to protect it. That month the Croats and Muslims resolve to co-operate against the common Serb enemy amid rumours that the Croats and Serbs are plotting to partition Bosnia between themselves.

By the end of the summer Bosnian-Serbs control nearly 70% of Bosnian territory while the Croats and Muslims attempt to stem the tide in Herzegovina, Central Bosnia, Sarajevo and Mostar. Bosnia is now at war.

John MacPhee recovers from a bout of pneumonia and is released from prison in 1992 vowing to enter the war. He starts to get himself in-shape and by July 1992 has convinced himself, his sons and the rest of his family that joining the Croatian cause will not be a suicide mission.

PREFACE

THE WAR AND JOHN MACPHEE

THE WAR

Never has there been a more vicious or bloody war than that which greeted the break-up of Federal Yugoslavia. Religious and political tensions polarised the Yugoslav Federation of Slovenia, Croatia, Serbia, Bosnia, Macedonia, Kosovo and Montenegro, erupting into war in the early 1990's.

Catholic Croats, Eastern Orthodox Serbs and Bosnian Muslims contributed to a unique shared history which, with the aid of the nationalist rhetoric of Serbian president Slobodan Milosevic and the simultaenous desire for independence in Croatia and Slovenia, contributed to a wholesale breakdown of trust between the region's diverse communities. Federal Yugoslavia, held together since the Second World War by the fragile glue of 'non-aligned Communism' under the semi-dictatorial regime of Marshal Tito, had won many friends during the Cold War.

Tito, a Croat, managed to achieve a semblance of peace in the area by giving all sides a say in the running of the Federal Republic. If a dispute between rival tribes emerged he would settle it by subtly altering the power base to give the impression of favouring one ethnic group over another without substantially threatening the Communist party's rule and the safety of the region. Effectively an enlightened dictatorship subdued all underlying ethnic tensions during this period. Throughout however, Croat remained suspicious of Serb, Bosnian Muslims felt threatened by both - villages where the population was evenly divided lived in an uneasy, but increasingly workable peace, until Tito's death in 1980.

Tito's funeral summarised the importance of the Balkans to European prosperity and peace. Every nation sent a delegate to pay their respects. Like the funeral of King Hussein of Jordan the future stability of the region seemed to be held in the hands of an old but respected diplomat. Once he died there seemed every chance that the ethnic fissures would re-emerge. But Tito, adept at covering up the past and prolonging the peace, left a void that proved impossible to fill. Still, inter-ethnic tensions failed to emerge until nearly 10 years later. By then a new generation of politicians had emerged and the notion of a Federal Yugoslavia seemed anathema to all of them.

The institutions in the old state (military, police, and government) were Serb dominated, engendering a feeling of alienation among the other states. As a result a groundswell of support for independence grew in Croatia. Slovenia did secede in 1991 and, amazing as it now seems, won their right with little bloodshed.

Croatia was a different matter however. The Croats and the Serbs had long running scores to settle. Suspended by Tito's 35 year reign both had brushed aside their role in the Second World War. However the dawn of democracy in the region heightened tensions on all sides. The Serbs accused the Croatians of siding with Nazi Germany during the Second World War and claimed that they helped to execute Communists, Jews and other non-Aryans while Croatia was under the Ustashe regime.

The Croats countered that far from being a special friend to the Allied forces, the Serbs had actually fraternised with Nazi Germany; using strategic cease-fires to better their own cause before further shaping their good-guy image with the Allies by secretly executing Croatian Partisans who fought against Nazi Germany. The Croats also believed that because the Serbian capital Belgrade had been the Yugoslav capital, and Serbs dominated the Federal Yugoslav Army, government and police, they had been stifled by the Serbs for too long. In turn the Serbs felt that every state around them had designs on Serbia and as a result the cause of nationalism grew, stoked by the bush-fires of half-remembered injustices, quasi-romantic history and unjustified paranoia.

In 1991 Croatian-Serbs began to arm, their cause fuelled from Belgrade by Milosevic's rhetoric and ill-concealed state aid. As town after town fell, a new word came into common currency - ethnic cleansing. By 1991 Serb forces were on the brink of breaking through to swamp the newly declared state of Croatia. Vukovar (on the Serbo-Croat border) was cut off, surrounded and shelled remorselessly. It has been estimated that

600 shells fell on Vukovar for every house in the town, yet the Croats held out for three months. Television cameras recorded the fall of the town. It became a symbol of resistance to unreasonable Serb aggression - a sign that the simmering tensions in Yugoslavia had boiled over into a war that no-one in the West had the power to prevent.

John MacPhee was one such viewer. However unlike the majority of viewers he didn't switch channels when the trouble started but became embroiled in it, seeing a parallel between the Croat fight for freedom and his own life which until then had struggled against enemies both real and imaginary. Within weeks of the fall of Vukovar he had vowed to join the Croatian cause.

JOHN MACPHEE

John Bulloch MacPhee was born the third of seven children in Glasgow on May 25th 1950. His father, once a proud, victorious soldier in the Blackwatch Infantry during the Allied conquest of Italy, was now unemployed and had become, if not quite an alcoholic, most certainly a drunk, while the birth of J.B. MacPhee had very nearly killed his mother Klara in child labour. John's mother quickly spotted the devil in the latest addition to the MacPhee family. He soon became known as 'the anti-Christ' within MacPhee circles, an argument that gained weight when, following his christening, the local church burned down.

From the beginning John's life was fraught with the realities of post-war Britain. Disillusionment stalked his father at every turn. The joy of the successful war for freedom quickly turned into drunkenness and cruelty as his father took out his frustration on John and his mother. John continued to take his father's rage in silence while his mother's frequent absences from their one room tenement flat in Glasgow served to further focus his father's rage on the child, so it came as little surprise when the violence meted out to the child became a hall-mark of John's entry into the rest of society.

Aged only four John took his first beating from the local police, a prelude to a life of mutual antagonism between the angry Scot and all figures of authority. It was also in keeping that his first word, following an early life bereft of speech, was not 'mama', or 'dada' but 'bastart' - the start of an angry life.

His story could and should have taken a turn for the better when, later that year, he boarded a ship bound for Australia. But Klara MacPhee fled the ship in tears before it sailed and the opportunity was lost. The result, while his brothers and sisters cried, was John's further retreat into silence. And, as the family disintegrated, the younger MacPhees were farmed out to children's homes; a prelude to John's incarceration during 31 of the next 38 years in one kind of institution or another.

Locked behind the bars of children's homes, prisons or within the strict discipline of military life John began to fight for his freedom, expressing his frustration in the way he had been taught as a child - through violence. The pain of the beatings meted out in children's homes welled up within him as he plotted his revenge; using the violence inflicted to build-up a tolerance to pain, adding determination to a plentiful reserve of hatred. Nevertheless, John had a brief taste of freedom when he escaped borstal to join the Swedish and Norwegian navy with the aid of a forged passport.

For 16 months he travelled the world, and while it was a kind of freedom he still found himself institutionalised by daily naval chores. When he was finally discovered he was sentenced to 7 days bread and water followed by 28 days solitary confinement in Wormwood Scrubs before being returned to Rochester Borstal, from where he'd originally escaped. A litany of crimes and misdemeanours ensued; violence, theft and daring each playing a part in an expression of hatred for society. For 10 years (1966-1976) he was a professional criminal, re-offending at the first opportunity. The death of his father in 1976, while John was serving a 7 year stretch for conspiracy to steal, meant that he attended the funeral in chains and, despite a compulsion to 'go straight' in memory of his father, the violence and mayhem was cranked up a gear later that year.

He was in Hull prison for the riot in August 1976 that was sparked by allegations of violence by prison guards on prisoners. John MacPhee played a starring role in the subsequent conviction of 12 of the guards in 1978 - his evidence appearing on the front page of the Daily Telegraph. Upon his release however John continued his cruel career in the underworld - one particular lowlight being the stabbing of a one-time associate of Ronnie Kray. Now suffering mental turmoil John sought help from the authorities to no avail - so carrying both a mental illness and post-prison traumatic stress he went into the countryside to commit suicide, however he and a pair of criminal associates wanted on drugs charges were followed and caught in possession of a gun - suicide averted he was sent down for another 3 years.

John had widened his criminal scope by this time. There were rumours of a connection with a Colombian drug cartel, allegations of his role as an enforcer for drug gangs, he fought against the Russians in Afghanistan, smuggled arms between Cambodia and Burma. In 1986 he was arrested for importing forged £20 notes and passing them on to the striking miners. He was involved in the 'Stalker affair' and was asked to explain how the conclusions of the Sampson inquiry had come to be delivered to his prison cell in Strangeways before official publication. At one time JB MacPhee was the most wanted man in Britain following his suspected involvement in the murder of a notorious criminal in London.

Brushes with the West Midlands Police ensued; helicopter chases and armed police confrontations became accepted parts of his everyday life - he led 200 police in a merry dance following allegations that he had threatened a police officer with a silenced pistol. A 'not guilty' verdict followed his arrest. But it was while he was inside that John heard of another fight for freedom. The crisis in former Yugoslavia was in full swing. Vukovar, on the border of Croatia, Serbia and Bosnia was being shelled incessantly. Television news reported the Croat fight for freedom and something within John MacPhee clicked.

Following a criminal career that had brought nothing but the worst excesses of society's punishment on John's head he finally saw the fuller picture. He had fought against society so violently that by 1991 the cycle of incarceration, release and re-incarceration had become predictable and dull. He was also ill, laid low by pneumonia and depression. In July 1992, having recovered, he raised the cash to fly to Zagreb. His knowledge of explosives gave him a way into the newly formed Bosnian-Croatian forces (HVO) and when he arrived in Croatia he experienced a real sense of life and freedom for the first time. He quickly became a respected figure within Croatia, was renowned as a determined fighter and found a love for humanity which the British authorities had long since believed impossible.

His cause was now war and freedom. He moved within all circles in Croatia, befriended the opposition nationalist party leader and became a frequent spokesman for the Croatian cause on British television. His travels as a freedom fighter have seen his 'talents' help with the struggle for Chechnyan independence, while offers continue to pour in from around the world - invitations from similar small nations who struggle for their independence in spite of the aggression of their larger neighbours. He has said that he found peace in war, something never accorded him in Britain throughout the formative stages of his life. His struggle for Croatia in Bosnia is the subject of this book for in his own words; "it is better to die in freedom than to be imprisoned and embittered within the chains of its loss".

This is his powerful story - a personal struggle for the freedom of a nation and his own battle for inner-peace within the chaos of the Bosnian War.

1 - A JOURNEY INTO WAR

ZAGREB - JULY 1992

As the plane touched down at Zagreb International Airport the sun blazed a welcoming heat upon the tarmac runway. The airport was quiet, which I thought unusual considering that a war was being fought in the vicinity. Then again the airline carrying me, Croatia Airlines, was the only one using Zagreb, they had loaned their stock of planes from Lufthansa, the deal being part of Germany's growing alliance with Croatia (Germany being the first country to recognise Croatia as an independent state). I looked out of the porthole and saw the reality of conflict - a UN transport plane was sitting on the tarmac. I suddenly found myself questioning my reason for coming to Croatia and abruptly realised that the fighting was no longer at arm's length, on TV, but that the action was only a few miles away - there was no turning back.

My feelings were in turmoil as I touched Croat soil for the first time before taking the airport transfer bus over to the smallest of the air terminal buildings. Once inside I relaxed a little in the departure lounge, cooling down from the intense summer heat. I remembered fragments from my previous life, jumping out at me from obscure corners of my mind - crisp, clear memories but they all held the same fear, all ended with the same inevitable conclusion, that I was walking to my death.

I was shaken from my self-obsession by a voice as I approached passport control. I was asked for my ID in Serbo-Croat. The man at the desk spoke firmly but respectfully, he had mistaken me for a Croat soldier and following our brief misunderstanding (I couldn't speak a word of Croatian) I was directed to the departures lounge for the next flight to Split. My mind wandered as I examined the runway, buildings and planes milling around outside. The harsh reality of war was yet to hit me; my initial fears questioned whether I was doing the right thing by coming to Croatia in the first place, never mind my imminent arrival in Bosnia. The bitter memories of my wasted criminal life returned. The 21 years I had spent in the English prison system, the 10 years before that in borstals and children's homes. This was my opportunity to make a mark for the right reasons, an opportunity to contribute rather than to take.

There was a dignitary in the lounge, Mate Boban - the President of Croat controlled Bosnia-Herzegovina. He was surrounded by a large entourage and was chatting casually. Despite his presence my mind quickly flitted back to the flight and how I would actually go about joining up with the Croatian army. In those moments I forgot about the President, although I later realised that I could have enlisted through him. In any case I decided that I would join-up by any means necessary, I didn't need a leg-up from the top man.

With renewed confidence I left Zagreb and as the plane rumbled on towards Split I put myself in a positive frame of mind by remembering the many times I had survived against the odds in Britain, Afghanistan, Cambodia and Burma. Yet nagging doubts persisted. I was 42 years old now, was I too old? Would a younger soldier make me pay with my life for my age? I didn't want to get too bogged down with the fatal possibilities but I did wonder.

I travelled from Split airport by bus to the city's dockside. Split was a bustling, friendly place - the warmth of the people struck me immediately, everyone appeared to be smiling which was unusual having lived most of my life in Glasgow and Manchester and even more unusual in a city that had only recently been cut-off from the rest of Croatia. There were a few sad, huddled, figures in the dockside however, refugees fleeing the conflict and it was seeing them that brought the humanitarian crisis home to me as I stepped from the bus into Croatian life.

A woman approached me at the bus terminal. She spoke in German, 'Zimmer, zimmer'

'Do you speak English', I replied.

'Nein, sprachen Deutsch'

'Ok,' I said trying to recall my sketchy German, 'Zimmer… ein nacht, wie wiel cost? Englesi punt?'

She held up five fingers, which I felt was fair enough for bed and board. So I followed her onto an Autobus, all the time she kept saying 'Dobra, dobra', the first words I managed to understand in Serbo-Croat - this apparently meant good. We got off the bus a kilometre on and reached a six-storey block of flats and went up to the third floor.

Her apartment was clean and tidy and with a gesture I was led into the kitchen to eat. She listened intently as I related my reasons for coming to Croatia while translations were made by the woman's daughter-in-law as the family continued to offer me food and drink until I was eventually forced to refuse, another early lesson in Croat hospitality. I was directed to a room that I would share with a wizened 60 year-old Muslim guy. He had something wrong with his fingers on one hand and a bandaged wound on his right leg.

The old guy told me his story: Serbs had attacked his village massacring all and sundry, killing livestock. They had tortured him, chopping at his leg with a machete and standing on his fingers until they finally left him for dead. As darkness approached he had managed to crawl to some woods nearby and stayed there half-conscious, half-frightened to death for 4 days before moving on with little or nothing to eat. He eventually found another set of refugees and they eventually found relative safety in Split. This was my first Bosnian tale – the story of Serb aggression, ethnic cleansing and barbarous cruelty would soon become commonplace, every non-Serb had a similar tale. I don't know how many similar stories I have listened to since, but this first one certainly made an impression on me.

Sleep came fitfully that night. Then, first thing in the morning I woke, had my breakfast and bid a thankful farewell to the old woman, her daughter and the old guy before heading for the bus bound for Tomislavgrad just over the border in southwest Bosnia.

Fear and anxiety overcame me once more as the bus moved toward the border. The evidence of the war was all around; machine gunned and burned houses were everywhere, the landscape desolate and desperate, all sense of hope shredded by the Serbian war-machine as military music blared from the driver's transistor radio – it made for a surreal entry into Bosnia. We eventually reached a port-a-cabin that served as a border checkpoint and my trepidation grew as we waited. If there was no turning back at the airport, I thought, there was even less chance of turning back now. Passports checked, we went through, and continued a few kilometres on before the bus broke down outside a roadside café bar. Another aspect of the Balkans to consider – prehistoric transport.

I got out and struck up a conversation with a couple of girls returning to Tomislavgrad when a passing soldier offered the three of us a lift to the command post at Tomislavgrad. So off we went. We passed the sign of the town 'Duvno', the old Communist name for Tomislavgrad (Tomislav was a former king of Croatia and therefore an unacceptable imperial symbol of the past under Tito) before we reached the Croatian Command checkpoint.

The Silent Cry

I anxiously handed over my passport to the guard and the guy left, only to return a minute later to abruptly tell me, 'you are too much', which I took to mean too old. He was an Australian Croatian, a non-combatant with a uniform. He didn't endear himself to me with his attitude, you would have thought that the Croatians needed all the help they could get under such pressure from the Serbs.

At that moment a tall guy, also in uniform, approached asking what the problem was.

'He thinks I'm too old', I replied, a little offended at the first guard's attitude.

'How old are you?', the guy asked with a Canadian drawl.

'42'

'I'm 39 – like you, the wrong side of 30'.

Without warning he turned to the Australian guy and said, 'you, go fuck a donkey' and directed me upstairs.

I sat down and told the soldier, who turned out to be the Tomislavgrad commander, my story. He made me feel right at home – offered me some peach juice and told me to ignore the Aussie on the gate. I explained my criminal past, my recent illness and the inspiration for my coming to Bosnia, finishing with, 'the truth is that there is nothing for me England. I was on death's door a few months back so I suppose I see every day as a bonus. I'd rather die out here fighting for a cause than languish in hospital for weeks on end. I have come to help you in any way possible'.

Hoping that I had impressed on him my desire and enthusiasm for the fight I was taken to a mess hall where I met some other HVO soldiers. Among them was a guy called Ante and a small group of Special Forces, they seemed like swell guys and made me feel right at home. The commander told me to hang about for a day or two in case I went off the idea of joining up, suspecting that I might go off the idea pretty quickly when I discovered what was at stake.

Later that day I was driven to Bucici village and given lodgings in a house with another two foreigners - this also bolstered my confidence, that others had travelled so far to join up was confirmation in my mind that I wasn't the only one inspired by the Croat heroics at Vukovar and that there were others prepared to risk life and limb for complete strangers..

BABICE - SEPTEMBER 1992

It was 7.20 am when the first of three 120mm mortar shells landed 15 metres or so from my makeshift bunker, scoring a direct hit on two adjacent frontline sleeping quarters. Within moments of the explosion I was up, running towards the cries of untimely, fateful death. This was it, my first action in Bosnia - I had moved into the hill only 12 hours ago and here we were within the earshot of death, screams known only amid carnage. This was death's destructive pause, the moment when a war-machine takes its inevitable toll. The dying and wounded were quickly within sight suffering agony beyond belief. I was not paralysed by shock at that moment but accepted death as a logical, if unjust, conclusion to the lives of my new comrades.

They were the fathers of 13 children, they had wives and brothers - tragic but true, they would leave the tears of their families on graves back home. Then I wondered why. Why had the enemy chosen our beautiful hill to satiate their lust for horror, despair and despondency? Then, hours later, I asked myself why am I not dead or at best dying? The very evening before, when we had arrived, I had been designated to one of the two huts that had just been hit.

But among the fatally wounded lay one Croatian soldier who had borne the brunt of that shell instead of me. The night before he had taken into account that I would be excluded from Serbo-Croat conversations and swapped places so that I could share with a German soldier and two other foreign nationals who spoke English - now he was paying for his hospitality, slumped against a tree stump, dead. Another who had loaned me his helmet while on guard-duty lay face down in the mud; from the buttock of one leg to the knee there was a huge wound, cut to the bone - he was also paying for his good manners.

The cries resulting from the explosion will always be embedded in my brain. The agonising screams spoke at face value of physical pain. On another level they could be regarded as the cries of the nation those soldiers represented, screaming at the injustices suffered by their homeland against a Serb aggressor, against the enormity and senselessness of man-made death.

There is no need to further relate what came into view that night as I scanned the area; my brain clicking like a camera in slow motion - images that still haunt me today. Around me shocked soldiers lay flat on the ground - not dead but numbed by the explosion. I couldn't feel for them; I screamed orders that they return to their AK positions and await

15

The Silent Cry

the next attack - it was harsh but the Croatians and other volunteers obeyed me. In effect I was trying to force an order on the chaos, later a Major thanked me for my reason and courage, but there was no reason or courage to the events that took place up in Babice during my first action in Bosnia. I was running on autopilot, attempting to exert some power even though underneath I was shocked by the deaths of our six colleagues on the hill. In the few days since my arrival in Croatia my doubts and fears had ebbed away as I found a new respect for the simple mountain people of Herzegovina. I knew their cause was life's freedom. The hate in my life, up until then such a driving force in my criminal career, had almost disappeared with the warmth of my reception in Croatia. Twelve hours before that shell had exploded we had embarked on a tortuous journey from the Tomislavgrad command base into these hills.

Shells pounded the road as our driver veered the jeep across the narrow track, pushing for extra speed to beat the mortars - my relief at reaching Babice in one piece had been tainted by the feeling that this was my first encounter with the real war in Bosnia. For the first month I had trained without a gun, then once I had satisfied them that I was not a 'glory-seeker' I had been flung into action in Babice, north of Tomislavgrad.

The Babice frontline was typical of most in Bosnia. Thick undergrowth protected us on all sides, which made getting through it silently impossible. Five small bunkers were set along the top of the hill as gun emplacements while there were a number of log barricades with apertures at chest height a little down the slope. The sleeping quarters were positioned behind the hill and consisted of a flimsy looking combination of polythene covered with branches - a covering which that first shell had had little trouble piercing. But there was little hope of surprising the Serb enemy on the Malovan Mountain opposite - we knew all about their positions and they ours. This was trench warfare First World War style.

The frontline was on a hill which sloped down to a town below called Suica. It had been shelled incessantly by the Serbs and was now completely abandoned, razed to the ground. Walking about down there the place was a ghost-town; a bombed out cafe, an eerie sense that people once lived there happily, as windows creaked above your head and doors banged in the breeze. Babice was a focus for much activity. It was a base to defend and from which we hoped to attack. I experienced joy and carnage, laughter and tears beneath the 4,000 metre high Malovan Mountains. But it was also a place of camaraderie as soldiers joked away hours of idleness or waited in trepidation as fraught seconds stretched one's sinews.

In the previous month or so I had been greeted with open arms; there were several foreign volunteers who had joined the HVO at about the same time as me and in a way this seemed to justify my long trip to Bosnia against the wishes of many members of my family. Now we were part of a great struggle for independence, for the right to self-determination and the natural right of all men, women and children - the human right of freedom. But the need to make real the rights of the innocent required the brutal act of killing for which I had volunteered.

There has never been any compunction in my life to continually take the life of another. However, here in Bosnia the stakes had been raised - now I thought, why should I care about inhumanity? Why should a soldier give an iota of consideration to the enemy? Life, in the cold act of killing, is to be taken quite clinically - once the initial killing has begun and a soldier has passed the weary stage of fear for the imminent battle, once you can no longer hear the zing of bullets or blast of shell and tank-fire directed at you from only metres away; smashing beside your feet, trembling the very ground you walk upon - then and only then can you be a cold and heartless killer. In heavy fighting your thoughts are mechanical and reasoned, there is something unearthly about it. It feels like some primitive point or aeon in a time warp, then you experience an inner excitement - a realisation that you are powerful and destructive, able to pierce flesh with lead.

Later that cold, heartless night within the mountain woods (following the morning that had seen the demise of six of my comrades) the frontline had slowly returned to routine. We were changing guard every two hours - it was a moonless, dark and bitter evening, a slight mist suspended over the whole area. My teeth were chattering. I don't know whether it was from the bitter cold or out of nervousness but there was something suspiciously quiet about that night. I could still hear the cries of the wounded and dying in the back of my mind and felt the painful realisation that only soldiers can understand - the shock of men who expect death at every minute, every hour.

Regardless of all that I quietly went up to the machine gun emplacement made of logs and boulders. The soldier beside me, a tall gangly Croatian farm hand, had received a mere four weeks basic training before being pitched into this cauldron. For all that he was a likeable character, if naturally a little nervous following the morning's events. When the shell had exploded they had been taken by surprise - I most certainly wasn't, being born to madness and its way, I expect the unexpected as the norm, as a law of nature. Wherever there is hell I'll be the first to open its gates. Don't get me wrong I don't invite trouble; I just accept it when bombs explode on my bludgeoned Scottish head.

The Silent Cry

Meanwhile in the emplacement I checked out my two Claymore mines, remembering the precise positions where they had been laid. Then I checked the 1943 German Eagle MG.42 machine-gun; it had probably killed more men than I could contemplate with its typical German coldness. As it would turn out German precision was what would be needed that night, and I patted it like a dog of war; it was now my mentor, complicit in my intent to kill all in our path. My teeth chattered, I became impatient for an attack, wanting someone to shoot-up my machine-gun post - seconds later they did. I jumped out of my skin, this was it - I was being shot to pieces - the cartoon was over.

I now remembered my aversion to fixed positions, the Serbs had plotted well and had got to within 50 metres or less of our frontline. Minefields? Don't trust them unless you lay them yourself. Chips of stone and splinters of wood spat into the night, as I clattered my machine-gun ripping the night to pieces - there were screams down to my right; the smell of gun oil and spent cartridges. I held the power of life in my hands, a survivor of all before me. I wanted to get out of the position to administer the kill personally, to make the enemy die like animals, to let them receive the cold steel of my bayonet.

Then to my shock the piece of history stopped in my hands - the German gun had jammed. I picked up a Bulgarian AK 47 and gave single shot fire to the edge of the nearest tree, the only place that could offer cover to any of the vermin out there. My sole intention was to survive, my fullest need to kill all and everything - but there was no panic. I was born to this as I shouted, short of breath, "Come on ya bastarts, take whits yours!"

Each bullet was now riding on autopilot, my tracers lighting up the sky - it seemed natural. They were firing all along the frontline now, my mouth dry from exertion. The bloke beside me looked amazed but more sure; even at this mad moment I felt for him - he was from these hills, had tended its fields of corn, now we were ripping his beautiful land, his mountains and forests, to pieces. Explosions everywhere - a grenade thrown to my left hit one of our lads in the neck. Shit! The bastards. Quickly, I un-jammed the MG42 telling the Croatian farmer/soldier to cover my front.

The smash of bullets gave confidence to all as the German scythe cut the undergrowth. The automatic rifle-fire was continual now but, I thought, it was pointless to throw grenades as the woods were to our disadvantage. Another 300 rounds expended I fitted another belt;.

It was useless to operate this old gun single-handed - the thing was jamming constantly, these guns needed a two-man team, one to feed, one to kill. As quickly as it began it ended. Some more sporadic firing took place before moans could be heard right in front of me. My comrade, sat beside me signalling, declined my invitation for him to go out and practise first aid on the Serb and I roared with nervous laughter. Soon everything was quiet.

As night gave way to dawn I felt a little strange. There was elation but also an inner fear - I was confused about my transformation from criminal to commissioned killer. I wasn't happy that I had killed for the first time in this war but there is a natural elation attached to survival - if I was to survive this war I would need to learn how to kill professionally and in cold blood - this was lesson one.

The sun reluctantly came up through the trees and still the cries and moans could be heard 50 metres directly ahead of us. I peered into the misty morning light with relief. Shouts all along the line of our positions confirmed that we had held our positions - as ordered, as expected. Only one man was down, seriously injured. As it later turned out the main attack had been directed at my post but of course the madness that morning was all theirs as I was awake - a Scottish soldier, a German gun.

I am normally teetotal - but a HVO soldier, who had worked at the hell and high-water position, was opening a bottle of 'Pivo' (beer) with his already broken teeth and handing me the bottle as a mark of respect. I guzzled it down like a bear and in one momentum had emptied every drop before I touched my forehead with the cold, empty glass - pure bliss and me a non-drinker as well.

Everyone was smiling and laughing now, through nerves or relief that they were still alive and in one piece I knew or cared not; who gave a fuck for death, we were still in the land of those who could pretend to live - then a single shot broke the laughter, a bullet took the bloke beside me to the ground, blood seeping from his left side as he flattened; in the middle of our jollity it was strange, like a film.

Instinctively I ripped AK fire into the face, neck and chest of the Serb in the aperture of my sights. The consolation was small however as I looked to see the blood bubbling from my comrade's mouth, his eyes pleading, as if he could not believe his fate - to be wounded by the Serb I had just this moment mown down. I gave credit to the enemy. Then as now I knew he fought us as a soldier and died a quick death, the kind deserved by a killer of killers.

Once the smell of cordite and sound of explosions had ceased I peered into the glade. What was there to see, to understand? I could see a mass of bodies, cold blood on the ground beside them. I was numb. Amid the carnage there had been a loss of respect for life, for some reason nothing seemed to matter any more. My fingers had squeezed the trigger

The Silent Cry

so many times and the result was there before me.

I also knew that I would have to continue the killing spree for many years to come - unless, of course, I too received my just desserts and was killed. Then I believe that there is more order in war than in civilian life. If you've ever been involved in a conflict then you too will realise the simple, natural order of things, the feeling that life is within your grasp.

Later I walked among the dead. Following the elation, the 'power surge' of killing in combat for the first time, I inspected the bodies and noticed that some of the eyes of the dead Serbs stared at me. They were only bodies now, carcasses in an open wood, but they looked alive as I walked among them, checking they were dead. One brave Serb, the guy who had wounded my comrade, had seemed to smile as his head disintegrated into pulp.

Standing there I was momentarily lost to all reason and compassion - my unconscious mind took over, protecting me from the shock of conflict but there was no shock as to how many I had killed. Blood soaked the soil here and there - death was not vainglorious, it was matter of fact - the soldiers were dead and gone, yet I lived - elation became experience. I stood and reflected on the harsh reality of battle: seeing in the faces of the dead all those that had frustrated my life's aim - freedom.

Bodies were checked for anything that might give useful information, right down to the country of origin on the chocolate wrappers, as we worked out whether the Serbs had received UNHCR aid or had looted supplies - if they had, this would also tell us where the Serbs had most recently been in action. My mind was alive with information, anything that could be used by us we took, the spoils ours to claim.

Guns, grenades, ammunition, the odd machete or axe, the killing knives; no money was ever to be had; their gold jewellery was always left behind at their base. Life went on and we were never bored, or at least I wasn't - I felt that it was impossible to be bored within a conflict, only a moron could venture such an excuse.

We checked the dead. Bodies were turned over by the use of a rifle-butt. I always bayoneted each by going into the solar plexus, and heart, or in through the neck and up into the brain. There was no degree of malice in this action, only the absolute certainty that one day one of the 'dead' wouldn't be as he first appeared - as sometimes you could encounter someone with the will to carry on even though they were maimed and on death's door.

Life force is life force, I never underestimate the power of this particular factor - they were animals, just as we could be, hell was their mentor as far as I was concerned. When that bullet had seared past my face and hit my comrade-in-arms I had little option but to shoot back at the Serb whose will to live was unbelievable; my highest respect remains for that soldier of the damned. We fought on equal terms, as rival soldiers on the frontline. He had traversed no-mans-land; dodged my bullets and tip-toed through a minefield before striking home at us - only to find me in a killing mood.

My need was my need. I had to continue to kill because I wanted to expedite the feelings, emotions and frustrations of my futile life. Now I was an equal with the ability and capability to destroy all before me, in this the first of many destructive sorties in Bosnia-Herzegovina.

JAJCE

Until October 1992 Bosnia and Croatia had agreed to work together against the 'common Serb enemy'. Politicians cemented this alliance when they set up a Joint Defence Committee on September 23rd. At the same time however Croatia negotiated with the Serb government for the relief of Dubrovnik (on the Southern tip of the Croatian coast) in return for Serb control of Bosanski Brod in North-East Bosnia.

This deal was greeted with dismay by the Bosnian government, who regarded it as an attempt by Belgrade and Zagreb to partition Bosnia between them. Despite these deals however the fighting intensified between Croatian and Serbian forces while the mistrust between Bosnian Muslims and Bosnian Croats exploded into fighting within weeks of their joint-declaration and finally resulted in war between all three parties.

It was at about this time, not long after returning to Tomislavgrad from Babice, that I met a Scottish girl and her boyfriend who were in the process of delivering much needed medical supplies to the Bosnian Muslims. At that time an enmity was growing between the Bosnian and Croatian forces, a division that would later find the HVO (Croatian-Bosnian Defence Force) fighting both Serb and Muslim forces. Meanwhile my job was to escort the white truck, laden with a ton of anaesthetics, through Croatian held territory to a Muslim hospital in Bugojna. Along the way the trail of destruction and terror became evident.

At one particular Croatian checkpoint in Prozor all hell had broken loose. I ordered the boy to slow the truck to 5 mph (any faster and we were sure to be shot at) in order to make sure that the Red Cross on the truck could be seen.

It was a bit hairy - a Croatian soldier approached us at the checkpoint. He had the wild, staring eyes of a madman and an itchy trigger finger. Only my HVO badge and my own particular brand of diplomacy helped avert a potentially threatening situation. Later that night we reached Rumboci, a Croatian hospital a little off the route to Bugojna, where we were given the traditional Croat hospitality - drinks all round and a slap up meal. Unfortunately for the Bosnian Muslims that particular ton of anaesthetics never did reach Bugojna - somehow they ended up at the Croat run Rumboci hospital instead - to this day I don't know how that happened.

I returned to Tomislavgrad to be told that my comrade Wilfey and another English volunteer had gone to the besieged town of Jajce in the hills farther north. In many cases I was given free-licence to roam and 'recce' on behalf of the HVO, so I didn't hesitate to make my way up there.

Upon my arrival in Jajce however I soon realised that death and destruction were close at hand. I had reached the town to find us in retreat. The Serb attack on Jajce, which had been steady for four or five months, was now nearing a bloody conclusion. We were being bombarded from all angles as an old woman handed me a ration pack through a blown out window - this left me grateful but a little confused. She knew me to be a foreigner in the HVO. I had the army badges to prove my allegiance to the Bosnian Croatian Army, yet she gave the food even though she was a Serb, as good and as innocent as anyone in this world.

She looked at me and smiled. Again this troubled me, it made me feel guilty, a little ashamed of being in the town where she had probably lived all her life. Her old, lined face was all the older for the experience of war; a war she and people like her had neither asked for nor needed. Myriad thoughts forced their way into my head - the dead and the dying coming to me in that instant. Civilians streamed about the streets, there was no pushing and shoving, just a frenzied hurry to leave the besieged town, to get away from the imminent destruction of their town. Shells were coming from every direction, upwards of 3,000 were hitting Jajce now every 24 hours, it is hard to envisage this kind of assault unless you have seen it. The explosions blew roofs off walls, erupted and destroyed the innards of buildings, depleting one's will to live.

There was little shelter, no place to hide; just an air of helplessness as people ran here and there gaining ground against the shells, running and stumbling to safety, before falling from the shock of a cluster bomb or shell explosion. Serbian jets thundered over the town, guns blazed at anything in their path, not caring whether they hit stone or human flesh - Jajce was a focus for all. I saw a child lifted into the air by an explosion and thud back to earth; my eyes and ears numbed by the sights and sounds. It was useless to try to help the child as I did, the little boy was dead. He might have been three, four or five years old. How could I tell? He could have been two - people of all ages were being prematurely aged by this conflict, why should a child react any differently? Again and again I tried to revive the child yet I knew he was dead and gone - he had lost his will to live as swiftly as I was losing my faith in everything.

George Bernard Shaw once depicted the explosion of an Anarchist bomb in a bullring in Barcelona. He saw many people and animals killed but Shaw spoke only of the animals and children being innocent. Everyone else was in some way partly responsible for the carnage in his eyes - just as in Bosnia something could have been done somewhere to avert the death of the boy who now lay dead in my arms. I finally looked away from the boy. Croatian soldiers fought on as they retreated metre by metre from Jajce - as a war machine we were stuck, bludgeoned by superior numbers and firepower.

A young soldier ran past me carrying an old woman. She smiled as she passed me in his arms - how could she smile I thought; perhaps she knew something I didn't, something the whole damned world hadn't yet figured out. Just then an explosion shook the ground and lifted the young soldier carrying the old woman from the floor - the boys legs seemed to leave him and, as I stared at them in horror, I myself was lifted by the force of the blast, my rifle collapsing on top of me as I tried in vain to turn over and avoid it.

Startled, I realised that a tank shell had smashed through the wall of a nearby cafe bar. 'Tea for Two' I thought. I was delirious - laughing, crying - it was like a dream that wouldn't go away, to this day it has never quite left me. I recovered and took cover behind an upturned car. The carnage accompanied my delirium as memories of my former life in England flickered in my mind. Debris - bricks, plaster, pieces of car - crashed to the ground as I ran into a doorway then out through the back.

I could hear screaming in the near distance as bodies lay all around me in a double-jointed mass of flesh, bones, broken teeth and torn clothes. Slowly my senses returned to normal and I began to function as a human once more. I wanted to get the hell out of it all again.

Later that day I found myself holed up in a top floor room. It was one of the few buildings that had not been set alight or destroyed by mortar shells detonated by Serb hands that itched with an enthusiasm for death and destruction.

Of course the Serbs had looted each and every building - taking everything of worth as well as that which was valueless to anyone but the original owners. Taking and looting had become an act of spite, a matter of morbid interest.

And I was there, scuttling about the streets of the town like a giant rat (just as all soldiers become when the chips are down). Once trapped within the streets and alleyways of Jajce there was nothing military or dignified about me. I just demonstrated a will to survive and, since I have always been something of a primitive realist, I lived here on a second-by-second basis. My feet dragged through the mud and slush of war; blood stained dirt lay on the hundreds of bodies in the street. The laughter of the victorious enemy could be heard quite clearly amid the carnage; the looting, the pillaging and the raping - specifics don't matter, only the animalism of that war.

I crept slowly along an alleyway - forcing my frame into doorways with only the stench of dead bodies for company. I could hear incongruous laughter as the sounds of Serb celebration lit up the tragic scene. Just ahead on the junction of a street I saw a makeshift spit and fire. A pig was still alive as the soldiers roasted it - I baulked for a second not only because I am vegetarian but because this was a sick and vicious way to treat anything, let alone an innocent animal that must now have been rueing the day it had been born. For now it was I who rued the day that I had ever set foot in Jajce, a location for the Winter Olympics less than 10 years before. Meanwhile hell played its game as I flitted through alleyways; flames shadowing the walled streets, the houses pockmarked with bullet holes, roofs collapsed and shelled. Just then a jeep roared down the street and halted before it turned to near where I stood.

Quickly I hid in a closed doorway - falling to the ground as if a lifeless presence - it would have been straightforward to have killed the six man Serb patrol despite the fact that they were armed to the teeth and keen to continue their killing spree. For days afterwards the Serbs executed stragglers who passed through the town - the UN and the UNHCR did little but watch the carnage - they were nearly as helpless as the civilians. Now, as the jeep slowed, it moved alongside what I hoped they would think was a dead HVO soldier.

Playing dead as the enemy scanned the human wreckage, my blood began to quicken; it raced through my body, disobeying my plan to lie low - seeking in its own primitive way the need to survive, to evolve, to find, as Nietzsche put it, 'the will to power', to subjugate the enemy who were now right on top of me. Finally the Serbs moved on. Slowly I turned on my side in time to see the jeep move and turn at the top of the sloping street - to the right and away. It was a patrol that searched for few remaining victims; clearly they regarded me as long since dead so they went in search of others to loot and abuse.

For a few seconds longer I waited before I rose and kicked in the door of the house where I had lain. The spider trick had worked once more, my reading as a child had taught me well - nature was a beautiful creature, perhaps even I had adopted some of it in my own brutal way -

the beauty that strives to be free and survive. A quick cursory search and I left a ground floor kitchen with a block of cheese, not thinking as to whether it was vegetarian or not (that thought only came later).

I conveniently forgot my vegetarianism for the moment as my quest for survival continued. Up each set of stairs I flew, inspecting room after empty room, not expecting nor finding anyone there. I finally brought an old dresser to the door of a top-floor bedroom and closed it, forcing it as silently and as quickly as possible to the outside world. But then I doubted whether a little noise could be heard in Jajce, the town was now full of the braying laughter and demonic celebration of the victorious enemy as they roamed the conquered streets.

Nevertheless, I cautiously knelt at a side wall looking out of a broken window and, as a whiff of smoke came into the room, I looked down and along the street one way and then the other before re-checking the opposite building again (it was one of the few buildings still erect and not in flames). Looking out of the other edge of the window and then up the street the opposite way; all was quiet, bodies lying here and there.

Slumping to the floor I awaited further darkness and a relief to the shooting which had become one-way traffic, leading to the uneasy conclusion that there was a winner of the town - the Serb invaders. My eyes closed and I drifted, drained and fatigued, to sleep - planning my escape through enemy lines.

My strategy again relied on nature, or at least the nature of the Serb enemy. I reasoned that soon most of the enemy soldiers would be dead drunk or at least drunk enough not to notice small movements. This enabled me to take my chances a little later - a calculated risk that also allowed for the extra cover of darkness. I also knew it was best to bide my time because, as with revenge, it is often better to wait for the precise moment - to time it when the enemy least expect it.

Burst pipes brought forth the sound of flowing water and that, for the most part, was all I could hear - the sound made me thirsty so I drank from my canteen while I gave myself time to rejuvenate as I ate at the stale cheese, breaking off small pieces of mould and eating the fresher bits underneath. I then relaxed a little as my blood pressure dropped and, with the odd crackling of automatic fire outside for company, I planned my escape.

A little later darkness fell. A full moon cast shadows within metres of the dense woods nearby and then petered into darkness. Burning fires were everywhere, crackling and spitting into the night. Screams and calls could be heard - audible indicators of the nightmare that was visiting Croats and Bosnian Muslims alike.

Then a Serbian truck appeared dragging a young boy behind it.

The Silent Cry

Laughter reeked the air as I held back my vomit, everything was sickly yet there was no 'horror'. This war had visited Croatia and Bosnia for too long, just about everyone was numbed to the horrors of war as they became accepted daily occurrences. The boy was barely alive from what I could see now from the top floor of a destroyed building; I kept back within the shadows as flames licked the building opposite.

The truck came to a halt. The bloody body of the boy writhed in pain as my mind reeled thinking of how to help. Quickly, I removed the pins from three grenades and crashed them down on the macabre scene below, before smashing my way downward - jumping stairs. A Chetnik (member of the Serb paramilitaries) confronted me at the bottom of the stairwell and, as he laughed drunkenly, I took my revenge for the boy - renting his head wide open with my 18-inch killing blade.

I hacked twice more in terror at the possibility of being captured by these torturers, these vermin. There was little or no time for thought other than instinctive reaction - to protect myself and kill the enemy. My Kalashnikov ripped right and left into everything in my path, the grenades I had thrown now exploded, lifting the truck into the air - my right eardrum bleeding with the noise as I was lifted from the ground with the force of it but, as I thudded back to earth, it was my soul that ached far more than my body. Staggering to my feet, I faltered then fell, dragging myself toward the edge of a small wood a few metres away. I toppled into a ditch, my senses reeling, blood pouring from my wrist, the pain was not immediately apparent as my adrenaline seemed to anaesthetise the blow.

Indeed I took on new life as I bounded through the trees. The truck had been laden with ammunition and explosives and the night was now alive with the ensuing explosions as I scurried into the dense trees and undergrowth. Bullets and shrapnel screamed all about me and I was breathless, my heart pounding as I stood up in anger and ripped more bullets in the direction of the buildings flaming brightly despite the thickness of the trees. Suddenly I became aware that there was no return fire, but that the bullets were coming from the ammo truck that had exploded just a few minutes ago. So on I went.

Further and further I crashed through the forest; tripping, falling, collapsing to earth, my arm numbed, my body dehydrated - as I continued to grip my Kalashnikov before - total darkness, my head spinning as if death had finally taken me... In fact I had collapsed from a combination of a loss of blood from my left wrist and the partial shock of the gruesome scene I had witnessed. For how far and how long I'd run I didn't immediately know although I later worked out that it must have been 7 kilometres or more. After I awoke and realised my position I got myself ready for another day behind enemy lines.

I ripped the field bandage from my injured left shoulder to bandage my bloody wrist but the pain was irrelevant, incidental. What was more worrying was the thought that I was going mad - 'off my head' - that this war was turning me from human to animal. I got to my knees. Then, putting one foot flat upon the earth, I forced myself up on both feet. I staggered briefly, my head spinning as I lent against a tree attempting to regain my balance and senses. Slowly, step-by-step, I recovered, gaining enough momentum to walk properly.

I could smell the air, the trees, the freshness of the morning's offerings - I was alive, a survivor - for a moment I felt that life was worth living. The roar of trucks and tanks could be heard nearby but then distances could be deceptive in the forests of Bosnia. I followed the noise cautiously and crawled to a ridge. I watched the enemy troops below as they sauntered toward the frontline with the casual air of advancing soldiers.

Jajce wasn't unusual in witnessing murder and mayhem on a large scale. Vukovar had experienced far worse but, as they trundled by 30 or so metres below me, it was as if there was no urgency to their movements. They knew that the Croat forces were once more in retreat, busily attempting to create a new frontline as Jajce was finally cut off from humanity. Later I was told of the full extent of the death and destruction meted out by the enemy on the innocent victims of Jajce. But then the fresh memory of the boy being dragged by the truck served as enough evidence to me and, as they swarmed about the road, I found a new hatred for the Serbs - something I never normally allowed to cloud my judgement; I always thought it better that my mind was clear in order to kill professionally.

Alas, reason is often lost within war and death, as are 'rules' such as the Geneva Convention and the other theoretical considerations of politicians, for they rarely if ever serve on the frontline of conflict and make laws which, though plausible to peaceful Western society, make little sense in a bloody war.

I quickly realised that this movement of the enemy was quite serious to my chances... I desperately needed to get back to my own lines and calculated that it would be better to do that now while confusion reigned and the enemy haphazardly advanced rather than later when the new frontline had formed and lookouts had been posted. Shells were exploding everywhere... the air was rent with the 'Ba-Boom' of T.55 tanks as they blasted the hell out of our newly formed frontline. Only woods and high ground put the enemy off while the ferocity of the fighting intensified.

Mortar shells crisscrossed the air. There was no mistaking the echo of 120mm shells as explosions reverberated up and down the valley.

The Silent Cry

I scurried back to the relative safety of the wood above the road. I was quiet. Checking my supplies I realised that my water bottle was nearly empty and the day had only just started, it was a good job that it was autumn, I thought, that would lessen the possibility of dehydration. Flitting from tree to tree I was relieved to see the Serbs halt and then disappear out of sight. Just as suddenly I seemed to accrue extra energy - a swiftness and agility returned to my hitherto stiff movements. My gun seemed to be lighter, as did the two spare 30 round magazines, one grenade, killing knife, boot knife and wire which formed the remainder of my personal armoury.

The bandage on my wrist was saturated with blood now, as the rattle of automatic fire opened again. The trees in front of me were being ripped and torn, smaller branches crashing down upon me as I took cover once more. At once I gathered the Serb's desire to continue the carnage that they had visited upon the town. We all knew about the death camps and former cattle sheds where the Serbs held Croatians and Muslims - and the last thing I wanted was a prolonged visit to one of them. I figured that they were firing either because they had spotted me or out of nervousness, either way it was better to be safe than sorry. So as the wham and blast of shells continued to echo up and down the valley and the air and ground trembled with the reverberations of Serb firepower, I took cover and watched.

A whooshing sound took the attention of all sides as a Serb rocket landed on the town below, scattering its fleeing population. Death was the unwanted prize for any that stood still that morning, yet still the machine-gun fire continued throughout the day. I soon realised I was helpless. Stuck behind the enemy, I would have to infiltrate the Serb lines and then, without an extensive knowledge of Croatian, find my way through my own lines in the middle of all this mayhem. Even if I did find a section of the Croatian line where English could be understood there was no guarantee of returning safely - so I decided to wait for nightfall. Darkness would at least provide cover and, since as a child I had always preferred night to day, it was my preferred course of action in most cases.

With the stealth of an experienced criminal who had successfully evaded the long arm of Scotland Yard for so many years (not to mention my on/off relationship with police forces around the world), I slithered and crawled through the remainder of the forest until I reached an escarpment where I laid low, awaiting nightfall. Before me the ground dropped before rising - the forest on the hill opposite acted as cover for the Croat army's temporary frontlines, that was my end goal. 'Crack, crack, crack' - the shots seared at me, the tree on my left bearing the brunt - "good", I thought, "at least my side are on the ball" as I beat a hasty retreat on my belly before, to my horror, small mortars began landing within metres of where I lay with my hands instinctively covering my head.

Splinters of wood ripped through the air as mortar shells exploded on the upper branches of the trees before falling to the ground around me - I briefly promised to get out of Bosnia and never return and came up with a million excuses in the moments while I lay there bombarded and helpless. Anyone would have thought that my own side were firing upon an army as an obscene number of shells were focussed on my little piece of the forest. Shrapnel and torn metal ripped the forest floor as my own mortar men guessed that I had fled deeper into the forest - so I doubled back and crawled to the edge again.

It worked. Suddenly the firing stopped and I lay there hidden, hugging the ground until the light faded and I was plunged into the darkness, the woods becoming eerie. However, I was more afraid of the Serb forces coming from behind than the threat posed by my own side up ahead. I knew that the Croatians would not attempt a counteroffensive, even though the Tomislavgrad command had recently sent up a reserve of about 500 soldiers, most of whom had fought in the unsuccessful defence of Kupres. Many of the Croat forces were mismanaged at this juncture in the war - but then war is chaos, order being hard or impossible to find under attack.

In many ways I believe the Croat commander who had ordered an early evacuation of Jajce had saved many thousands of lives even though later reports claimed that only 16% of the town was Serb controlled when he made the evacuation order. Teenage Croatian soldiers had fought bravely until the Serb encirclement of the town was complete and, once the last road had been cut off, the Serbs exacted revenge upon the several thousand civilians left behind Serb lines.

In the days before Jajce's fall, ammunition was prevented from reaching our frontlines providing further evidence of a growing mistrust between Muslims and Croats - a mistrust that would result, a few months later, in the creaky alliance between the two finally collapsing.

Meanwhile the outside world cried openly for the Muslim plight but little for the Croatian cause, although both suffered equally at the hands of the Serbs. Only together could we stem the Serb onslaught. Unfortunately our common enemy was soon forgotten as Muslims and Croatians fought against rather than with each other during a period when we were supposed to be allies.

Now, however, the firing intensified as gun, tank, mortar and artillery fire was quickly exchanged at a terrible rate. Blast after blast came from the town and its surrounds, the Serbs closed their lines on the

The Silent Cry

perimeter and we hit back with what little we had - our forces knew the bitter consequences of letting the enemy through. Tracer fire scored the sky as explosions lashed the heavens on both sides of the frontline. Fire was all about the town; smoke billowed from wrecked buildings prompting a feeling of elation and horror at the same time. As the buildings and tanks burned I imagined the soldiers fighting, having limbs torn from their bodies, eyes blinded, souls taken.

I heard a rustle in the undergrowth from deep within the woods - "oh fuck", I thought, "this is it"... Turning to face the advancing enemy patrol the hairs rose on the back of my neck. The enemy appeared a little too casual in their movements however. They made a lot of noise and, as I checked my ammo and changed my bandage, I felt confident awaiting the imminent skirmish. Now I was ready and went quickly toward the noise that had stopped 100 or so metres away. I could hear laughter and the unmistakable clink of bottles and estimated that there were maybe 7 or 8 Chetniks in the patrol. I got to within 20 metres or so and quickly fixed my last grenade that had a 4 second delay. Withdrawing stealthily, or so I thought, I heard a shot. Briefly I thought "shit I've been too clumsy, now I'm going to pay with my life".

Throughout my life I have always considered it foolish to underestimate anyone - never mind a fool - and now I had broken that golden rule I was sure I would pay. Slumping to the ground I heard the drunken shouts of Serbians. Despite their clumsiness one of them knew my position and the shots were aimed straight at me and, as another burst of shots ripped through the woods, the enemy crashed clumsily onwards.

Then a blast forty or so metres behind me sent the ground trembling beneath my feet. The night was alight as my own side started to blast mortar shells into that area of the forest - the Croats reacting to the thought that the attack was aimed at them - it was understandable and inevitable. Of course I was in between a rock and a hard place now and had nothing to lose as I decided to reveal my position by ripping AK fire at the Serbs.

Three or four of my bullets caused a scream as I hit the 'flash' of their rifles - one Serb was a split second too slow to react as I rolled away to another tree, smashing my ribs on a small tree stump, I let out a cry which brought forth a further crack, crack, crack from beyond the trees. In the dark it is preferable to give small bursts of fire without revealing your position but with my ammo low and with little idea of how I was going to escape I decided that sure-fire single shot was better than a scattergun approach.

Then the blast of a 120 mm mortar shook the air. 'Wham!' there was a loud crack beyond belief and a second later the cries of what was left of humanity could be heard as the enemy took a direct hit - the moans of death emanating from the forest were awful and familiar - in death everyone sounds the same. It was all but a split-second later that I was up and running and, as our mortar men heard the firing cease, I contained my dash toward the cries so that I could make sure that I eliminated what remained of the Serb enemy.

"God in hell", I muttered - the carnage was terrible.

Pieces of body could be seen as parachute flares lit up the scene. There were at least three of them still alive - one immediately in front of me - a metre or so away - the other two still breathing nearby. I remembered the deaths of my six colleagues on the hill in Babice - when the first few hours of my part in the war had shown the horrific extent of this particular conflict. One Serb had his arm torn from his shoulder; his face blackened and gashed ... eyes staring ... mouth mumbling in Serbo-Croat. A cold pity came to me as I put my AK over my shoulder and pulled my knife. As I walked up to him, knife in hand, a pitiful pleading came from his eyes... his legs and stomach were open to the bone and entrails - how on earth could he still be alive?

Then I realised that we were both instruments of war - the pawns of politicians - had the mortar fallen a little short our roles could so easily have been reversed - I respected him, envied his brave death, if not his pain and suffering - we are, after all, all the same in the end. I swiftly moved within inches of him, took out his cigarettes and placed one in his mouth and, as I lit it, he coughed and spluttered - that was the cue for me to sink my knife into his neck and up into his brain.

His death was swift and merciful. I grimaced as I pulled out the blade and his head lolled forward, the cigarette falling onto his stomach. Turning, I heard a gurgle from a destroyed face and neck - another Serb had been watching me all along - one eye out of its socket. I couldn't pity him for long however as I spied that his right hand held a gun - his finger poised on the trigger as he struggled for the strength of revenge. Instinctively I crashed my foot down on his wrist, snapping it with a violent crack.

The flare grew dim and darkness returned, taking me by surprise as I wrestled with the half-dead Serb, whom I then realised was mortally wounded, my knife sinking into a gaping wound in his stomach before he gave a final sigh and was dead. Then all became blackness as I was knocked-out - the third live Serb grabbed me and, as I found out when I came round, had died in the act - leaving both me and him sprawled on the floor.

I woke some hours later. There was a terrible stench as I felt the dead man's hand on my neck - it was cold, cut and broken. Struggling free from the dead bodies I needed to urinate - this was war and death - the result of political need - was I really the barbarian? Shouldn't some blame be attached to the men who pitted neighbour against neighbour? Then I will admit that many times I acted in accordance with the most basic human attribute - revenge. Having witnessed many atrocities and the aftermath of needless suffering it seemed natural at the time to even the score - not on innocent civilians but on the colleagues of those I decided were guilty.

I collected my thoughts. From the dead bodies I took two water bottles, a third was half-full with Rakija (plum Vodka) - I gulped at it in haste and spat it out quickly, it would only dehydrate me further. For some strange reason I brought all the bodies together taking a Skorpion Pistol, umpteen AK 47 magazines and a machete which I soon threw away as it was too heavy. I also discarded some emergency meat rations but kept the American veggie ones which had either been captured or surreptitiously sold to our enemy.

I knew from experience that arms were being supplied to the Croatians from Russia (the Serbs main ally) and it was plausible that the Americans could be supplying the Serbs with food rations. Bosnia was a big game and all the Western powers liked to exert a little control on all sides - it stored up vital brownie points for them in the future.

I looked at the bodies again and felt a self-loathing and a loathing of all 'normal' society - a soldier quite often has to decide when life has all but gone - not playing God, just easing the pain by death. The same rules apply when you must kill one of your own men, to know you must do it and not allow them to be tortured - which were commonplace fates for captured men in this particular conflict. Conscience had no bearing and I lost little sleep as a result of my actions. I just hoped that this would not be another day of waiting. Patrols were sure to come to both the frontline and no-mans land from both sides to 'recce'. Basic military knowledge told me that I wanted to be long gone when the patrols tried to piece together events in this part of the forest.

I was now far steadier on my feet. Again I cleaned and re-strapped my wrist from clean bandages found on the dead Serbs and ate and drank before heading off toward the edge of the woods a few kilometres away, my arm throbbing with pain. There I laid low for the day, keen to avoid all contact with the enemy nearby. From the edge of the forest I could see the task ahead of me. There was a three hundred metre stretch of rough, open, rocky terrain - it was now late afternoon and relatively cold for autumn. Gun-fire was still all about ; bullets and shells zinged and blasted the air while tank fire and the familiar crash of 120mm mortars continued to make life difficult for our frontline.

Thankfully, the sky was heavily overcast and rain was imminent so I waited, working out my best route home through the rocks and hollows of the terrain. By now my left arm was almost useless so my best hope was for a deluge of rain to cover my route back. Visions came to me of a sopping-wet homecoming and the relief that this past few days of madness would be but a memory. My arm felt numb from hand to elbow but that was the least of my problems - suddenly the heavens opened as thunder and lightning shook the area - my opportunity to survive this hellish journey was at hand. It was still light but so heavily overcast that it wouldn't be long before darkness fell - then down came the rain.

Once my guns and ammo were covered I found myself laughing at similar rain-soaked experiences in Glasgow and Manchester - this was the glorious rain I loved when the chase was on - police, enemy soldiers, whatever, I loved the hunt to evade capture against all odds. After the initial euphoria of the rain, however, I was freezing, my teeth chattering, my arm felt like it was on fire. The injury had inflamed - but I still regarded it as a minor irritation.

Now it was almost completely dark again so I slithered into the clearing, moving forward metre by metre only to discover, to my horror, that there was a small bunker emplacement directly in front of me. I froze for a moment expecting a bullet to strike me at last. But the moment lasted ten seconds, then twenty as the rain lashed at my face. I was amazed, there was no way, even in these conditions, that I could be missed. So I peered over the brow again with the concern of a bank manager looking at his losses. Nearer and nearer. There had to be two in the OP bunker - something drove me nearer and still the rain lashed down smashing my head, back and legs. Muddied..a sight for sore eyes..I was now naturally camouflaged.

Peering even harder. I couldn't see a gun in the aperture, nor a discernible face as I should have done - now, under the cover of a storm, would be the perfect time for a soldier of skill to sneak up on the Observation Post and hurl a grenade in there. Yes, I was sure it was empty. I pulled myself up and over a log, forcing myself in through a gap that was barely wide enough to take me. Crash! I went flying into an empty ammo-box. Crash! Not a shot... no shouts, no calls nor anything by my own side to ascertain as to who the hell was out there. I steadied myself in the shelter and watched the outside world.

If there is a God he was undoubtedly on my side those three days and especially that night. Slowly darkness overcame my eyes as my mind tottered and failed - it switched itself off. As it turned out my uniform and unit-arm badge saved my life. The next thing I knew I was being dragged from the emplacement and onto a stretcher. Just before first light two of

The Silent Cry

our soldiers were checking along the lines for anything worthy of report and had shone a torch down upon me in the emplacement.

Now the sky had cleared and I was being carried, my eyes blinking. I was exhausted from three days' exertion and a loss of blood, but a drip soon fixed the latter and I emerged from hospital within a few hours. My survival had involved a great deal of skill and luck; being in the right place at the right time was a knack I seemed to have acquired.

Following my three-day adventure in the hills around Jajce I discovered the true extent and effect of the Serb onslaught in the town. A Croatian doctor later told me of the atrocities; refugees were machine-gunned in the road, napalm and cluster bombs had been dropped on Jajce while the Serbs also shot up ambulances. As I discovered, their route to freedom was particularly harsh and unforgiving.

2 - THE ROAD FROM JAJCE AND BEYOND

I caught up with the stream of bedraggled humanity as they dragged themselves along the mountain tracks and roads from Jajce. Each and every face regardless of age, size or personality knew the pain of life. They were filled with the tears, strain and pain of existing in this living Hell.

Artillery fire reached out to the column of humanity still - shells crashing down on the mountainside and into the refugees. Explosions sent rock and earth into the air and down upon them as people scattered, trying desperately to cling to their string wrapped bundles and plastic bags that contained all their worldly possessions - the sum total of lives now wrecked by war. An awful sadness filled the air and could be seen deep within their eyes. Yes, it was a bedraggled, torn and bloodstained people that trudged their way along the road from Jajce.

Communist jets scored the air - bombs were dropped before the jets roared into immediate visual contact and rockets blasted out scattering all humanity - the refugees mixed with the retreating Croat forces. Some fell to the floor, others toppled over the edge of the mountainside, some managed to keep going with a reserve of strength and determination that seemed unimaginable to me - they were cold and starved in most cases. In others too old, young or feeble to look after themselves, yet they maintained a will to survive.

You could almost hear the pangs of hunger within the column. After five months of siege upon their town - constant shelling, the scream of attack jets overhead - death was visiting them once more as they fled for their lives. Eventually, after a time, the Serbs were checked in their onslaught as they slowly realised that they didn't have the resources to maintain a forward momentum of invasion. Many breathed a sigh of relief at the temporary lull in this region.

But the lull merely heightened the mistrust between the Croats and Muslims. Initially, the two sides had worked together against a common enemy - but leading up to the Serb invasion of Jajce Muslim checkpoints had taken up the habit of checking Croatian military and medical supplies - disarming individuals and preventing Croatian ambulances entering the hills. For nine days or so a stalemate ensued and, as a result, Jajce fell to our mutual enemy. Following the fall of the town we were unsure whether the Bosnian army's interference had been directed from Sarajevo or whether it had been carried out by rogue units - either way the result was an inevitable victory for the Serbs. In turn the Muslims accused us of deserting Jajce too quickly - it was the beginning of the end of our alliance.

The aftermath was terrible. The atrocities carried out by the Serbians here would not have looked out of place in World War Two, but this was Bosnia in 1992 - a mere 2 hours flying time from London. Still, the enormity of the situation remained beyond most people in Britain or the rest of the Western World for that matter. As a result, only a desultory force of United Nations 'peace-keepers' was present. The lowest paid of these officials, a truck driver, was on £700 a week plus expenses - these were not fighting or medical staff but drivers. By contrast, as a soldier in the HVO I earned £3 a week in the first five months of the war, and they called me a soldier of fortune! Screams, moans and cries could be heard in the anguish of the refugees' pain - God how those people suffered.

As the enemy jets soared back toward the Serb positions, bodies lay strewn about the road and just over the edge of the mountainside - the survivors hiding behind rocks or any cover they could find. The wounded were tended by the person nearest to them - there were very few medics among the fleeing civilians and retreating soldiers. Tractors, carts and makeshift prams conveyed belongings and human cargo on a struggle toward Tomislavgrad or any town that would shelter them from the storm of conflict. Medical aid would be given along the way but resources were scarce and casualties high.

Kilometre after kilometre they trod that bitter, bloody road as they fled their homeland. It was some hours before the gunfire receded from the ears of those marching away from the trouble - too tired and exhausted to think, they barely realised when it was safe and when it was not - only when a generous host extended a warm hand of kindness would they again put their faith in humanity rather than war.

The conflict had sealed many of their fates already. Loved ones had died and suffered within the burned, bombed homes they had left several days before. And although trucks loaded with bread and water began distributing relief to everyone, it was very little in reality and barely enough to sustain them on their long journey. The lined faces, dirty and drained with bitter experience, stared into space and time - all eyes devoid of humanity, an emptiness apparent to anyone who witnessed it.

Finally the old men, women and children came to a halt to eat the freshly baked bread and drink the cold, clear water. The food came from nearby Croatian and Bosnian villagers who also provided blankets; with winter fast approaching every spare cover would be needed up in the mountains. Then the tears came as a realisation of relief and pent-up emotion surged out. They realised they were now in safe hands but after the five month strain of defending their town they still found it hard to accept that their army was between them and the advancing Serbs.

However a lull in the fighting at least allowed them a chance to reflect and, as the many considered what their land would look like in the future, few could picture it at peace. They were safe for now, their journey at an end and soon they would be given temporary shelter in Bosnia but on all sides the fighting rarely stopped as the war continued on all fronts.

Official reports of the exodus of civilians from Jajce note that it was, at the time, the largest forced evacuation in Bosnia. The town, bombed incessantly by Bosnian-Serb forces with equipment left them by the Yugoslav Federal Army, had been under siege for five months as Bosnian Serbs attempted to create a link between the 'mother state' of Serbia and Serb enclaves in Western Bosnia. This forced 25,000 Croatians and Muslims to flee; the Muslims to Travnik, the Croatians to Tomislavgrad where John was stationed.

In Tomislavgrad the local populace had been annoyed when barbed wire had been erected around the new UN base there, they regarded it as an affront to their friendly intentions. So in my capacity as an unpaid spin-doctor for the UN I tried to give a Scottish explanation for the barbed wire, claiming that the local Croatian children were so fierce that the British had to protect themselves from them. A look of consternation greeted this suggestion and although the locals seemed to trust me they still burst out laughing as they walked away shaking their heads.

Admittedly a few shots had been fired in the direction of the UN base, especially after a few bottles of Pivo but in the main, with the exception of three shells that landed on the British compound, the UN had little to fear from the local population. Those three shells had caused concern among the British as they sized up the damage and calculated that they must have been fired from the HVO frontline! Once again I don't know how or why that happened.

On a gentler note I approached the Tomislavgrad checkpoint at the UN base, after my chat with the locals, resplendent in a Blackwatch kilt and sporran. The British UN Royal Engineers checkpoint was 'manned' by two very attractive, young female soldiers. It was no surprise to find women at the checkpoint - the HVO had several gallant female warriors and, in my experience, they killed as well as any male soldier. Reaching the two camouflaged ladies I was asked the nature of my business and showed them a wreath, a mark of respect for the Welsh soldier Wayne Edwards who had been the first UN fatality in Bosnia.

A phone call was made to the main block, a former school that had been a refugee station prior to the UN's arrival. Several minutes passed with light banter while the elder of the two girls attempted to feel under my kilt, to ascertain whether I was hanging 'free and wild' or whether army shorts covered my decency. I foiled each attempt as I didn't want every female I happened upon to start chasing after me to discover the contents of my kilt. 'Please Jock, let me see what you've got under your kilt', the elder girl pleaded again. There was no way I could shock this girl or her younger colleague so I told them that if they showed me 'theirs' I'd show them mine. That deal was predictably declined so a further attempt was made to assault my person.

Enough was enough so I shouted, 'you English bitch get yer hands off or I'll slap yer face'. Laughter greeted this threat and as I blushed I told them the real size of my kilt's contents 'the glory of Scotland, 203mm capability!' The girls laughed even louder upon hearing this (the God's honest truth) before a call came through to escort me over to the command centre.

Naturally they argued about who should escort me, after all I was at my physical peak, a fine figure who would put Sean Connery to shame. So I tossed a coin and the younger girl won. I arrived at the main hall of command and handed the wreath to a miserable Captain who accepted it without thanks. It had cost me the equivalent of a month's HVO wages, although in relation to the life lost that was nothing. The Welsh soldier had come to help the innocent and had ended up a victim himself - 'c'est la guerre'.

These were about the brightest moments to be had in Bosnia. I was greeted by catcalls and wolf-whistles on my return to the checkpoint and, as I continued on my way back to the Croatian command post up the road, I found myself laughing as the girls waved me good-bye.

It wasn't so light in mood when 15,000 refugees from Jajce arrived in the town a little later. 10,000 of them headed for the safety of the main town, the rest finding safe haven in the surrounding villages. Thronged with refugees, Tomislavgrad was awash with the dispossessed of Jajce. They congregated around the monastery while clothes, shoes and food were distributed. They had lost their homes and had arrived owning only what they stood up in, but I felt they must be given their dignity and a sense of purpose.

The Road From Jajce And Beyond

Makeshift refugee shelters were erected to ensure that Croatian and Muslim refugees would have a roof over their heads. At times, in the first few weeks following the fall of Jajce, their accommodation left much to be desired - but what could be done when 10,000 people descended on a town the size of Tomislavgrad that had a population of only 17,000 to sustain the influx?

Day-by-day the stories emerged of civilian killings. Some people I met had retreated from Jajce in the very final days. Torture and rape were the order of the day - the Serb forces were into their practised routine by October 1992, performing their evil ways once more just as they had during their invasion of Croatia the year before. Just across from the town's hotel I went into a local shop and bought a loaf of bread before making my way along the main street a few metres to where an old woman sat on a wall with her family - all had fled the horrors of Jajce.

Looking at the old and withered face before me I could see that she knew the pain of loss, a pain brought by the terror of war and the degradation of military action against civilians. They had had peace wrenched from them by military conquest - all the refugees looked bewildered by the force railed against them. Handing the fresh loaf to the old woman I looked into her eyes. She returned the look as I pressed the equivalent of about four pounds into her other hand. She turned to someone I assumed was her daughter and tears streamed from her eyes onto her dried skin. She looked to the sky briefly and, from what I was told by a translator, she thanked God for the first fresh bread she had known in three months of siege, for the first money that could buy more bread and told me that the loaf itself was 'manna from heaven'.

I can still picture her face to this day. The sadness turned to joy in her eyes, the transformation from a look and sense of hopelessness to one of tearful expectancy and hope. I was humbled as her daughter and grandchildren also cried while they stared at the loaf and the small amount of money. It was further translated that the UN had not come to give their blood in defence of the Croatian or Muslim people but that I, a Scot, had left my children behind in England and come because I believed in the freedom of others.

It was within this group of refugees that I met a girl. She was perhaps fourteen years old. Amid the confusion of conflict my mind cleared as to the reason I had travelled the 2,000 miles or so to Bosnia - it was to be here on this day, to look upon troubled, pained humanity. The girl and her friends looked at me and smiled. I felt a tear well in my eyes and a lump in my throat as I reached into my holdall and gave the girl a leather jacket.

The teenager was a Madonna, another reason to fight, shed blood and struggle. She accepted the jacket with a nervous laugh and put it on after I cajoled her into wearing it. Then she began 'modelling' it for her friends while I sat back and laughed at the joy on their faces. It was a small, temporary respite from the conflict and as we stood next to the shelled remains of the Tomislavgrad monastery, I'm sure God shone a little light on us as the sun emerged from behind the clouds, illuminating our little group. 'Dobra, dobra, dobra' the girl called out, as tears welled in her eyes before trickling down her face onto the dry soil below. It was like beauty and the beast, as my hardened face smiled and I turned and walked away.

Meeting the old woman and the young girl gave me great purpose, a sense of fighting for a cause; a fight for freedom for the people of Bosnia. For years the war ground on, making people like the old woman and young girl victims, but throughout the conflict whenever I remembered them I remembered why I was there.

JOHN MACPHEE - TV STAR

Soon after arriving in Bosnia I became in demand as a commentator, an expert on the war. I was one of the few English speaking soldiers not attached to the UN and as such could speak honestly about the Croatian cause and the state of the warring sides. One such encounter was with ITN's Peter Sharp. He was putting together a piece for News at Ten about the recent fall of Jajce and agreed to meet me outside the monastery in Tomislavgrad where the refugees had stayed since arriving in the town. He was a flamboyant character, a confidence in himself coming, I take it, from his years of experience interviewing people in difficult situations around the world. I turned up, as arranged, my arm still in a plaster-cast and sling and he told me he needed ten minutes to use for that evening's broadcast. It was a straightforward business with no skulduggery, although changes are always made during the editing process.

On another occasion Bob Greaves interviewed me on 'Granada Tonight' and from the response I received upon my return to Britain I was told that I had got the message across about the situation. It all seemed worthwhile when a youngster in Market Street, Manchester told me that I'd made him see that there were more important things in life than being a criminal. To me that was exactly why I was fighting and the reason, of course, that I had first volunteered to fight in Bosnia.

It was strictly upon such a basis that I went and not as a mercenary, there was little or no money to pay a foreign soldier - my £3 a week pay proves that. There were many other TV interviews; some of course were done by 'cowboys' who tried to twist my words to suit the TV company. Then there were times when they edited me right-out other than stating that I was a criminal fighting in Bosnia in an attempt to undermine the Croatian cause.

The reality (that I was fighting for a belief in freedom, for the rights of children to sleep without the fear of imminent Serbian attack) didn't appeal to TV producers who wanted to make entertaining news. Eventually I didn't have much time for the media. Most lacked the courage to get right in there and film or report. It is true that many were killed by shelling or Serb snipers, but their deaths didn't mean much to a soldier. They were highly paid individuals whose families would be taken care of by their colleagues and the companies for whom they worked. Death might have been unusual in the west but it was commonplace in Bosnia.

More important were the old, the women and their children. They were not paid actors on screen, they had no choice in the matter - they and their families were the real victims in that war. No tears could ever be shed by a soldier for a journalist - life went on. There were never any reports that our side killed or wounded members of the press or TV. Yes, they were a pain when they reported what I knew to be a twisted opinion but we resisted the easy target of an unarmed journalist. The Guardian newspaper was one of the worst culprits - a paper I'd bought and read since a teenager but which I vowed never to read again. That paper gave the Croatian forces a hard time with little evidence.

I believe in freedom of the press, a matter I once wrote to Andrew Neil of the Sunday Times about; in defence of his right to expose the Pergau Dam scandal. And although I might disagree with the Guardian's coverage of the war in Bosnia, I would also admit that their support and reproduction of Bosnian Muslim propaganda was their right in a free country, it was one of the rights for which I was fighting. But my regular TV appearances also had an unwelcome side effect. Serbian intelligence received all Western TV and I swiftly became a target, it was another reason to lie-low - it's one thing being a bit of a personality in Britain, quite another to be a specific target in Bosnia. As a result I quickly returned to my real purpose - fighting the Serb enemy on the frontline. I was summoned to Babice once more as the Serb forces had consolidated since the fall of Jajce.

The Silent Cry
BACK TO BABICE

The Lada jeep roared into life and steadily made its way down the short track onto the road that led to the Tomislav-Mostar Highway. It was a bright start to the day as the sun rose on the horizon; it was just before 7 am. In the immediate distance church walls were lit with this joy of light - the shining sphere giving the corps of life and a feeling far more important than warmth - hope. We all hoped that the long promised counteroffensive would start soon, that it would batter at the Serbian enemy over the mountains to the east of Mostar and north of Tomislavgrad - that Kupres would return to the fold of the people of this beautiful land.

Unfortunately, for the remainder of that summer that was not to be. The raised hope of the counteroffensive would remain just a hope. Tanks and weapons were not available to make that dream come true. More than soldiers and strong morale would be needed to take back Kupres and Jajce. The echo of a 120 mm mortar shell reverberated through the valley as it whooshed along before building up for an explosion. The air erupted in the valley below shattering more buildings in the ghost town of Suica and, as the tiles of a roof flew into the air shattering an otherwise quiet morning, smoke spewed into the blue sky, flames following in its wake.

A blast and another shell tore at the sky as we passed more Serb positions above - the exaggerated sound of ripping silk jarring all within earshot. The jeep was being targeted from a Serb mortar position somewhere near the Malovan Mountains, the threat of their mortars had hung over our hill positions for too long. The advantage of our frontline position in Babice was that it was set in a wooded area that acted as useful camouflage, which meant that we were not in direct sight of Serb mortar positions.

While we were out in the open in a jeep however the mortars landed with ferocity and it was to the safety of those wooded emplacements that we now scurried. Our driver, a miserable but nonetheless likeable former Legionnaire nicknamed 'Charlie', sped on in fear of a lucky shot from the Serbs who continued to bombard us with shells from directly ahead. I broke into nervous laughter as Charlie's face constricted in near terror. My laughter was not a matter of cowardice or bravery but an attempt to hold my insanity by a perversity of emotion. Since I had known the reality of death on this frontline it mattered little to me whether I died. Within that particular theatre of war I had already been hardened by the deaths of six of my comrades.

Some soldiers grow in stature in the crucible of war - I had, unfortunately, been one who had hardened as a bitterness grew within my blood. The memory of our dead comrades in Babice gave me the courage to go on, to fight and defend their children by whatever means necessary, to visit carnage upon the enemy and all who stood in the way of Croatian freedom. 'Smash', the pounding shells hit the road and ground to our right and left.

It was madness that we had to run this gauntlet each and every time we went to our frontline position, to patrol the ghost town or even to communicate. The shelled and holed church steeple of Suica could be seen clearly as we neared - then 'whack', an explosion to our right blasted debris on to the jeep, the sound of sheet metal, rocks and chips of stone peppering our ears! The jeep lifted slightly for a second at the blast rocking the five of us heavily laden with ammunition. The little English guy in the back of the jeep winced - who could blame him.

War is not a human pursuit but this little character found it especially hard as he was just not cut out for conflict. He was emotionally unsound and had a serious drink problem. So much was building inside him during his weeks in combat that those who talked to him when he first joined the HVO could now no longer stomach him. I felt pity toward him. I awoke from this thought quickly as outside the vehicle some bastard began gunning for us - it was then that I thought of the reality of that expression, I would never ridicule it again - as if it mattered to the enemy. They wanted to mangle us up - to give us, simply, what they would get from us later.

We didn't look like a command vehicle.... Charlie was a major of sorts who trained recruits. He was not active in the strictest sense. His training and years of French Foreign Legion service were now being put into practice for his own people - to teach them the Legionnaire way of killing - simply and brutally! Fortunately death was not for any of us that day. We skidded side-ways (quite a feat on a dry road), before Charlie regained control - a credit to his driving skill. Meanwhile at the back of the jeep the English lad shouted that he wanted to walk the rest of the way - 'it'd be safer' he complained.

We laughed and then grimaced again as our driver increased his speed and we took another bend at full pelt and headed up the last part of the road in the enemy's vision - already the road and earth to either side was pock-marked with old mortar explosions.

Suddenly and without warning, Charlie stopped in sight of the enemy and began to turn around!

For a split second I thought 'he's gone off his rocker'. But no, he had forgotten to deliver the secret codes that had changed only thirty minutes before. They had to be delivered by hand so we were forced to run the gauntlet once more. This was hilarious to all of us except our passenger in the back sitting on a box of grenades and squashed by foam bedrolls.

On the way back, a shell from a smaller calibre mortar shook us off the road to the right and on to the verge; fortunately it didn't knock us to the left otherwise we'd have shot down the sheer face of rock and landed at the bottom of the valley. We tottered on the edge of the slope then swung back and onto the smashed-up road. This was a nightmare. More laughter rolled around the car as under my breath I cursed the driver who had put us through a rerun of this hellish drive for the sake of a lapse of memory - to my mind the mistake was all his; an officer should be calmer than his troops, not the other way around.

Foreign Legion discipline should have adjusted him to these kinds of conditions, in a war this shelling was routine. Still we had to return. Tree roots shattered, smoke choked the air. Whack! Something shattered our windscreen as pieces of roof from a burned-out warehouse came down on us with other debris.

We took a detour to Suica where the streets were deserted - sandbags here and there at cafe bars. Soldiers were inside, out of the way of this present bombardment. Our jeep slammed to a halt, stalled then erupted in a roar that gave life to the engine, as we took off again into the air and landed with a crash shaking the springs, the suspension and us before we scrapped into and alongside the church wall. A funny looking Italian-Croatian priest came running out of his house next to the church. He was going mad at our driver for scarring his already battered church further and, as we all jumped out, Charlie pushed the priest aside. The devil, I do believe, was mentioned in the priest's dispatches as we sheltered inside the house.

Ah! I could smell spaghetti bolognese or something similar while outside a piece of metal pierced the sandbags protecting the walls of the house. My right ear and my nose bled from the shattering sound - we were all numbed. The priest, undeterred by the shells exploding outside, was more concerned about his already decimated church, the result of six or so mortar or artillery shells which had been launched at the priests place of work in the past five months or so. I followed the stupid bastard out as he would be sure to get himself killed and I didn't fancy doing his next service for him!

The tower had been hit again and our dear friend was jumping up and down waving a pontificating fist at the devil Serbs up in the Malovan hills, I threw him to the ground as the shells whistled into the church. Once the skinny priest had cooled his temper at blaspheming the Serbs (he made a point of telling God that only 4% of their population were ever christened and as such they were unworthy of firing bombs on any church) I asked if he could fix me up a little breakfast - vegetarian of course.

The look was worth a thousand reigns of the Pope. The guy went off it, especially when I told him that I was a Pagan. Now to be a mad Scotsman he could relate to as he was a mad 'spaghetti eater' but that a Pagan had invaded the house of God and demanded breakfast - well the priest couldn't believe it. He was a Catholic of the old school. He checked his throat a few times to make sure that it was still intact and once satisfied that I had spared him, he sat up in the street and agreed to feed me. People began emerging from the doorway to check what the priest and I were up to. They must have been surprised to see us sat out in the road in the morning sun. The weather was glorious as the rays of the sun hit the walls of the church - a last outpost of hope in a hopeless situation.

It was then that I questioned what the hell I was doing in this land of destroyed churches and mad priests. Was I as mad as people said I was, trudging about in this war zone? I concluded I must be approaching the edge of insanity but I truly felt a kinship with the Croats and Muslims, our allies at the time. My criminal life was exhausted back in Britain and Croatia and Bosnia-Herzegovina had taken its place. Fate is fate - this was now part of me. I loved the sun drenched faces, the old and the young.... they were my reason for being here.

Yes, there I sat outside a church with a priest and he was promising to make me spaghetti and some sort of sauce...life is stranger than fiction. Once fed, I told the skinny little Italian that I was off with the other soldiers and that his food was shit. He had a fit at that... then I laughed and told him to calm down as I was only joking. We parted on good terms and arranged to talk another day; he wanted me to punish the Serbs for what they had done to his church. If there is a God then God bless that skinny priest. Up the hill again we wandered, but this time only one shell landed as we delivered the codes to our listening post on the other side of town without incident.

Finally, after successfully running the gauntlet several times between Tomislavgrad and Babice, we were positioned on the frontline. But that night, what a night to remember; the moon flitted behind the clouds creating momentary shadows, a light, cooling breeze moved nothing of any consequence, but just enough to give even the most battle weary and professional of soldiers the jitters.

All was quiet before a rustling of the undergrowth could be heard to my left, directly within my scope; a noise like that meant there was someone out there. There was movement and then silence - this could only mean that the movement was human; an animal would have carried on regardless, oblivious to the surroundings of war. A noise that becomes stationary at its point of hearing can only be a soldier; a killer with intent, or at the very least a 'spy-out' - a recce for a future attack. This night was no different and as I keened my senses, peering into the darkness and sniffing for the enemy at the same time, I listened intently. Another noise and then nothing; was an enemy out there hoping and praying not to be spotted or realised as a threat?

'Fuck You', I said, blasting the night apart - aiming roughly at the spot where I sensed his heart pounding, his sweat pouring. As I fired into the tree and bush so did the other itchy trigger fingers on the frontline, copycat fire was launched at an astonishing rate as we opened up on anything in our field of vision. Then the scream. It was a heart-rending gurgle familiar to the hardened soldier; an instinctive reaction when a man is hit. I had little envy for the Chetnik on the receiving end as at least one of my MG 42 bullets struck home as required.

Once our side had begun shooting it was difficult to call a halt to it, at least anyone out there would consider twice before continuing their 'recce'. There was no way they were coming through this sector; let them try further along the line to our left where our soldiers had an even greater advantage of height and light. Orders were carried by word of mouth to halt firing unless a definite target was identified. This was a vain hope however as the itchy fingers continued to twitch with adrenaline. Then I crawled out toward the 'scream'. A moaning sound was all that could be heard forward and to my left - a Croatian came close behind me while I tried to remember the position of our own mines.

A moan came from the trees; all that could immediately be seen was a shattered leg poking out from behind a tree. Moving on a little further I could see a Serbian sat against a tree, his limb broken and torn, protruding into the night - I signalled to the Croatian to go to the left as I moved to the right. But the Serb was going nowhere fast. His limb was shattered, blood seeping onto the forest floor. But there was little or no fear in his eyes, just a pained expression mixed with the shock of having been spotted and fired upon. My comrade brought a knife to his neck, as he looked to me for the OK to kill him.

'Let's look at him first, Ante' I said, 'then we can kill him or take him in for questioning'. I checked his condition further. Feeling his stomach I realised that the Chetnik was nearly dead in any case. Where there should have been guts there was now just a hole, his blood came in spasms and, as I felt its stickiness on my left hand, I continued to search with my right. His gun was a few metres away from where he lay, useless to him now, as I decided what to do with his life as it ebbed away through my fingers.

The Road From Jajce And Beyond

We found nothing of any consequence and decided that to move him back to our lines and then to a hospital would have been pointless and a waste of petrol, he'd be dead within hours. So a primed grenade was placed under his good leg. But he showed no fear, he understood it was his choice. It may have seemed crazy that he could have moved his leg and blown all three of us up. I told the Croatian to pull back in line with the tree and while I slid around it I took my hand away from the grenade. As we retreated we remained flat to the floor, hoping for a Serb to come back and check the booby-trapped body of his dying comrade.

It all seemed to no avail as we watched his position. Ten minutes then twenty passed and still all was quiet, not even a moan could be heard from our man by the tree. Then an eruption as the grenade exploded. It created a deafening sound in the stillness of the night. A flash of light from the tree, dust and debris filling the air - fortunately the tree had prevented shrapnel coming in our direction. So Ante and I trooped back to the lines and into the bunkers, laughing nervously at the strained sinews of war. The difference was that we were still alive while the Serb was dead. That is all that matters in war - kill or be killed. Fate and care had carried us through another night, as our eyes, ears and nerves screamed into the woods.

It was hard to sleep that early morning. The enemy's attack had failed and despite the re-assuring fact that we had seen off the Chetnik we knew that the Serb forces, intent on revenge, would probably launch a mortar attack at first light. My decision not to take a prisoner was based on two thoughts. First, the memory of the loss of 6 good soldiers on this part of the frontline only a month or so ago was still fresh in the minds of our men and they and I knew that the Serb had come from the direction of the mortar emplacement which had launched that fateful attack. The temptation of our men to prolong the suffering of any Serb would be great when one bore in mind the carnage of that particular evening. Second, I reasoned that the Serb was on death's door in any case and medical aid, a scarce enough resource for our forces, should not be wasted in vain on the enemy. So we left him to play God with his own life, allowing him to decide how much longer he wanted to reflect on it before exploding the grenade. Morning came and as expected shells rained over and upon us; the Serbs had 2 years' worth of ammunition for their mortar tubes and they were trying to avenge the loss of their man.

Once the blasting had stopped figures started to emerge from their bunkers, up and out into a sunshiny day as the mist lifted from the mountain and valley. We looked as if we were tinkers or at best a ramshackle assortment of dishevelled humanity. Fires were lit and hot water made ready for morning tea, or more likely bitter Croatian coffee.

The Silent Cry

The truck was late with the breakfast, which typically consisted of small tins of meat paste, supplemented with cheese bread, boiled eggs and jam. Our daily morning tea was red, thick and sweet but I always enjoyed the taste, especially when there was no milk to spoil it.

Soldiers chatted here and there at each campfire in a timeless morning banter that mixed relief with fear. The Ustashe, who had patrolled these hills 50 or so years before, would have gone through the same daily frontline routine. In effect we were no different from them, we just had higher calibre weapons but essentially the conversations, hopes and fears were the same.

Within two years Croatia's army could turn from defence to attack. All we needed was a reasonable stockpile of ammunition, arms and tanks. Then the Serbs would realise how lucky they had been when the odds were in their favour while the full might of the JNA had been at their disposal. The scene looked surreal, like a picnic. In small groups some of the Croatians played cards; claims of cheat could be heard as they traded German Marks. A Slovenian girl laughed as a soldier chased her into the trees and bushes near where I sat on a tree stump eating breakfast - for a brief moment life seemed wonderful.

The captain of our sector had gone to Tomislavgrad to report on that night's activities. He was a drinker and at first I had held a natural hatred for such an authority figure, but as he began to trust me I grew to like him, my heart went out to his day-to-day problems, he might have liked a drink but then so did nearly everyone on the frontline. I could make allowances for certain drink related matters after the deaths of our six colleagues on this hill a month ago. Everyone had learned the hard way from the death of their comrades - in the end it turned out to be a lesson well remembered; now they stayed in the shelters and did as they were told.

Another day done some of us headed off to bed while the rest took guard duty... and hated it. The Serb offensive continued on Babice well into the next day, making it impossible to get any sleep. Us off-duty soldiers were holed up below ground as the shells came in...

BUNKER MENTALITY

Each soldier stared into a void - perhaps into the distance and experience of their lives. Their faces spoke of the grime of war; streaked with sweat they conveyed the inhumanity of conflict. There seemed little left in life for the men in this hellhole, they had taken life so many times; what were they doing underground? The simple answer is that they, like me, were fighting for their loved ones, for the respect and right of freedom.

A metre underground the occupants of the bunker listened intently to the smash of mortar and artillery fire - the vibrations causing shock waves, a smell of cordite and smoke reaching into the bunker. We were shaken once more as a 120mm mortar landed sending dirt down into the hole; there was no fear, just an acceptance of the shelling. It was hard to hold onto this particular sense of reality after a while.

There was always the possibility of shell shock, the prospect that the lunacy of war would manifest itself and take you as a victim. Within one twenty-four hour period a soldier heard so many explosions that if you listened intently to each one you would surely turn loco; that was why a soldier had to develop a lack of fear, he had to take the fear out of his brain and resolve not to care whether he lived or died; in my own way I had come to terms with this mind-set over the month or so since my first action in Babice.

I remember walking in a wood one night while shells exploded in the branches of the trees all around me. It was then that I realised that I had become a walking zombie. True, I kept my head while others lost theirs, but to the average human being I must have seemed insane while I calmly carried out duties at which normal civilians would have balked. As ever there was a method to my madness; I realised that the break-up of Yugoslavia and the resulting wars in Croatia and Bosnia were not five month affairs like the Falklands or the Gulf War - the conflict in Croatia lasted six months, the Bosnian War three and a half years. If I were to survive in the long-term I would have to accept the daily possibility of death and ignore that which was not directly aimed at me.

HVO Special Forces had a limited range of weaponry. We did not have the arms or air support available to the SAS or US Special Forces. We were alone in every sense; satellite intelligence seemed like it was from another planet, computerised weapons systems a myth invented by Hollywood. In this way the Bosnian War was fairly basic. We killed the opposition before they killed us - every time we killed we reduced the chance of losing one of our men: it was that simple. This was the way soldiers on all sides fought - there were no complex rules to us on the ground.

Back in the waterlogged bunker we were under fierce attack. We heard a distant 'wham' before a huge and much closer 'crump, crack' shook us all - a shell landed just outside the bunker sending lumps of earth, debris and shrapnel down upon us. My right eardrum was perforated again; blood ran down my neck, I was deafened for minutes as I felt about for the lamp to check out the condition of my fellow soldiers.

A Croatian voice from outside the bunker inquired 'is all well' and as soldier by soldier we answered we felt relieved that we had escaped without casualty. Then there was total silence as the next eldest soldier after myself failed to answer. He was lightly covered by earth and as I felt for a pulse I quickly removed my fingers to see them covered in blood. He had a gash in his neck below the jaw-line and, as I shone my torch into his face, I could see that it was about eight or nine centimetres long and about three wide. Opening his left eye-lid, I discovered that his eye had rolled back in the socket and, though he was barely alive, he was clearly about to give up the ghost. A fellow soldier, Ivan, applied a padding to the wound while another went to seek a medic as I helped place the wounded man onto a stretcher.

Ivan had more reason than most to fight in this war. His wife had been one of the first victims of the Serbian onslaught against Croatia in 1991. Now he fought for all that he had left in life - his country and his freedom. He was a fit soldier; quick, authoritative and calm under pressure, he was about 24 years old and his experiences made him cold and calculated. Meanwhile the soldier's life ebbed away before our eyes. A fellow soldier will always try everything to save the life of a comrade. This is partly because it seems important to the living that they would want to receive this kind of treatment if they should ever catch a bullet. Now we scurried around the dying man, fussing over him, making sure that he knew that he was dying among his comrades and not alone.

A Morphine Syrette was plunged into his arm to ease the pain and, although he may have been dead by then, a drip was fixed to his arm when he reached the makeshift ambulance. The Syrette would accurately determine the time of death, a small consolation to his family. Meanwhile the shelling continued regardless of this drama and we forced our way back into our bunkers. Swearing and cursing in broken Croat I persuaded two of the soldiers to follow me to the mortar positions so that we could unleash our own shells on the Serb enemy. Initially my words fell on deaf ears but after a few moments of broken rhetoric a few men volunteered to follow me to the mortar emplacements. Quickly we ran up the slope and trained the mortars on the enemy, beginning a ruthless assault on their hill opposite. We were loading them quickly enough so that while one was exploding on the ground another was already following it over the two-kilometre distance to their frontline.

We had sent twenty shells or more when we realised that the Serbs were not returning fire. Minutes later I could hear shouts of excitement and it was related to me that we had intercepted a radio message to the effect that the Serbs had lost five men with another four wounded. We had caught them on the hop again - I don't think they believed that we could hit back at them so quickly. Of the shells we had fired two had scored a direct hit on the complacent enemy, while another had hit a field ambulance, which already contained some of the wounded from the original explosion, killing another two.

Was it luck? Certainly it was fortunate to be that accurate with a shell. But knowing the Serb mentality it was almost certain that a number of them were drunk on their frontline, they made many mistakes that way - lost men who would have survived if sober. Serb hatred was later directed at the deserted town of Suica - meanwhile we returned to our bunkers waiting our next turn at guard duty. Outside war continued to rage, fires blazed and tanks fired, as another day's duty came to an end.

TIME OFF

During the lulls in fighting the HVO were given a few weeks welcome leave. The free time was vital to give our brains a rest from the constant shelling, calculating and fear. On these occasions I returned to Bucici village. It is built on a slope that extends upwards toward a hill and was a peaceful place even during the war. There the smoke flickered to the sky from houses that, remarkably for Bosnia, remained intact. The houses were made from local stone hewn from a quarry a few kilometres down the road toward Mostar - Bucici made a pretty home away from home.

Another village, the name of which escapes my memory, lay to the north, its church steeple and graveyard clearly noticeable by the stark whiteness of its walls against the greenery surrounding it. A number of graves had been added to the cemetery since the start of the war. So many times had I walked in and around the place that I had come to think of both villages as home, just about all the local villagers were friendly and would do anything for you - sometimes they would overdo it. Once invited into their homes they would overfeed you in their eagerness to show appreciation, it was their way of thanking you for being there, for giving your time and, on some occasions, your blood. As any land the soil was more than eager to soak up the blood offered by civilian or soldier.

The Silent Cry

A few metres down the street stood the local school behind which the schoolmaster and his family lived. He had two teenage children; one, a cannabis-growing son, was an anti-war protestor who would complain to us about the war and killing in general. A sardonic smile would come to my lips whenever I caught the young guy going on with himself. He had an opinion that no soldier could appreciate. Within any war there is little room for this kind of sentiment but with regard to the situation in Croatia and Bosnia at the time it was, I thought, a little dangerous for a man of fighting age to share such dangerous beliefs. I believed that people in Croatia and Bosnia should defend their lands. That young guy had a mother and father, for example, and they really appreciated our efforts - they shared in the sorrow of war and took pride in the defence of their land.

During my years in Bosnia and Croatia I rarely met a man, woman or child who did not welcome me with open arms. They appreciated that I was a volunteer, knew that I was there to do what was necessary and that the volunteers were willing to shed blood so that they might live in peace. They were also aware that we were underpaid and overworked. I mixed with the locals because I needed to meet those I was risking life and limb for. The local villagers, both young and old, gave me a reason for being in their land, many other volunteers came to Bosnia out of boredom or dissatisfaction with life in their own country, there were very few who came just to kill. In the end I must have visited nearly every house in the village at some time or another, everybody knew one another and I got along with all of them.

Life was good in my lodgings above the one room school in Bucici; there was plenty of hot water and a spring that filtered down from the rocky hill behind the school into the basement. The 20 children at the school were very polite and respectful, which surprised me as a Glaswegian. They would smile as I handed out chocolate and oranges and then thank me in German - considering that they were living in a war-zone they were the best-behaved children I had ever come across.

On Sundays the local church was packed, it was almost impossible to find a space on the church steps such was the dedication of the people to their religion; it was the same at the monastery in Tomislavgrad. Loud speakers were used to convey the morning service to those unlucky enough not to get into the small chapel and it was the same wherever I went in Herzegovina. The entire population was devout a result, I understand, of the banning of religion under Communism - on most occasions I was the only non-believer in the village.

It was always sad to leave the area even for a few weeks and I would always try to obtain a few items for the locals to raise their spirits: toiletries, jewellery, perfume. I will always remember the people of Bucici, they took me in as an orphan of the conflict and all but one of them appreciated my efforts.

One early summer morning in Bucici I woke to the sound of a jeep making its way toward the house. It stopped outside in the alleyway that led to the main village further up the hill. There was some shouting outside my front door and I cautiously peered through the kitchen window. There were three HVO soldiers - two were strangers to me and another one, a German, looked worse for wear; they had all just returned from a disco in a nearby town.

The jeep finally backed-up to the building opposite, a sort of wine cellar that had been left unfinished for tax purposes. A man in a ripped uniform was man-handled out of the jeep by the three soldiers and hurled onto the loose stone chips in the road as several kicks were aimed at his head and body forcing him to curl up in a ball. His face, nose and mouth were already red with the impact of a previous 'kicking' and, as the blows continued to rain in on him, he lay there like a human football before he was dragged by his feet into the doorway of the cellar.

The man, given a few seconds respite, protested in English, he was in fact Swedish and as he feebly attempted to grip the doorframe he was finally kicked and dragged into the first of the two large rooms in the vault. I quickly dressed myself and ran across the street and into the building; the young, skinny, Swedish guy was trying to run on the spot, there was some blood on the grey, concrete wall behind him at eye level.

The German guy looked a little bewildered; it emerged that he had had a fight with the Swede a few hours earlier at the disco and was quickly sobering up at the sight of blood, a little shocked at the treatment being meted out. The Swede was naked, his clothes ripped and torn around him and he had shat himself. He hit the concrete floor as his legs were taken from him; he struggled to get up and was kicked, punched, jumped on - the crunch and crack of fractured ribs and arms as the boots rained a maelstrom of blows on his torso subduing him once more.

I waited for a lull in the violence before asking, 'what's all this about? Has he killed anybody? Is he a traitor?'

'Yeah Jock,' the German replied, seeking to justify his crony's actions, 'the bastard was giving information to the Muslims, we caught him in the act.'

I looked again. The Swede was no friend. I had spoken to him the day before and warned him to leave Bosnia. He was a drunk and had gone to the disco the night before with men who wouldn't bat an eyelid at killing their own, let alone one they suspected of conspiring with the Muslim enemy. As a result he lay curled up on the floor - both arms broken. I could do nothing to prevent his inevitable death but promised to return with a Morphine Syrette that I left on a bench outside the vault.

Meanwhile the strangers continued their work - smashing his face and body against the wall, the Swede crying for a respite, hoping to be spared. Accusations of him being a spy continued to rain in on him, he begged for a final cigarette before he died but to little avail. He finally tried to raise himself from the floor but his arm gave way on him, his broken limb piercing his forearm as he slumped to the floor. The thinner of the two strange soldiers finally relented a little and used the Morphine Syrette. The soldier struggled to find a vein before ramming the needle into the guy's arm. It looked like he would finally be unconscious, unfortunately there wasn't enough morphine to cover all the injuries he had suffered and send him into a coma. Now he was going to have to experience every painful blow before he died.

I looked on hoping that the Swede would die quickly. I wasn't convinced that he was a spy or a traitor and, as the needle was removed from his arm, the Swede called out for one last cigarette but held his arm out as if inviting another injection. The same, thinner stranger moved over to the Swede so I said 'give him another pain killer, he's in agony and the other one isn't working.'

Suddenly the larger of the two soldiers said, 'alright we'll give him another..' and without warning took a fast-bowlers run up and booted the guy again. This was ridiculous; the Swede was helpless, not even attempting to protect himself. Finally the thinner animal stopped his mate and proceeded to inject more morphine into the Swede's battered and broken body.

Resigned to the guy's fate I left the gruesome scene. Of course a reader of my role in this incident could claim that I was cold and callous. A liberal might claim that I could have intervened, risked my own reputation and accusations of traitor to save the drunken Swede.

True, there was the possibility that I could have done something, but at that stage in the war, when tensions on all sides were at a height and the threat from our estranged allies the Muslims was great, my intervention would have been seen as treachery. If there was one iota of truth in the allegations I would, by saving the guy, have invited similar punishment on myself. I have seen death in all its guises in Bosnia. The Muslims were burning and raping Croatian civilians at the time and this one guy's fate was connected to all that. This was one incident, the prolonged death of a guy that I had advised to leave town the day before, but compared to some of the worthier causes to risk a kicking for this seemed pointless.

A little later, while I lay in my bath, voices could be heard again before the jeep roared away. I took my time, looked again at the scars and wounds on my body and thought myself lucky in war, the fates must be with me. Eventually I went over to the building again. There was little evidence of what had taken place, a little blood on the floor, but all four men had disappeared.

A day or so later I found out from the remorseful young German that the torture had only really begun when I had left. The two strangers throttled the Swede with a rope until he was blue in the face, his eyes bulging and starting to bleed. His face, already cut and bleeding, was pounded again before he was executed, without the benefit of a court-martial. I walked with the German kid over the hill as he related the whole thing to me again. The Swede's final half-hour was gruesome; the two strangers had attempted to garrotte him but still he moaned and grunted with life. Frustrated, the two strangers laid out a tarpaulin in the back of the jeep and lifted the Swede's cold and battered body onto it. They took him to a grave, a little way along a track off the main road. He was still alive.

The German pointed out the whereabouts of a makeshift grave which would go unnoticed to passing traffic - these men, cold and murderous as they were, must have been professional killers. A year or so later, while we were fighting the Muslims in Gornji Vakuf, the young German responsible for the Swede's death (if not every injury he suffered) was fatally wounded in the head and died after a long struggle in Split hospital. Was it justice that that bullet had sought him out? Sure he was a good kid at heart but circumstances had overtaken him after his drunken fight with the Swede.

Rumour has it that the other two soldiers also died. The skinnier guy was stabbed to death and burned to ashes in a house near Gornji Vakuf. The larger of the two was knocked unconscious and trussed up like a chicken by a Muslim brigade. His eyes blinded by acid he was apparently dragged behind enemy lines and tied to a tree. When he was found both feet had been bayoneted and a message left next to him in Croatian to the effect that this was his punishment for killing and raping.

True or not, fate has a way of catching up with you. The three perpetrators followed the Swede to an early grave - the Swede, by the way, was said to have been buried alive although his body has since been exhumed and returned to his family. I remain the sole witness to those events, a gruesome example of what can happen when soldiers turn on one another and an example of the particular tensions between foreigner volunteers in this war.

In the breaks in the fighting and during our time-off, the HVO soldiers used to congregate in a Muslim run cafe-bar in Tomislavgrad. It was a stop for all kinds of characters, the kind of opportunists war attracts. Sitting in the local bar/brothel were a few foreign nationals. I was in deep conversation with Klaus 'the man from Berlin'. A thickset German he professed to be an explosives expert but I knew differently. Indeed I had probably known more about explosives while I was a 15 year-old boy soldier with the Royal Engineers bomb disposal unit in Chatham, Kent than he knew then.

Klaus was not your average German soldier. They were typically eager and capable, with little or no real fear. Klaus, on the other hand, was a bit of a con man with a work-shy attitude. After a few drinks his lack of knowledge shone through. His tongue loosened, he started to ask me about how to construct a Claymore mine and how best to lay it as a booby trap instead of operating it by manual control - this was basic explosives knowledge and too much for me; here was a guy who had professed to be an expert and who had been teaching Croatian soldiers the highly dangerous art of laying explosives.

As it turned out Klaus had gleaned an inkling about explosives from some American soldiers stationed in West Berlin many years prior. He had bluffed his way into the Croatian army and always made himself unavailable each and every time that he was asked to go to the frontline to lay mines and Claymores. In reality Klaus was a hazard and a real danger to his own men. After this conversation I let it be known that he was a rank amateur.

A few days later I escorted him to the outskirts of Tomislavgrad to see how he performed setting-up a practice trip-wire Claymore having explained to him how to do it. I had to tell him to rig it up with a live detonator as a practical trial but the fool started to connect a live homemade Claymore and even then he got it wrong - I quickly disconnected it to save both our lives.

He soon understood the effects of implosion (an explosion having a greater effect the tighter the casing) understood that is after I had shown him in a real-life demonstration. I was hopeful at one stage that Klaus would keep close to the trip-wire to which I had attached a length of wire so that the mine could be detonated at long range. My German friend declined my offer to trip the wire at close-quarters. In his own way Klaus was alright even though he was obviously a con man. After his lessons in mines and anti-tamper devices we returned to the bar and his interest turned to the barmaids who doubled as prostitutes at a basic DM 40 per twenty-minute session. There was negotiation and laughter as to what some men wanted - Klaus became a little angry when one of our men, quite correctly, told the barmaid that the German was likely to explode a little prematurely.

The Road From Jajce And Beyond

I had met Klaus just once before when he had butted-in on a conversation I was having with Colonel Brown, owner of the American 'Soldier of Fortune' magazine. A former US Special Forces officer and ex-Foreign Legionnaire, the Colonel was a good guy and helpful in his own way, so I passed an hour or so with him sitting at the same local bar. As an acquaintance of our own commander I'd been asked to accompany him if and when our own Colonel was called away to Zagreb.

Klaus took offence at our chat saying that I was talking too much about the Croatian 'military', inferring that I was passing on secrets to an American. Quickly I dragged Klaus out of a side-door of the hotel and put a knife to his throat before he had had a chance to blink. He was shocked at the ease with which I had dragged him from the bar with one arm (the one that had been wounded on two separate occasions). I was tempted to cut his throat but, as I pressed the blade against his flesh I quickly calmed down and put it away as the Colonel told me not to bother on his behalf - but there was no way I would allow the American to be insulted as if he were a spy. The Colonel was well capable of looking after Klaus himself but I acted out of respect for a man who had been through it all. Respect was his due.

It was in this same cafe bar that I met a local girl called Almira. She was a slim girl of about 26 and we developed a relationship during the lulls in fighting. Our initial courtship was difficult. She spoke little English in public, but seemed to know more than she let on in private and day-by-day our conversations improved.

For a number of months we exchanged trivialities and generalities with each other, about the war and the way things were going. Almira was always cagey in her responses, preferring to whisper her thoughts and beliefs in public. She was a Muslim originally from Jajce but had left at the start of the Serb onslaught. Gradually we became involved. It was almost as if the pair of us clung to each other after being thrown in the deep-end. We needed the comfort of one another, the company and conversation was a way of escape from the war and the threat to both our lives.

But we also knew that the war was about much more than survival. We loved life, enjoyed freedom and talked about our hopes and fears - our relationship continued like this for some months. Some months later, after a lengthy absence, I met Almira at the cafe just before I was due to head back to see my family in England and sensed that something was wrong. She was not herself and, as I sat with my back to a wall trying to make pleasant conversation she tried to avoid eye contact, lowering her head as if she were ashamed. After a few minutes of a one-way conversation she ran into the back room of the cafe.

I looked at the Albanian cafe-owner, a friendly character that had taken to me from the first time I set foot in his bar. He grimaced back at me, 'Problema Scot, big problema'. He spoke quietly to me and put his right index finger to his lips. 'Come back later when Almira is gone. I will tell you all about it' was all he was willing to venture. I returned later when I knew her shift was over and the Albanian took me into his office in the back and sat me down with a pot of coffee and a glass of water.

He looked serious, there had been a terrible incident and, even now five or so years later, it still pains me to recall it. Almira had gone up to Bugojna to see some friends and there had been an incident. She had been raped. By whom she didn't know or wouldn't say, and now she was in despair, at a loss as to what to do about it.

Immediately I felt a twinge in my heart as my mind searched for an answer, conveniently falling on a simple act of revenge - resolving to make the rapist pay with his life. The cafe owner, Almira's uncle, reached out and put his hand on my shoulder and after a few minutes I had recovered slightly and left the cafe in a daze. I went for a walk, turning the event over in my mind, thinking about the incident, trying to come to terms with her feelings and what I should do - before I knew it I'd walked the 18 kilometres from Tomislavgrad to Bucici, the village where I lived. The next few days, before my return to England, I attempted to contact Almira but to no avail, it would be January before I returned.

I searched for Almira again when I returned and finally got to speak to her privately on her bus home from work. Immediately she broke down in tears and I held her to me, but all I could get out of her was 'no possible, no possible'.

Her life, like mine on previous occasions, had been ripped apart. It was impossible for her to think of the future even though I tried. I explained that we could both go to Scotland, there would be no problems for us there, no shame, we would be just two people in a country where all people are respected. She was having none of it and said that she would bring great shame on me, pointing to her stomach - then it hit me like a ton of bricks. She had not only been raped but was pregnant because of it. I was at a loss once more, my head spinning as she gasped and sobbed.

Another few hundred metres on and the bus stopped and we both got off. As it sped away I held her again but she tried to struggle free and eventually started to walk away. I called to her that we should talk it out but she continued on. My mind was in a whirl thinking about what to do, I stood at the roadside and thought before returning to Tomislavgrad. In reality there was little I could do. She didn't want me to go after the guy or guys who had done it and wanted to forget all about it - so I tried to by taking my revenge out on the enemy.

In reality my relationship with Almira was made impossible by the situation at the time. As Croat and Muslim forces turned on each other there was little long-term hope for us in Tomislavgrad - we belonged, whether we wanted to believe it or not, to different sides.

3 - THE SILENT CRY

By January 1993 the former allies, Croatia and Bosnia, were waging a full-scale war against one another. Matters were not helped by the recriminations following the fall of Jajce (where both sides claimed that the other had betrayed them) or the sketchy terms laid out in the Vance-Owen peace plan. Under that plan Croatia was offered Herzegovina in the southwest of Bosnia, roughly the area of the self-declared Independent state of Herceg-Bosna, or 27% of Bosnia as a whole. The Serbs were offered about half Bosnia territory, even though they had only a 34% share of the population, leaving the Bosnian Muslims (the most numerous group in Bosnia) with less than a quarter of their Independent state. Effectively the 'peace-plan' led to more intense fighting as the forces of all three sides attempted to secure more territory before renegotiating the terms of the agreement.

The Croats were the most pleased party of the three and accepted the geographical agreement, the cease-fire conditions and the plans to demilitarise the area within weeks. The Serbs remained defiant however, clinging to their long held belief that Bosnia remained a part of 'Greater Serbia' while the Bosnian government had most cause for complaint as it lost more than half its territory to what it maintained were 'invading forces'. By the New Year John MacPhee had joined Bosnian Croatian Special Forces and was ordered into the fighting near Gornji Vakuf, an area that later became synonymous with some of the worst excesses of ethnic cleansing.

All hell had finally broken loose since the Prozor flare-up in October - three of us, all of course volunteers, got a lift from Command Headquarters in Tomislavgrad to Congorji at the base of the hills and from the first HVO checkpoint we began our journey by thumbing a lift.

I told the MP at the checkpoint that one of our number, an English volunteer called Tommy, had a drink problem - I was only joking but within seconds of me relating this guy's weakness for drink, the guards they were showing Tommy into a hut. The checkpoint MPs had brewed their own particular form of Vodka called Rakija; it was a renowned cure-all for the Herzegovina locals. Minutes later Tommy emerged coughing and spluttering from the hut to the general amusement of us all - he'd been forced to down a spectacular amount of the brew and was staggering around trying to regain his breath and curse me at the same time.

Our second form of transport arrived shortly after. It was a small white Renault whose driver looked a little reluctant to help us out. But the HVO guard was soon inspiring the driver with Croat rhetoric that left him in little doubt that it was his national duty to help us reach Gornji Vakuf. In truth the road to Gornji Vakuf was going to be a nightmare for him either way - it twisted and turned through the mountains of Central Bosnia with the constant threat of sniper fire and or shelling.

At last the guy reluctantly agreed and the three of us wedged ourselves into the tiny car, each of us loaded with weaponry - a lethal arsenal that would terrorise Attila the Hun. Guns, grenades, rocket launchers and some spare ammunition took up the space in the car originally intended to carry families and shopping. The two volunteers with me - Tommy (still recovering from his drink) and Wilfey were reliable types, both had trained in the British Army and were conscientious in battle. So, as the journey continued up the hill, we entered into banter before I realised that we were not moving.

The car, weighed down with a ton of ammo, ground to a halt - so I got out and, despite my health problems, decided to run up the hill and wait for the car there. The two Englishmen meanwhile were 'volunteered' by me to push the car up the hill. I clambered in again and the car seemed to have adjusted to our weight at last as it zigzagged through the mountain passes without a problem. We passed convoy after convoy of food and medical supplies as they made their way toward central Bosnia. The roads in central Bosnia were the arteries of the people - during the war it was the only way to get aid to villagers cut off from the rest of humanity. Yet there was a beautifully sinister feel to the mountain roads that day as all three of us (and especially the civilian driver) remained aware of the possibility of a Muslim ambush. The Vance-Owen 'peace' plan was foremost in people's minds up here and they were prepared to attack anything - a little white car would make an easy target.

Soon we passed the British UN base in the hills. HVO soldiers were particularly jealous of the luxurious conditions and rations afforded the UN presence in Bosnia - but their position during the conflict always seemed confused. They could neither defend nor attack, I felt no animosity toward them - they only annoyed me when their trucks got in the way. We drove on, past dark, foreboding woods that would surely contain enemy forces (Muslim extremists had ambushed four of our men up here a few months before) toward the lakes of Rama before we briefly halted at a checkpoint just outside the woods.

The Silent Cry

The views overlooking the lake are spectacular, reminiscent of Scottish lochs and the English Lake District - even in the middle of a war they offered a distraction. On we drove along the perilously high mountain track, a treacherous journey made worse by the need to overtake slow trucks before we finally reached Rumboci, a large village with white, red tiled houses dotted over the mountainside. The guards on the checkpoint were nervy. They stared at our 'military' vehicle with a mixture of amusement and fear, took our military passes and phoned through to Tomislavgrad to confirm we were HVO. After a tense ten minute wait the commander returned shouting 'Scotlanda go!'

A little later we approached Gornji Vakuf with heavy hearts. There had been rumours of the extent of the brutality and animalism in the Bosnian hinterland and I don't think I ever truly thought about it, but now we were here you could sense that the area was rife with the scent of revenge and human decay. Looking down and to our right we could see a small village that had recently been destroyed. Some buildings were completely gutted by mortar shells, from a distance you could see the thousands of pockmarks made by bullets and shells, there were so many roofs destroyed that it was easier to count the houses still standing. What a dismal day, I thought; smoke trailed the air, some of it wispy, some of it charring the overcast sky and suspending a haze over the area. A light rain also fell on the village, merely adding to the gloom.

HVO forces had reached the village in great numbers and were stood watching fifteen refugees as they in turn watched the ruins of their village. We drew slowly to a halt near to a group of nine or so civilians; men, women and children with strained faces and an air of hopelessness, they were a mix of Croatians and Muslims.

Our immediate attention had been diverted from the town of Gornji Vakuf to this small village on its outskirts. We had travelled from Tomislavgrad swapping banter and jokes - but there was no laughter now. The group of villagers were standing around a young girl and as I eased my way into the group I could see she was lying on a number of drab, torn blankets. It seemed that an ambulance was on its way from Rumboci hospital, but one look would tell anyone that it was too late.

I reached down and lifted the girl into my arms, her blood seeping onto my camouflaged uniform. She might have been 7 years old, and in appearance she looked almost Scottish - she had long, fair hair and a freckled face. A pulse was barely discernible from her limp wrist as blood seeped from her ears and nose - her face pale and devoid of life. I took her into a dimly lit room in a ruined house nearby. My gun slung over my shoulder, I entered the sparse room and laid the child on the bed; the room testified to her family's grim existence - these people seemed to be stymied by a higher force, unable to break out of 50 years poverty which had culminated in war.

The child lay upon a patchwork quilt covered by my camouflage jacket. She was surrounded by her family as I watched trying to hold back a tear. Briefly her eyes opened, the lids fluttered before she finally passed away - I only hoped that she thought she was passing into sleep. Around me the old and young of the village looked like they were used to the pain of death. Loss had visited their village so many times over the past months that another seemed inevitable to them. Theirs was an ingrained, experienced pain the like of which I had never seen or, should I say, sensed before.

For me the war was a simple matter of kill or be killed. For the grieving villagers the war was a battle for a different kind of survival; they knew only the pain of suffering, starvation and the death of their sons and daughters, mothers and fathers. Did these people ever know a smile of happiness or laughter? They were certainly steeped in the ways of 'Balkan' madness - it seemed commonplace to them as they stood grieving another death.

Croat tears have been shed so many times in that nation's war-torn history that it is no wonder that as a people they are God-fearing Catholics. And, as they surrounded the bed, clasping their hands in tearful prayer, I was handed my jacket. I turned to leave when a Croatian girl, who could have been the elder sister of the dead child, pulled my arm and through tearful, pleading eyes said 'my name is Ivana. Go out and kill those who have done this'. For once I was lost for words. There was little else to do so I nodded and left vowing to avenge the girl's death. But first we had our orders. We pushed on towards Gornji Vakuf with instructions to force the enemy Bosnian forces beyond the town. Their 17th corps had been released from the Serb concentration camps and fed hatred and revenge directed by misleading propaganda. As a result the most distressing factor in this region remained the inhumanity with which our new enemy treated civilians.

This changed many mild-mannered Croatian soldiers into animals - the death and mutilation of children, old men, women and whole families was not unusual. True, many of the deaths were caused by incidental artillery or gunfire, but in other cases the treatment meted out seemed entirely out of proportion to the grievances of the enemy. During this period ethnic cleansing appeared to become a military aim for certain Muslim elements. Day and night villages were shelled incessantly as people hid in cellars or behind sandbags and logs.

That night however we returned to our base, a school converted into a hospital-cum-Special Forces barracks. I thought of the girl again -

The Silent Cry

she and other young victims like her could have received their education in that building, could have played in the playground, perhaps could have helped restore peace and prosperity to their land after the war. Instead she was just another innocent victim of this depressing war.

But worse was to come. As a Special Forces soldier it was my duty to command groups into areas only recently vacated by the retreating Muslim army - one such patrol took us to a hamlet near Gornji Vakuf...
We had worked our way steadily toward the edge of some woods near a rocky covering. Underbrush covered much of the ground as we kept watch before moving as quickly as possible closer to the burning village while one of our men covered the 12 houses for a sign of the enemy.

I was in charge of a squad of eager Croatian soldiers, but this was one mission I could well have done without. As a soldier one accepts the possible consequences of war - seeing the death of a comrade-in-arms is disturbing but inevitable. The death of an enemy soldier makes one smile nervously; it isn't so much a matter of being genuinely pleased, more a sense of relief that it wasn't you.

But what we were about to witness was something entirely different. As I approached the village I could smell death, sense the genetic memory of decay. Nearing the houses I could see the bluebottles and maggots, the eerie quiet broken by the occasional buzz of an insect - nature's embalmers here to claim their bounty. Stinking, rotting flesh was everywhere. Nature, birth or beauty never was - one house was left standing in the hamlet, in it were piled 37 dead bodies. The other houses were smouldering, razed to the ground.

As I approached the house the scene made me retch. The other soldiers following me ran from the dilapidated house and were sick themselves, turning back I regained a little composure and assessed the situation. The thirty-seven bodies were piled up in three separate rooms. A baby in a makeshift peasant cot had had its throat slashed, its neck hanging by a strand of muscle. Children from four to five were torn to pieces - raped. An old man lay in the doorway of the house, his left leg shattered, the sharp point of a broken bone piercing his skin and muscle.

'Good God' I cried 'for what, for why?' My belief had gone as I screamed at my comrades to find the enemy who had done this. I quickly realised that I needed to get my act together, after all I was leading this patrol into hell - but despite my attempts to calm down there was no professionalism about me now.

Children lay torn to pieces at my feet, as my thoughts turned to the enemy - they must suffer I told myself, as my heart pounded at my chest with a rhythm that sounded like 'kill, kill, kill'. My eyes pained as did my chest, my simple fuckin' brain, through all of this I could hear vomiting outside.

I had crossed a divide. I hadn't witnessed this kind of revenge killing in all my years in Afghanistan and Cambodia; even in those countries I never witnessed the sight of 37 deliberately raped civilians. Lifting my torch I shone it further into the house and went toward the bodies of two mutilated children, covering the corpses with a bed cover I was now on autopilot as I ordered a young Croatian to burn the house.

Then two enemy soldiers were captured. Guilty or innocent I knew that they had to die. I fixed my bayonet and before I knew it one of them was beneath me in the death throes. My hand was ripping at his flesh, my fingers gouging his eyes, I was becoming worse than an animal - survival and death was my goal, my aim to kill and go on. I bit into his face, blood poured down my chin, my 18 inch killing knife stabbed and chopped and slashed, I, no better than they in my rage.

I speared my bayonet into his neck one final time and lifted his quivering body into the air with such force that it broke the bayonet, his body finally slumping to the floor in a gory mass of blood and teeth marks. They shot the other enemy soldier before I could lay a hand on him. The other soldiers confronted me as I sat slumped by the dead Muslim, covered in blood and gore. But I was lost to the world, amazed at the depths to which this war had dragged me.

Getting up again I walked back to the house and set it alight, a little of my soul burning as the flames consumed man's inhumanity to man. It was then that I realised that my hands and face were covered with blood. I tasted it on my tongue where my teeth had ripped into his face: I was delirious.

What was there in life for me now? I thought as I came around in hospital a little later. I could write about the experience but how could I come to terms with such a savage incident in my mind. I have thought about this incident many times in the intervening years. Often I regret losing my cool, more out of the need to accurately assess the situation and report it to the UN War Crimes Tribunal than out of sorrow for the Muslim soldier I maimed.

The scene was horrific and had a great impact on me during the remainder of the conflict. Again, like my first action in Babice, it was a form of initiation into the war. It was the first time I had witnessed this particular form of extreme violence and mutilation against innocent civilians. In other wars there have been innocent victims, but in Bosnia the crimes against humanity had an intensity and wilfulness about them that defied normal belief. That day in the village near Gornji Vakuf changed my outlook not just on the war but also on human existence itself. Croatians were butchered for no other reason than the fact that they were Croatian.

It's true that as the house burned a little of my soul burned with it - the scene of carnage could never be witnessed, the victims had already been brutally murdered, I felt they should at least leave the planet with a little dignity.

The bloodletting continued into the spring of 1993. As a result HVO soldiers were ordered into Central Bosnia to clear up the dead and dying...

We wore surgical masks as we lifted the bodies from the truck; moving the stench of rotting, decomposed corpses was a gruesome chore that even the most cold-blooded of us found tremendously difficult to bear - how could any human stand it? An undertaker would balk at such a task. Some locals watched us, numbed and shocked by all they saw - as they tried to recognise their own flesh and blood as we laid the bodies in rows for identification.

We were up in Konjic, South-East of Prozor, where Muslims had massacred a number of civilians and these were Croatian dead. They had also been mutilated. Once a Serb prisoner had told me, during his detention at Tomislavgrad hospital, that if I thought that the Serbs were animals I should wait and see the work of Muslim extremists. At the time I thought this was another piece of Serb propaganda designed to drive a wedge between us and our then allies the Muslims.

But I also knew of the history of the Ottoman Empire and its killing machine throughout the hundreds of years of occupation of these lands. They had massacred Serbs and Croatians during uprisings and now, it seemed to me, their barbarous culture was visiting the 20th century. The Arab world had also suffered at the hands of the Ottoman Empire - their Sultans and Pashas. The Serbian people had lived with these fears for years and you could see the results in Konjic. The Muslim influence was all around. They had desecrated Yugoslavia; it didn't seem to matter to the Muslims whether the victims were Croatian, Serbian or Montenegrin.

The villages in the Konjic region counted their victims now. At Kruscia upwards of 50 dead lay about - butchered, tortured, raped - the evidence gathered by Croatian Medical and other staffs attests to such, it is undeniable; the graves attest to such; the word of mouth evidence supports these claims; it is enough to make any civilized person's blood run cold, make them shiver at the merest thought.

A list was posted in the HVO command centre that totalled the estimated number of Croatian civilians murdered, dead or missing.

PODHUM	100
GORA	100
KALE	120
JASENIK	100-150
BARE	NOT YET KNOWN
SLAKOVICI	" " "
DOBVILEVIC	" " "
ORLISTE	" " "
MRKOSOVICE	" " "
LUKSIJE	" " "
BUSCAK	150
TARCIN	POW's held in grain silos by Bosnian Army

So many deaths and I was there as the list came over our command radio; our commander related and wrote on the blackboard as to place and estimate the dead and missing. As the HVO retook villages mainly populated by Croatians we discovered more butchery. Initially the Serbians had been driven out or wisely left of their own accord - then it was the turn of the Croatians to be driven out and ethnically cleansed by Bosnian forces. By the time we returned there was little trace of human life, just a pile of rotting, mutilated corpses and rows of burnt houses.

We moved out into Central Bosnia to clear up more of our dead. We came across another ethnically cleansed village - a small hamlet near Konjic called Gora. As we approached we remained extremely cautious, there was a high probability that the buildings were booby-trapped or that the road was mined - the Bosnian Muslim army had large supplies of explosives.

Looking down was a nerve-wracking experience however as we were unsure whether there were any enemy left in the village. Hell, for the umpteenth time, visited my senses - the reality repeated itself - new images made for my future nightmares. Tears came no more for my mind had hardened itself beyond belief - yet I was not cold enough to keep out all the atrocities that were before me now.

We fanned out, watchful and wary of what lay in store for us in the village. Each building was barricaded in, it turned out, a futile attempt on the civilians part to protect themselves from the onslaught. To no avail, the slaughter, hatred and mayhem had continued despite their attempts - the thirst for blood satiated again.

Smouldering beams of wood and other debris were noticeable to us all as we searched over each remnant for signs of life, looking in the hope that a child might have escaped to live through this nightmare. But even the survival of a single child would have been a double-edged sword;

what was there for him or her to live for - in the event there were no survivors. Our faces were as grim as the reaper that had recently visited the village, that had bludgeoned more lives in Bosnia. Some bodies lay naked and blackened by mud and flames; it had recently rained and the houses were smouldering rather than burning - the wind was also building, blowing into our faces and adding to the miserable scene we witnessed.

Who were we to be alive when all about the innocents died? On we searched in hope, against expectation. Animals lay about - dogs and pigs had been hacked to death, their entrails hanging at their sides, their innocent brains smashed to pulp. There were no chickens, which was unusual in a village like this but what constituted 'normal' was open to debate, the dogs had been wounded before they were killed - the pigs brutalised like the people, tortured and killed.

Again I thought no true Muslim would do such a thing, there were sick, sick minds at work - even hatred did not justify this destruction. True, I had once seen a Croatian soldier shoot a dog and that had shocked me, but never did a Croat kill an animal without good reason. Dogs in war were dangerous, as on that occasion the animal had, in its innocence, brought attention to our position and had to be shot so that we wouldn't be.

Charred burned-out houses were all about, only a few had been left standing. The few left untouched were undoubtedly Muslim homes, and there was no doubt that, innocent or guilty, they would have been wise to have left by now. We brought the bodies together for either burial or transportation. If we buried them here the chances were that the same Muslims would return and desecrate the remains - this, after all, was not war but deliberate genocide. I looked at my fellow soldiers and saw the pain in their eyes as they tried to keep a grip. The losses were felt by all of us, but more especially by them - they were burying their own kin, Croatian civilians.

A few of them had tears running down their faces. Realising the difficulty they were having a German volunteer called Hans announced, 'Helmut, Scot, we three shall set out the dead while the others guard the perimeter of the village'. Both Helmut and I nodded and grimaced in Hans's direction - there was nowhere to run and hide for us now as we went about our morbid work. We just had to blank our minds from the scene, move the bodies to one place and pretend that they were not human, which was impossible of course.

I picked up a child and it seemed to breath. Of course she wasn't alive, it was gas coming from her stomach and through her mouth, a putrid smell that made me feel sick. I returned to another house and saw a baby of a few months old with its mother. The mother was half-lying under a smashed door; she had probably been trying to protect the baby as the door was smashed in, hitting them both at the same time. It seemed strange to me and I began to look at the situation like a forensic scientist, attempting to piece together what had happened.

My inner-will was protecting me from the reality of the situation by now. I remembered a book I studied while in Long Lartin prison in Worcester. It was called the 'Anatomy of Human Destructiveness'. All this was a way of distracting myself while I attempted to control my emotions but it didn't work and still hasn't (my eyes are filling up as I recall these events years later). I wrapped the baby in a burnt towel and set it beside the other bodies. Hans put his arm around me and said 'John, leave it to Helmut and me. I shall take care of the dead - you go with the others - it is best, you have seen too much since you've been here'. But I insisted, 'No, Hans, I'll help you. It's bad for all of us, I can see it in your eyes'. So we carried on with our grim chore. We performed robotically, bringing body after body to the site, the rain washing off the blood and mud. Brothers were rested next to sisters, mothers next to fathers and grand parents before finally we had finished. Helmut and Hans brought blankets to cover the bodies as best they could.

Then a noise could be heard from between two of the houses, I lifted my gun. In a split second I realised that it was one of our own soldiers, a very tall Croatian guy called Draga walking in a trance-like state, his AK trailing in the mud and the blood by his side, the strap broken. The rain intensified as I looked at Draga. He stared at me in hope, but I shook my head communicating silently to him - 'no Draga there were no survivors'. He fell to his knees and began to pray. For some reason he knelt beside the woman and baby that I had taken from inside the wrecked house that had barely been touched by fire or bullets. He mumbled in Croatian as another Croat came over and led me away from the carnage. 'He' the Croatian started, 'he back there, Draga, was brought up as a child by the woman - it was his close friend's wife. The husband is killed by Serbs whilst defending Muslims at Mostar... now he sees baby and woman murdered by Muslims!'

Hell, what could I say in such circumstances. It was useless, these Croats felt more pain than I could in such circumstances. There were upwards of fifty bodies. 'Not one a soldier' I thought aloud. 'What you say, Scot?' asked the guy beside me who I didn't know that well. 'Nothing' I replied. 'OK' he said and we quickly set about taking up better positions while we waited for the trucks to take the bodies away.

Radio contact was established and we were told the transport would take an hour to reach us. It was a wise move to take the bodies from the village to be buried behind our own lines. Turning I saw Draga still on his knees, now making the sign of the cross and ripping the chain from his own neck. For some reason I remember a link of the gold chain flying off into a puddle as he wrenched it from his neck. He placed the cross under the towel on the baby's chest, looked for some moments before covering the baby up again.

None of these guys wanted medals - this was not the well-organised and well-equipped British Army. We had no medical back up or helicopters. Only at the very end of the war were we offered air support once the HV (regular Croatian forces) had grown in sophistication with American help. In 1993 it was a matter of survival - to try and retain some state of humanity, so that we could possibly live with ourselves after it was all over. The war in Croatia and Bosnia meant that men's souls became forfeited for the armed struggle which, in reality, all sides lost regardless of nationality.

Presently the jeep arrived to cart off the corpses. Helmut, Hans and I did not return with the others but decided to stay and ambush those who had done this to our people. We borrowed a jeep - a Russian one armed with a mounted .50 calibre Browning. Getting our own back on the forces who had perpetrated such an act was foremost in our minds - the temptation was in our minds to even the score on a Muslim village but we knew that that would be worse than what they had done. We would only kill their soldiers. Hopefully we would get one of those responsible for this act in a nearby village. From now on this would be as it should be - no prisoners taken - a fight to the death, the enemy's or ours.

The Croatians in the main were far too Godly and civilised - there was too much honour riding on the whole conflict for them to hit back like this so we, the foreign volunteers, did it. Time after time I saw Croats save fearful Muslim civilians as they ran about in Mostar while shells fell and bullets searched for targets. Always it seemed to be an old Muslim guy of about 80 who was saved by a HVO soldier risking life and limb to run out in the open and pull him back from the brink - Croats were too brave to know any different.

AHMICI

The Muslim cause, by this time, had attracted the support of the West and Middle East - as a result the Bosnian army felt confident enough to take on the Croats (if not the Serbs) and fought tooth and nail to retain disputed territory in their central Bosnian strongholds. A particularly contested area between Vitez and Kiseljak led to reports of both Muslims and Croats taking part in 'freelance ethnic cleansing', action stimulated by the Vance-Owen plan. But Central Bosnia was also of interest to the Serbs in 1993 who prospered from the Croat-Muslim enmity. From their stronghold further north in Banja Luka they had pushed south in 1992. Now, however, both Muslim and Croat forces had arrived in strength and the Serbs were largely outnumbered but that isn't to say they were disinterested in the conflict...

I was patrolling in Kiseljak not far from a village called Ahmici. Our task was to recce the area and assess the strength of the two enemy forces, a task that soon became an exercise in survival...

Shots came toward where we lay. There was no return fire from us, we just waited as I watched trying to fix the enemy positions. Being outnumbered, the greatest care was being taken. Eight or nine Serbs lay out there although two of their number had already bitten the dust. Yet still that did not deter them, they were as experienced as any soldiers in this war, regardless of two of their number having already paid the ultimate price for the laughter they had given when we ambushed them several minutes ago. Shouts could be heard from the Serbs as they started their outflanking moves to left and right, edging ever closer.

We knew they were well equipped as we could hear the crackle of their radio. We also knew that regardless of our own radio communications we could not call upon air support or a helicopter airlift to take us out of this mountain forest - we were out on our own! We were several kilometres beyond Kiseljak and possibly two or three kilometres from the village of Ahmici (which has since become infamous for the alleged killing by Croats of Muslim soldiers and civilians).

An hour or so before our ambush of the Serbs we had come from that direction and heard explosions in the distance as we traversed the forest floor while continually watching for booby traps and mines (all but an impossibility at times). Our going had been tough - in keeping with the HVO motto 'Rougher than Rough and Tougher than Tough' and hell, we had to be as we trekked up and down those hills.

When we had ambushed the enemy it had happened all of a sudden - it took place with an abruptness and, (hardly a minute or so before we struck) trees and undergrowth had delayed our positioning and prevented us from having any great advantage other than surprise. And, although trees covered us from return fire, the enemy also had those same advantages. So as relaxed laughter continued to come from the enemy we waited; our itchy fingers trembling upon the triggers of our AK 47s.

I privately estimated that there were ten or more as we gently squeezed our triggers second-by-second; a coldness flashed my skin as beads of sweat broke out upon my forehead. Another minute passed and then all hell broke out within our small neck of the woods. Blast after blast could be heard as bullets whacked into the first two soldiers who were almost upon us several metres away. The whack of bullets scored into the trees out there, while our enemy recovered from the initial shock of ambush.

An English volunteer soldier, Wilfey, lay a little to my right. He had cut down the first Serb and shot him to pieces with a burst of automatic fire from his RPK light-machine gun. All four of us (two Croatians, Wilfey and myself) gave it to what we were to moments later discover to be Chetniks - die-hard, experienced soldiers that you normally never meet. Anyone would be forced to respect their ferocity and unbelievable determination.

One other Chetnik had dropped dead with bullets from all four of us - another was possibly wounded - his scream was evidence of such. Our mini-fire fight really took off now as we were being forced back toward the edge of the wood. We could not afford to be there as once we were out in the open we would be doomed for sure with the probability that Serb reinforcements would come to the Chetniks' aid - we were most definitely on our own without a hope of outside assistance.

Now at least two RPKs were barking their metal at us while 7.62s began raking at us and the trees and bushes we crouched behind. 'Shit'. The ambush had reversed on us - then out of madness or plain stupidity all four us opened up on our enemy; blasting their approximate position in an attempt to stem the charge. Really we knew we were 'in it' this time and had to bring it to this, to give us any chance of escape - capture was an alternative we all knew was out of the question.

Initially we forced the Chetniks back thirty metres or so then they held fast, recuperated before they shot us up once more, in an attempt to keep us tied down. Our ammunition was diminishing fast so we knew that our escape had to be quick to alleviate us from this predicament. Reflecting on our error I realised that there was no way we should have ambushed men in such numbers. They were in such a thickly wooded area, but it had all happened so quickly that our decision was made without due care and we all now assumed that we were about to pay the price for our over eagerness.

One Chetnik called out to us to surrender and said that we would be treated fairly under the terms of the 'Geneva Convention', which prompted a little morbid laughter from his colleagues out there. A rustling of leaves could be heard as two or more of their number began outflanking us.

'Zjelko, Zjelko' I whispered over to my left and some metres forward, 'they're on the move to your left'.

'Ok, Ok Scot I'm on to them', he replied

'Englishman' I called to Wilfey.

'I know Jock. They know we're foreigners talking about the Geneva Convention' he replied.

'Hah, hah Wilfey and you believe them?'

'No fuckin' way - they'll cut our balls off'

'Hey Wilfey boy - have you got any!' I shouted back - laughter came over to us from the Chetniks.

'Iz good English - Geneva Convention iz good by Chetniks... You believe us, Croats lie to you'.

Our two Croatians laughed loudly. It did not matter that we were giving our positions away, the enemy knew where we were, those bastards could tell from which direction you breathed. No one underestimated the guile, cunning and deviousness of the Chetniks and their innate ability to kill - as adversaries they were mean and more than capable. 'Whack' a bullet flew inches away from my neck as if to support this last thought, as down I went onto the forest floor hugging the ground; wanting to bury myself deep and hide forever, wishing I was far from these woods, a million miles from the madness of the hills, mountains and lakes and within the safety of a stinking concrete jungle.

They blasted at us again as all four of us held check for several moments before sneaking a look out to where we knew the enemy were lurking, awaiting the kill. They were waiting for a time to strike; to shoot and wound us then play games with our bodies before cutting our throats and gouging our eyes out, it was their custom and I have film to prove such, a three hour film documenting the atrocities exacted upon the Croatian people, their churches and hospitals.

I threw a grenade into the thick under-brush some twenty or so metres away. This was, in hindsight, a stupid thing to do as I watched in horror as the thing glanced off the edge of a nearby tree and bounded back toward me like a fuckin' boomerang.

The explosion deafened my ears as pieces of branch fell upon me, shrapnel scoring the tree I hid behind. My ears rang as I lay there prone, hands to my ears as the ringing continued in my brain, immobilising my will to power, my need to protect myself from certain death. Then, just as quickly, my senses and survival instinct returned as I rose to a crouch and began blasting toward where the grenade was intended to land. There was a yell, then silence followed by a barrage of return fire. A Serb could be down dead or at least wounded or then again it could be a ruse to give us a false confidence that there was one less of their number to contend with.

Laughter wreaked the air once more, coming from the same direction where I had just fired that short burst of automatic fire. Calls and signals were made between us four (Zjelko to my left and Goran and Wilfey to my right a few metres away).

'Jock', Wilfey called once more, 'have your pants changed colour? Hah, hah'

'You mean the grenade - English boy'

'Yeah Jock, that's it'

'It's hard to tell, I'm sweating so much.. Who knows' I replied.

A dense canopy of branches and leaves covered us, yet the sun still shone through. There was no way we could wait for darkness, we'd be dead or captured by then. Only one real hope existed for us and that was to lay down the small shoe polish size 'Pasteta' pressure mines; and this we did. Holding fire, Wilfey and I prepared the mines. Then all four of us crawled about positioning them where we expected the Serbs to come through.

Zjelko indicated that he would put two down, the position of which he relayed to Wilfey and he on to Goran. At a hand signal us middle two fired at the enemy before us. Short bursts of automatic. Throwing an extra magazine at Wilfey who lay nearby so he could use it in his RPK. At this moment the two Croatians pulled back some twenty metres to cover us as much as they could as we also withdrew in line with them. As Wilfey pulled back, I quickly fixed a grenade tripwire to a fallen tree near where I had lain. Then we ran, turning back only to give short bursts of fire in the general direction of the enemy. I was sure the Chetniks would waste little or no time in their relentless pursuit.

Then to my horror my foot got caught in the root of a tree on the slight slope that I was running down. Over I went, tumbling and crashing into a bush, cutting my face and numbing one arm as my full weight fell on top of it. Bullets zinged and zipped above where I lay entangled and trapped in the bush for several seconds.

It was really on top now. Then came two successive explosions from behind me. One was definitely the tripwire grenade - it had erupted along with one of the small pressure mines.

Gun fire tore the woods apart as the four of us ran, the further we went the more the density of the trees protected us - on and on we ran, crashing through the undergrowth, falling, stumbling to our feet and it must have been a kilometre or so further before I realised that I was not being fired upon. I was alone. Stopping suddenly I could hear rustling over to my right ... I gave a short sharp whistle and after a moment it came back - Goran emerged from the woods. Then another return call from just forward on my immediate left where Zjelko stood up, he was smiling broadly - then it occurred to us that Wilfey was not with us.. A silence overcame the three of us as we began to search the immediate vicinity while listening for the slightest movement or sound. But we could hear nothing, only the buzz of insects.

There was a grimace on all our faces - it was a foregone conclusion that Wilfey was lost to us, he was probably dead back there. It would be foolish even to contemplate returning to look for him as a few kilometres behind us the Serbs would be swarming all over the place and, even though they had lost four of their number, rage would be all the incentive the Chetniks needed to hunt us down.

There was no time for further thought, there could be no recriminations as it was a fact of circumstances and war that Wilfey, the little English guy, was gone and lost to us. "Tis life Scot - we play the game, I only hope that he is dead and not wounded or alive for the Chetniks to be 'caring' for him', Zjelko said. He was saying aloud what the rest of us were thinking, 'Let's head toward Ahmici I've checked out the compass reading and terrain - it's over those two hills there about a kilometre away'.

In the distance, where he pointed, we could see smoke and hear explosions; with all the haste we could muster we ran toward the smoke that trailed up into the clear blue summer sky. The sun blazed down as we left the woods looking over the landscape before continuing our run. No houses or hamlets were within our vision, which was a godsend; we had to hope that no soldiers - Serbian or Muslim - had us in their sights.

It was now 2 pm and the sun was scorching our backs. Most of our ammo was expended but at least we were close to where we believed our own Croatian forces to be - the main problem was that fighting between the Bosnian Army and our own had erupted and was still on-going - both sides working on a hit and run basis. Atrocities had been carried out by Muslim forces against both the Serbians and us. It was a most bitter and bloody war ... seldom could there have been one like it before - only perhaps in the Dark Ages had the Balkans witnessed these kinds of atrocities and they, after all, were the root causes of this present conflict centuries later.

We took a few minutes respitewhile we rested and took water, hidden for the moment while we sat down, ever watchful of our harsh and hostile surroundings. Not a word passed any of our lips as we sat and peered around - hoping against hope not to be seen or shot-up before we could regain cover and eventually return to our own lines. This particular area, near Kiseljak, was heavily saturated by Muslims hell-bent on eliminating our smaller population and army numbers.

'Scot, Zjelko, let's move on and get somewhere safe, this sun is too much for us', Goran urged as he got to his feet and adjusted his equipment. He moved on, gun at the ready. All three of us walked for some hundred metres or so before we broke into a trot at Goran's insistence. The sweat pouring from us as we went.

Life had meaning in these moments as I reflected again on the plight of Wilfey, hoping he was dead rather than captured, his skinny little frame would find it hard to withstand much torture - he would suffer more than most, the fear of capture held on to all our thoughts, even the most hardened of us feared it; but then it was always an underlying consideration in Bosnia, a fate worse than death.

I remembered the occasion when Wilfey and two other foreigners had left a man named Silvio, a young Croatian guy, thinking that he was fatally wounded near Jajce when they withdrew from the monastery area in October 1992. Later we found out that he had been taken to a Serb concentration camp.

The two other foreigners, one English and one Danish, were later wounded - the former was hit by shrapnel on both feet and the tips of his fingers from a small mortar shell - everyone else in the vicinity had heard the shell coming apart from its only victim, this often happened in war, as the saying goes 'there's always a bullet with your name on it'. Both soldiers eventually recovered after extensive treatment and were sent to a convalescent's home on the coast near Split for about seven months having refused to enter a Croatian military hospital, their stay on the coast being much longer and more relaxing.

Up the first hill we struggled. At the top we rested for a minute or so before continuing, peering over the ridge we suspiciously scanned the ground below with binoculars to seek out any form of life near the foot of the opposite hill - that hill was the last obstacle between Ahmici and us. Smoke billowed up just beyond the hill we were about to climb while gunfire could be heard several hundred metres beyond us. We got up knowing we had to cover the distance as quickly as possible, but now we were severely fatigued and down to our last mouthfuls of water which was warm and almost unpalatable. Regardless we hurried down the hill, the momentum building as we ran, doing all we could to avoid tumbling over and injuring ourselves.

Barely glimpsing each other as we concentrated on our downward run we were still sharp enough to look about for signs of an enemy. Then onwards a few hundred metres to the foot of our last objective and using our momentum we initially surged uphill several metres before slowing almost to a halt.

Loose boulders and stones lay everywhere as we forced our way, foot by foot, winding more as each step was made - on and on - I stopped for a few moments, as both Goran and Zjelko urged me on; my lung and heart problems were beginning to tell, my health and earlier lifestyle taking its toll - and how I suffered for it. But I forced myself to go on, to catch the others up, my Scottish determination working for me. Goran and Zjelko continued to wait for me crouched behind a boulder, scouring the land behind us to the right and left, watching and waiting for a sign that we would be noticed by an eager enemy.

They urged me on and moments later I finally reached the pair of them. Only forty or so metres remained but the others gave me a few welcome moments to recuperate and get ready for the final push. I forlornly sat down, wedging both my feet against a boulder. My head sank as the sweat poured on to the rock and dirt below, my heart pounding as if it was beating its last, then six, seven minutes passed as I coughed and spluttered bringing up no more than a thick watery substance.

The sun shone its relentless beat above as I sipped the last turgid mouthfuls from my canteen. Then, looking to the others, I nodded that I was ready to force the last distance to the top. Sounds of gunfire increased as we made the last metres to the ridge, repeating the same procedure as before upon the other hill. Goran crawled to the top on his belly as Zjelko and I followed suit, easing our way to either side of him - Goran fixed his binoculars on the village of Ahmici below. Houses were burning, machine-gun fire was almost incessant as both sides fought it out.

I took Goran's binoculars and peered down upon the scene; houses were ablaze as our men withdrew, running from buildings as the enemy pushed us back. There were a number of civilians lying prone, probably dead. The terror was apparent in Ahmici. We were certainly in a predicament: our only option was to join in the fighting. My mouth dried as I'm sure my comrades did; we were going into the unknown. Death, I felt, was here in all its severity, all its gory endgame.

Zjelko made radio contact after a couple of attempts and it was ascertained that HVO were pulling out as Muslim fighters were being reinforced, Goran translated all of this to me. Down we went, arranging a meeting point with those fighting their way out of the village's immediate area. On and on to the edge of the village, over the rocky terrain avoiding boulders and debris here and there. Everything was on fire; houses blazed and screams could be heard; cries that I took to be for help, or just in sheer agony. As the village burned, the stench of burning was sickly, unbelievable. I'd known the smell before; buildings, rubber, flesh, clothes, and lastly wood; it is still distinct to me.

Bodies, civilian in the main, lay strewn, shot and dead - my senses faltered, even when shots were fired in my direction - everything was 'Helter Skelter' - thoughts of Charles Manson and the Beatles raged in my confused brain; jumping projections, visions, weird sounds - then the harsh reality of a war-zone hit me as I returned fire. Back to war and destruction - no crescendo, it was just there; a simple reality that meant the termination of life. Nearby I could hear the distinctive roar of a truck engine or two.

Goran and Zjelko were carrying an old Croatian woman between them, blood poured from her head - she had been cut with a large knife or machete. I will never forget the scene, that old woman with blood pouring down over her eyes and face, was in shock, her eyes quite glazed. She seemed to me to be in her sixties, or had had a hard life - what made me think that I'll never know. "Keep covering us Scot - the bastards are everywhere," Goran shouted, as Zjelko screamed, "Left, Left!"

There was a Bosnian soldier in the direction he was pointing. I shot him, holing his stomach, he fell to the floor. Shots were being fired as we ran. Zjelko went down, a bullet hitting him in the left calf. Plaster and pieces of masonry splattered us as we ran past the last house in the village - bullets zipped by us, this was all far too close for comfort.

Goran slung the old woman over his shoulder as I took Zjelko's arm and helped drag him up a small hillock as we threw ourselves to the ground, the pain immaterial as we thumped down on the loose chippings and earth. Goran was now shouting at the old woman in Serbo-Croat, and as I tore at Zjelko's combat trouser leg he winced in pain. Fortunately the bullet had seared through the calf muscle missing the bone. I staunched the considerable flow of blood with a bandage that I wrapped as tightly as possible around his leg, there was no need for Morphine considering our very real predicament.

A light machine gun barked out over our heads - it was then that we realised that it was our own men giving covering fire. At that Goran tended the old woman's head wound, a green field dressing was placed on her gashed head - she was mumbling deliriously as she was tended but this was no time for civility. It was instinctive for Goran to repair her. To prevent a further loss of blood as we assessed our situation and worked a way out of the seemingly hopeless circumstances in which we found ourselves.

The fighting was getting heavier now. The sheer propensity of bullets flying over our heads and hitting the top of the hillock made us keep our heads down - as Goran radioed for help. We had lived second-by-second from the hell in the woods until now. But this seemed to be a more severe situation. We had lost one man in the woods, another was wounded, we had a delirious old woman for company and little or no ammunition to defend ourselves. The village was overrun by Bosnians and our forces were retreating quickly, at that moment I reckoned our chances had all but gone.

That was until we heard the roar of an engine to our left and rear as three jeeps appeared - the first mounted with a .50 calibre Browning machine gun. Its bullets whacked out at Ahmici and its surrounds ripping all and sundry within its path, the other two stopped nearby as soldiers from a local unit jumped out and helped Zjelko and the old woman on to the jeep.

Two of the locals opened up on some enemy soldiers who had been busy blasting the hell out of us - then a shout went up that we were getting out, Goran and I jumped in the second jeep as the one equipped with a gun continued to fire at the enemy. My last memory or rather vision was of the blazing village of Ahmici. Mortar shells could clearly be heard as we escaped, in those moments I didn't care who they were hitting as long as it wasn't me, I had survived and was completely exhausted with little will but to succumb to a rough sleep. The jeep pelted hell for leather along the road toward Kiseljak and relative safety. Gunfire and explosions receded as they terminated another chapter of this war and I drifted into an exhausted sleep.

When I awoke in Kiseljak my Croatian comrades told me of Wilfey's survival. He had been picked up by a passing HVO patrol and, amazingly, he was safe and on his way down country to Prozor and then Tomislavgrad.

'The lucky shit' I thought to myself, it was typical English luck that confined itself not only to World Cup draws but also war - but then I thought he wasn't a bad guy at heart. Soon after he left Bosnia. Many volunteers gave their blood and, in some cases their lives, fighting for Croatian freedom. Some of their graves remain unmarked - I hope their families realise that their struggle was not in vain, that they were part of a greater cause. I feel sad when I remember the many foreigners who never returned; German, French, Swedes. One Swede in particular lies in a grave somewhere out there. That soldier was another part of the Bosnian War and its tragic loss of life as soldiers fought and died on all sides for the love of land and freedom.

Not all Serbian soldiers or civilians were as bad as the UN paint them - it is too easy to say they were all monsters. Many were honourable soldiers as were many in the Bosnian Muslim army - but the ordinary people - Croatian, Serbian and Bosnian Muslim - were the real heroes of this war in many cases. While we as soldiers were merely the pawns of a higher power, of a political struggle for power.

The Silent Cry
DEATH VALLEY

Zenica was always a town of great contention between Croat and Muslim forces. The Vance-Owen plan did little to dampen what was already a great underlying tension that had simmered bitterly and which flared into out and out conflict during the spring and summer of 1993. Nearby Busovaca was no different to Zenica; it was there that fierce fighting first broke-out in Central Bosnia. Blame was continually placed upon the HVO forces when in all reality it was the Bosnian Muslim army that, in most areas other than Western Herzegovina, outnumbered our forces. This factual reality was helped by Muslim knowledge of our positions because we were former allies - they took advantage of this while we were simultaneously fighting the Serbs.

As a result, during 1993, the two armies fought us into defensive positions time after time - in this period the considerable Croat population fought for their very existence in Central Bosnia. We felt, at the time, that the Bosnians and Serbians were involved in an unsigned pact against us as they continually made unproven allegations to the western media about our activities in the Lascva Valley, which later became known as the 'Valley of Death'.

In my own way I tried to redress the balance. I wrote letters to the Guardian, the UN and New York Times in an attempt to impress on the outside world the reality of the events in that region and in Mostar (another area where HVO were accused of war crimes).

The problem with all these bodies was that they never saw the conflict on the frontline. Their reporters never lost children in the conflict or buried the charred remains of their loved ones. I saw many atrocities perpetrated on Croatian people - the crucifixion of a HVO soldier in Slatina in East Prozor, the rape and murder of children and their infirm grandparents in a village near Gornji Vakuf.

I understood that no sensible Muslim would be involved in such attacks and that these actions were the work of extremists - but it was the same with the forces and people of Bosnian-Croatia. At such times the Lascva Valley was alight; houses, shops and cafe bars raged with fire - tit-for-tat fighting went on day and night as whole villages were razed to the ground - it was indeed the 'valley of death'.

In those days I left my HVO Special Forces brigade saying I was going back to England for a week or so when in reality I had joined up with HOS units who were unrelenting in their pursuit of the enemy. When our people were being slaughtered on an almost daily basis it seemed the logical thing for me to do; HOS stood for Defence of the Land and that is what we tried to do.

An example of HOS's way came shortly after the HVO commander in Zenica was said to have been tortured and then killed - at that time that is all we knew. We were under no illusions as to the way Muslims fought. It was April and the Muslims had been reinforced by Mujahadeen fighters from Afghanistan and the Middle East. The Chetniks did not have a monopoly on torture and humiliation. What they had inflicted upon the Muslim population at the start of the conflict we knew would be repeated on us by the Muslims - it is the way of these things.

As a result we decided to take out the main Bosnian army headquarters in Vitez. The plan was to drive a truck full of explosives into the enemy command centre - it was a simple plan for which there many volunteers. The irony of the situation was that the explosives used had been captured from a shipment bound for Bosnia from Libya. We were outnumbered in the area six to one, owing to the release of refugees from the Omaska Concentration Camp after international pressure as a result of a story about it on ITN.

So that was that. The bomb was driven right through the Bosnian positions - showing an audaciousness and nerve beyond belief. In fact it was nearer bloody madness but it worked perfectly - as the explosives detonated, destroying their base wiping out a considerable number of their forces.

To be honest it was an action we didn't relish. We should have been fighting the Serbs, but that was not to be. These were desperation tactics, the kind used in any conflict when the enemy far outweigh your own forces; regardless we caused much devastation and it was a serious blow to the Muslims.

Within days of Vitez's centre being blown to kingdom come it was also discovered that the Muslims had just taken delivery of a fresh supply of explosives when the bomb exploded - the result was a bonus for us. In the end however there were no winners in that action, beyond perhaps the arms dealers and racketeers who made their living in Bosnia.

Several days after the Vitez action, at Ahmici village a few miles away the war took more victims. It was later claimed by Colonel Bob Stewart that the casualties found there had been caused by Croatian hands - in fact I had arrived in the fighting just as we were pulling out from the Muslim onslaught (see Kiseljak above).

Bob Stewart was a character I had run into before in Rumboci in the autumn when several British Land Rovers blocked the small narrow road that wound through the town. It was not long after he had made scurrilous remarks regarding Croatians. The alleged massacre at Ahmici was a chance for Colonel Stewart to appear heroic on television. He told British people of the murder of the Muslims, the vicious nature of the Croat forces (we were all Ustashe apparently) and conveniently ignored the many Croat dead in the village.

He continued to espouse the Muslim cause on TV making political mileage out of a tragic situation rather than conveying the real horror of war in Bosnia. Colonel Stewart took TV crews with him wherever he went, spouting the official line of the Bosnian government. As a result the Croats were painted as the bad guys in 1993. I was at Ahmici but arrived in such a hurry, under heavy fire, that all I saw was the result of a recent battle.

The mosque had been blown up, there were dead bodies lying everywhere, some had died violently, others from shrapnel wounds. Houses were burning and there were a number of Croatian and Muslim soldiers lying dead in the village. Twenty or more HVO soldiers evacuated the village as we arrived. There were a number of mercenaries that I hadn't met before and haven't seen since. Afterwards Croat soldiers returned to the village and took away the civilian and military dead from our side. But when they returned there were Muslim civilians still in the village when reports had told us that all Muslims had been killed. Perhaps the absolute truth about Ahmici will never come out - in either case it will not bring back the dead on all sides. This was an example of the precarious nature of life in the valley of death. It didn't matter which side you fought for, your existence remained on a knife-edge.

Not only did the Serbs ethnically cleanse Croatians but so did the Muslims and when they did it there appeared to be an added violence to it. Much of this violence seemed to be directed at the young, 'kill them before they reach fighting age and that is one less soldier to worry about', appeared to be their way of thinking. The summer of 1993 was long and hot - throughout I associated myself with HOS further north away from my regular unit. Foreigners were, in the main, excluded from this organisation but they made an exception for me. It was do or die for us. We fully realised the dire consequences if we failed to defend our women and children.

Our losses were greater in some respects against the Muslims than the Serbs - the world didn't seem to care about Croat civilians in Bosnia or when we were outnumbered seven or six to one - in Vitez some of the frontline conditions bordered on those seen in the First World War. Later HOS members were ordered to return to the HVO and we re-took trenches in a counteroffensive against the Serb-Muslim enemy. We battled it out over central Bosnia and down into Mostar where we counterattacked to the shock of the Bosnian Army, driving them over the Neretva river and onto the east bank. Our refugees continued to flee the area however, making their tearful way down toward Tomislavgrad and finally into Croatia.

MISTAKEN IDENTITY

In a Bosnian village we were under fire, being sniped from a top floor window. A camouflaged cap and shirt appeared. The shot rang out, a body toppled. What could I do to reverse the death? I looked closely. She was perhaps 25 years old. An enemy true enough, she was dead, now only a memory, another victim of this war. This was the way in the Balkans, as we continued to fight our way through the village killing anyone in our path.

The carcass of the young woman was dragged away to lie in a line with the others. An old Croatian guy approached me.

'She had no gun, she was not a soldier,' for a moment I reflected that hindsight was a wonderful thing.

'Yes Tomis, you are correct but our people die day-by-day, night-by-night. She wore an enemy shirt and cap' (as many did).

He looked and nodded in dismay. Thinking, possibly, why a hardened enemy soldier would walk into the open when under fire. Also, he probably thought that I'd used my x50 binoculars at 500 metres distance and killed an innocent on purpose.

I recalled the occasion when some of our soldiers had hesitated when they spotted a Muslim soldier on a hill aiming an RPG launcher. It is true to say that he who hesitates is lost, whereas I state, 'if in doubt kill first, ask questions later'. Our soldiers paid for it. Three former Legionnaires ended up, like that young woman, as victims of the war.

At this time I remembered the 37 dead in the village near Gornji Vakuf. At least the young woman I had just killed would be given a decent burial – her body was barely marked. By the standards of this war hers was a peaceful death. We had recently witnessed the actions of Serb and Muslim units on Croatian villages and were aware that they could be cruel beyond belief.

The reaction to the girl's death was immediate. A barrage of shells were launched in our direction. It turned out that she was the daughter of the Army's local commander. The earth shook; I slammed the old soldier next to me to the ground. To be a soldier you shouldn't ever cry over spilt blood, this was no ordinary war, it was Bosnia and now I believed it, I knew it and grew to love it.

The Bosnians had managed to get hold of a lot of shells, I thought as I hugged the ground with my old comrade. They couldn't have got them solely from Serbian arms caches. The ground was hard and it made the earth shake with every explosion in the vicinity. You couldn't dig into this unless you had a JCB, this made the shells far more effective and far more dangerous. Time after time I'd been put under such fire and, as it intensified, I decided to make a break for some better cover nearer the edge of the village. But the enemy were upon us. All nine of us in the squad knew it was time to be live cowards rather than dead heroes – we definitely didn't want to die in or near this enemy village.

One by one we split up. The Muslims had a spotter who was training the shells on us, and now we were being bombarded mercilessly. The old guy decided he would chance his arm with me. Just then a shell exploded, blasting the air from my lungs, making my ear bleed and I laughed, trying to give the old guy next to me a little confidence. We ran on and I fell, deafened and numbed by the explosion.

This old codger could have left me but came back; he was the type of Croatian I loved. I was stunned by the blast, but he returned and spoke in broken English, trying to work out whether I was hit. I had blood coming from mouth, ears and nose – he had a point about me looking out for the count. I wiped a grimy hand over my mouth and saw the blood. It was dark, almost purple in colour.

He was egging me on the old soul, praying for me as I attempted to recover, forgiving me for the death of the unarmed, female civilian. That old guy really believed that I took her out on purpose, thinking that I knew she was an actual civilian. After that experience I could no longer condemn soldiers in such fraught circumstances – there is a fine line to be drawn in the heat of battle and often the way you react then is not something you would contemplate doing in the cold light of day.

The fine line between sticking to the rules of combat and breaking them becomes blurred. Restrictions are for those who never have to make the split second decision, never have to weigh up in a nanosecond the rights, wrongs and potential dangers of the enemy (or what looks like an enemy in a camouflaged cap and shirt).

For those not conversant with death or any type of tricky military situation the subject seems black and white. Instead try and look at those who place a soldier in these positions, the men who order other men to kill, train them to commit murder legally and those too incompetent to keep the peace – there is no complaint along these lines from me, a volunteer.

The zing of bullets whistled by our ears – the top of my old comrade's helmet was holed – boy did he thank God for looking after him. The shells ceased and we quickly realised that our men were covering us. The enemy came looking for us, a mistake, as it turned out, as our comrades picked them off one-by-one, they were fuckin' swell guys these Croatians. War brought out that need, that love of humanity, a love that children can not inspire – it is a special bond among soldiers who fight, live and die for one another.

We retreated and were forced back into Muslim territory. Our best soldier, Ante, covered us with his light support weapon, shouting in Croatian and English for us to retreat. I looked to him and respected him. He was a soldier of great character, a former Foreign Legionnaire who'd left in a hurry in 1991 at the start of the crisis in the then Yugoslavia. Just like our commander Glasnovic he was a soldier's soldier. I nodded my thanks to him and ran on. He was a diamond; he stayed while my group retreated.

Later we lay under a makeshift cover and rocky overhang watching the rain pour down on the forest. Rain was the only sound in our otherwise silent, tense hideout. Thirty-minute guard stints were agreed upon as we pulled out our ration packs and ate in silence.

Ante had not caught up with us. The probability of his death was real. He had known the risk of staying behind of course and he had all the skills to get himself out of most situations, as calm and as cool as all in Special Forces had to be – if anyone could get out it was Ante.

We ate in silence. We looked at one another, our grimy faces betraying the fears for our friend. Down below in the valley, about a kilometre away, there was considerable movement. But we were well covered in our sloping forest hideout. I sat and thought again about Ante – there was little doubt that he could track down a Red Indian let alone a group of tired soldiers.

Allowing for the downpour it would be all but impossible for him to track down our position – he knew, I was sure, that we would pick a spot somewhere near to the river as it turned toward Mostar. So a decision was made that we would give Ante another hour. But as 4 pm. approached there was still no sign of Ante.

As the time ticked toward the appointed hour our nerves were strung. There was to be no arguing, we would just have to leave him behind – he knew the risks and anyone of us would have traded places with him – this was a soldier's war. I was proud to be with these men. They were human, real – freedom was freedom – as each of our men would die the rest would keep their memory alive to tell their families and friends, a part of the fight for Croatian freedom.

Just then there was a crashing noise below and hell did we jump out of our skins as a wild pig came bounding into our little area. A few men, attempting to release a little of the built-up tension, tried to capture it. 'It's a spy' one of them said chasing it, forgetting the tension of the situation we laughed as the little pig ran gave our men the run-around. The rain continued to fall and we filled our water bottles with its freshness and roared again as another of our number went scurrying after the pig in the mud. One, two they were knocked down in a heap, left lying in the forest covered in the mud and leaves, the finest camouflage I've ever known.

Then off it went. As a vegetarian I was glad and rebuked the Croatians for their stupidity, and in turn they started to take the piss out of my Scottishness, referring to my kilt as a skirt. Then they told me a story about how a Stone Age Scotsman made the caves in France. Apparently years ago a Scotsman went to France to seek a little culture and some French Celt threw a penny down a hole. The Scotsman, as tight as they come, dug and dug trying to find it making these particular French caves – they all scattered as I brandished my knife and slashed the air with it, growling at them all.

But the fun and games stopped abruptly as mortar shells came over from near the river. They were from the Serbian positions, the exact location of which remained a mystery, the talk about them being as rife as a rumour in a fishmarket back at base. We knew that the shells were coming from 120mm mortars and clearly they were firing upon fixed coordinates, perhaps they were aiming at the village that we'd just evacuated? Two or three landed some distance away, then one exploded half way up our hill – it shook us up, confused us. No shell could fall that short unless, of course, it was aimed at us or was a dud.

Seconds later we saw the target of the Serbian assault. There were 2,000 or so Bosnian Army soldiers and vehicles below: the war was most definitely on for them – they hadn't taken cover and the Serb guns and shells were landing now with precision in the path of the advancing army. We felt a pity for those below. They clearly hadn't taken cover as the shelling was far from the road. At first there had been a few hundred or so Bosnians some of whom seemed to be refugees and civilians, then this main phalanx of soldiers.

We needed to get across that road now. Jablanica was to the north, Prozor to the west – what was going on? I thought. It was an assault of some significance but we had to get through nonetheless. I scanned the lower road again and could see that there were bodies everywhere – the road was strewn with wounded, several of them refugees. The rain continued to pour as if to wash the carnage away. Our real enemies were not those being pounded below but the animals in the hills to the east – the Serbian monolith that we would dearly like to come to terms with.

High above us a jet flew, perhaps it was UN or maybe Serb, breaking the no-fly zone with ease. Gorazde and Srebrenica lay to the east but did the West care? The jet soon departed with a roar and a decision was taken to cut short our party and head home by the shortest route. We had to cross the road barely a hundred metres behind the bombarded Bosnians.

We struggled down to the roadside as quietly as possible, no mishaps or close shaves, a clear run and then over the road and onto a small, waterlogged slope. Our own frontlines were now only a few kilometres away but night was falling and shells could be heard in the near distance, so we trudged our way through the sodden soil, keeping back from the road in case there were any stragglers.

That mass of Bosnian soldiers and refugees were heading for one of our towns, Prozor, as we'd been pushing them back and were holding them on the hills by the damn and tunnel.

Meanwhile Serbian and Croatian shells bombarded Mostar, an unfortunate alliance between ourselves and our hated enemy, the Chetniks. All of us, to a man, were sad about that. We alone wanted to fight the Serbs and our schedules and ammo were being expended down there against those that ought to have been our allies. Our best were lost to one another: ammunition, medicines, brothers, sisters and girlfriends...

I made my own tearful journey from a burnt village soon after. I had heard that something had happened to Almira, the Muslim girl I used to see in Tomislavgrad. I emitted a silent cry, the kind I had heard from countless grieving refugees over the past year or so. It was a cry of rage, of pain, but which produced no audible sound - my vocal chords could not convey my true feelings despite my attempt to scream into the universe.

Amid the ruins I walked in a numbed trance. I looked but never really saw. For some minutes my mind was blank, concentrating on the pain growing in my brain, battering at my soul. Time after time I had walked amid the dead and bereaved in Bosnia and had known the pain of personal loss after the death of my father years ago. But now I could not shed tears, yet continued to scream in silence, trembling with rage and grief as I finally fell to my knees.

Both bodies, the woman I loved and her baby of six months or so, still smouldered - burnt and blackened. A sickly, melted mess - my pain had become painless, flashes of light struck in rage at my brain, my eyes red and swollen, the veins on my neck pulsing and tense.

'You bastart! you bastart!' I finally burst out, calling to God or anyone who could hear. I tried to pick up the charred remains of my loved ones, but their collapsed, shrunken skeletons disintegrated, falling from me as I fell to my knees again - punching the ground in frustration. I looked at Almira's body again. She had been tied with wire around the wrist. 'No, no, no' is all I could say - dehydrated, tears still flowing regardless, falling like acid onto the Bosnian soil.

Few people knew that we were lovers, that we cared for each other and that she had a child. All that mattered to strangers was that she was a Muslim. Her child, so free of hate, enmity and the damp dross of life, lay nearby. The woods grew eerie as darkness engulfed us, taking me over. It was almost as if I was floating above it - looking down on all three of us as I lay there upon the burnt embers of the house which had been such a comfort, the only place we could love and care for each other, but which was now just a smouldering ruin.

Revenge was on my mind, of course. Its light shining like a beacon in my soul. It was my only hope; to find those who had taken my loved ones - to kill them up close and personal. Being burnt to death must be the worst way to go. But to inflict it on a mother and child...Again I picked up the remains and staggered over to a nearby wood. The trees would shelter them there, I thought, would look after them while I wandered the earth attempting to avenge their deaths.

I would govern the lives of those who had done this. I was death now; only I could extinguish the black flame flickering in my soul. I stumbled, fell to my knees and held the bodies for the last time, my tears falling on burnt bone and charred flesh, briefly hoping that my tears would bring them back to life - I looked at their eye sockets, the eyeballs burnt out - there was no way back. I don't know for how long they had suffered.

Behind me an old woman kept her distance. I turned and looked at her clear blue eyes - she was life, the grandmother of the girl I loved, that I still love. The great grandmother of the child I held now on my knee. I turned and met her eye-to-eye. Both of us wavering as we continued to look beyond life, to question why.

'Muslimani...Muslimani' she called, pointing her aged rheumatic right hand toward the bodies. Muslims had killed their own, my loved ones. A numbness overcame me. I lifted the bodies and carried them both deep into the forest - deeper and deeper until I was alone with them. I buried them. Only the grandmother would know their precise location, a private burial of her loved ones.

Step-by-step I walked back to the village - there were only seven buildings in the hamlet, all had been damaged by shooting; three burnt out completely, all related to the girl who had been a part of my life.

The old woman, I later found out, had hidden in the woods when they came. But she had told me enough, that it was her own people who had done it. As I dug their graves, I thought of retribution - only the grandmother remained in the village. The rest had flown, their houses deserted - fear was in the air - fear at the possibility of retribution - it would be done, I vowed - it was done.

The memory of that morning is never far away. Among the myriad deaths, tortures, charred remains and assorted tragedy of the conflict this one returns most often to haunt me. And when I remember it, I remember the silent scream and there is no other sound - the low, high-pitched, loud, quiet sound of grief and pain - the kind of noise I had heard many times in Bosnia but which you only understand once it comes from deep within yourself.

After I had buried her I walked away in a daze. Should I carry on? Where do I go from here? Why should I live? Should I take my own life? Am I a coward for deciding not to? All these thoughts entered and exited my mind as if it were a revolving door.

I finally returned to the old woman again and handed her some chocolate bars and the remainder of my water bottle and left in silence. I have seen her once since that day. When I walked up the pathway of her new home it was the longest walk of my life. But she was there. Waiting, ever watchful, knowing that I would one day return - how or why neither of us could explain - but we knew all the same.

A doctor at Rumboci hospital said she was well known to the locals. She returns to the house every Friday and can be seen talking to the walls. The house itself is now covered in poppies. The story had been related to a French aid worker who was so moved she scattered some poppy seeds there - always when I see one of Monet's painting of poppies in a field I think back to the softer and then harsher feelings of life, and remember Almira.

4 - THE DIVIDED CITY

OVERVIEW

As the newly formed Bosnian Army suffered defeat after defeat against the Bosnian Serb forces and associated paramilitaries in late 1992, countless refugees were forced to flee central Bosnia. Most of them made their weary way down toward Jablanica before finding their way to Mostar, Bosnia's second city.

Mostar lies in a valley and straddles the Neretva River. It is situated in the south of Bosnia and during the war was equidistant between the self-proclaimed Bosnian Croatian region of Herceg-Bosna (Mostar was the self-declared capital of Croat dominated Herzegovina) in the south, the Bosnian Serb forces to the Northeast and the Bosnian Muslim dominated capital, Sarajevo. As a result all three forces had a vital interest in the city.

According to the 1991 census Croats made up 33.8% of the population of Mostar, Muslims 34.8% and Serbs 19%. So to all sides, but in particular the Croats and Muslims, it was a matter of pride and morale to secure the city on behalf of their people. The population figures might be misleading however as, following the Bosnian Serb invasion in April 1992, many Croatians fled further south into Croatia. The later arrival of Muslim refugees therefore increased the Muslim share of the population.

Mostar's basic infrastructure had been blown away in April 1992 when the Bosnian Serbs invaded the city. But by June of that year the Bosnian-Croatian HVO had driven Bosnian Serb forces back into the surrounding mountains. At that time of course the Bosnian Muslims and Bosnian Croatians were allies.

However, the main problem in Croat controlled Mostar during the winter of 1992/3 was the influx of Muslim refugees. The sudden rise in population was of great humanitarian and political concern to the local Croat commanders so a decision was made to allocate the refugee families to deserted Croatian property on the West bank. The spare accommodation was offered to refugee Muslims on the understanding that it be returned to its original occupants should they return. Naturally, once the HVO had taken full military control of the area, many

Croats returned placing further strain on the city's already fragile infrastructure making conflict between returning Croatian civilians and displaced Muslim refugees inevitable. This tense situation was not helped by the announcement of the Vance-Owen peace plan in January 1993.

The Muslims were the most aggrieved of the parties as, under the terms of the treaty, they were to be awarded less than a third of the territory of their independent Bosnian state. As a result the Muslims in Mostar became bitter and paranoid with a reason based upon some truth - that the international community was effectively, in the words of US president Bill Clinton, 'rewarding ethnic cleansing'. By offering the Bosnian Serbs 50% of the territory of Bosnia the Vance-Owen plan, under the auspices of the UN, had effectively frozen out the Muslims. They were quickly becoming the minority force in their own country.

As a consequence many Muslims believed that the Croats and Serbs were plotting to divide Bosnia between themselves and, as rumours of partition by their neighbours mounted, many Muslims began to take a more aggressive stance. By April 1993 this bitterness spilled out into all-out war between the Bosnian and Croatian forces and the now divided city of Mostar was its focal point.

Our new enemy made initial successes as both of us fell into a trap set by the Serbs. In truth the enmity between Bosnian Muslim and Bosnian Croat had been brewing for a while. The siege of Jajce in October 1992 had been a litmus test of the alliance between the two - upon its fall each side blamed one another.

Within weeks there was a flare-up in Prozor south of Gornji Vakuf where a HVO guard was gunned down at a checkpoint. Bosnian Muslim forces then compounded that felony by slaughtering 36 HVO soldiers as they slept in their barracks in east Mostar. That was too much for us - how could they do such a thing to those who, at the time, fought alongside them? We gave them ammunition, food and medical aid - their soldiers were treated at our hospitals, Croat and Muslim doctors and nurses worked side by side. I had befriended many Muslims at Kuruga Old hospital in Mostar and found them to be decent types but certain elements on their side seemed determined to start a war against us.

As a result weaponry and lives were thrown at the Muslims rather than the Serbs. Serbian TV urged us to fight, warning the Croats that the real enemy was not they (despite the fact that it was the Serbs who had initially attacked Croatia, bulldozing cities, raping, looting and degrading civilians) but the Muslims who they termed 'fundamentalists' - the kind of Muslims that would rape, slaughter and loot just as the Serbs had. Indeed some of the actions of the Muslims were treacherous - certain events, which I have related in this book, took place which defied belief, but a lot of the rhetoric was just that, before we started fighting I had few qualms about our alliance with them.

The Silent Cry

In Mostar the enmity between Croat and Bosnian manifested itself in tit-for-tat fighting. Eventually we forced them back to the East side of the Neretva River and from then on we kept each other at arm's length. In the meantime of course there was the problem of the returning Croat refugees to Mostar. When, in early 1993, it had been the turn of the Muslim refugees to move from their temporary homes, the Bosnian army caused a great fuss claiming that HVO forces were ethnically cleansing the city - this is utter nonsense.

I spoke to Muslim doctors and nurses who admitted that their hospital could never survive without Croat assistance; they shared the security of Croat controlled Mostar and its frontline. As a result of the fuss the world's press tended to believe the Muslim's side of the story, leading the IMF and UN to threaten to withhold aid from Croatia proper. This diplomacy fell on deaf ears on the ground in Mostar however - the sons of bankers and politicians in the West were not being carried away in body bags from the frontline, their homes were not being burned and looted, their daughters were not being raped. So when the fighting between Bosnian Muslims and Bosnian Croats turned into a full-scale war the fragile agreements crashed to the floor to the sound of Mostar's falling masonry.

The victims of the fighting piled up on both sides. It was hard not to feel sorry for the civilians of Mostar; their beautiful city, their lives and livelihoods ripped to shreds for the sake of duplicity on both sides. But the press reports coming out of Mostar belied much of the truth. Much of the reporting by the Western media was inaccurate to the point of propaganda and only served to inflame an already tense situation. Absolute viciousness was meted out on both sides and, for a time, such actions became the norm. One thing was for certain; people died - there was no media bullshit about that.

Meanwhile, on the ground, I became dedicated to survival. It was all about will and determination to overcome the odds - to survive for families and brotherhood by any means necessary.

The political game played out in Sarajevo also had a big impact on the situation in Mostar - Muslim refugees were directed by their government to come to Mostar. This put pressure on the Croat forces when we already had a refugee crisis. As a result some of the refugees entering the city were forced to go to Croatia which in turn led to an increase in taxes and provided a further drain on an already stretched war economy. And this was another reason to disbelieve much of what was being reported. If the Croatians hated their Muslim neighbours so much why did they allow them to cross into Croatia? 300,000 refugees passed into the motherland on their way to Hungary, Italy or other parts of South-eastern Europe. Croatia's policy was to appease their former Muslim ally so that they could eventually join forces against the Serbian War machine which, by common consent, was regarded as the cause of the whole conflict.

Then there is the question of the Bosnian role in the initial Serbian invasion of Croatia in 1991. The JNA were allowed to attack Croatia from Muslim territory. Obviously the Muslim army was in no shape to oppose such a force, but throughout that war the Bosnians gave the Croatians no assistance (for instance intelligence reports), indeed the general feeling among Bosnians remained that 'our comrades in Serbia will not attack us here in Bosnia'.

As a result, from the start of the Bosnian conflict, the only opponents to the Serb onslaught outside Sarajevo were the Croat forces - Bosnia didn't form a nationwide army until the summer of 1992 and then concentrated their efforts on defending Sarajevo, so the Croats defended Muslim lives with their own. Once the political game had backfired on the Muslims, the Bosnians were forced to arm themselves - a situation in which Croatia once again aided them.

This was the background, although from my point of view it was all water under the bridge - under the Stari Most Bridge in particular. Stari Most was a symbol of Ottoman controlled Mostar. Built in 1566 it had seen invading forces come and go and its eventual destruction at the height of the fighting upset the world's press greatly (indeed they seemed to be more upset by the destruction of some bricks and mortar than human flesh).

I remember the night of November 9th 1993 as our artillery observation post sighted a number of Bosnian snipers taking up positions on the eastern side of the river - our patrols had infiltrated the Muslim sector and reported back that there were large movements on foot and that they were surreptitiously moving toward the Stari Most which at the time was the only bridge connecting east and west Mostar. This was all the invitation the HVO needed and we began a barrage of artillery fire upon it as that is where the enemy would have the best chance to build-up for a full frontal attack on our position.

Shell after shell crashed into the bridge at the far end from us - a field gun officer laughed and offered me a chance to load and fire and I did twice. Eventually the old structure gave way, the ancient stone and masonry falling into the river, cutting the enemy's attack off as our own reinforcements came up and all hell broke loose again. The destruction of the bridge appalled many who compared it to a war crime. This is of course nonsense. At the end of the day it was an ancient way of getting from one side of the river to the other and if your life had been at stake I'm sure you would have expected your forces to do the same.

The Silent Cry

The real war crime was the inactivity of the UN and their 'don't know' attitude toward the war - the Vance-Owen peace plan was a result of their inability to understand the conflict - which was one of many reasons why the Muslims and Croats had started fighting. Hatred and mistrust led to fighting, fighting led to more refugees, many of whom had fled to Mostar in order to escape the conflict elsewhere in Bosnia. Far from running to safety they found themselves slap-bang in the middle of it all again. The casualties piled up - the hospitals and morgues of Mostar became full to overflowing. The survivors rarely ventured out of doors. When they were forced out to look for food and water they often perished in the crossfire or received shrapnel wounds from the shelling.

Day and night the bodies were dragged away - sometimes the dying were unintentionally helped on their way when soldiers tried to carry them to the hospital and wounds were wrenched open when they were lifted. I saw this happen often in Mostar, but educating soldiers to be gentle is a little difficult in a war-zone. As the battle for the city continued prisoners were taken and, inevitably, many press reports remained inaccurate. But the very fact that we were taking prisoners showed that some form of humanity still existed between Bosnian and Croatian forces when you consider some of the extreme fighting taking place elsewhere.

Reports that the HVO held upwards of 2,000 Bosnian prisoners may well have been true but again it shows that they were taken rather than shot. It is easier to kill a soldier than take him prisoner. Prisoners tie an army up, yet they were taken. Civilians were not taken as prisoners as many have suggested. They were offered accommodation as refugees - was it not better to take the enemy's civilian population away from the frontline fighting in the city?

The whole of the city was at war - it was a terrible sight. The Serbs enjoyed all this from their vantage point in the mountains surrounding the city. From their lofty position they could shell either side at will with little chance of retaliation. For them the city must have seemed like a big game. They could relax and look down on the bowl as Croats and Muslims fought street-by-street for the city, reducing the numbers opposing them. So Mostar, for most of 1993, was the eye of the storm - all three sides were represented in large numbers, all had a reason to believe they should control it and all had grievances stoked up by the Vance-Owen plan.

Comparing the behaviour of the Muslims and us is also revealing. Bosnian POW's were incarcerated at a former JNA camp in Mostar. This was sensible as the place was well structured, secure and had good sleeping and toilet facilities. Croat POW's taken prisoner by Muslim forces in Konjic during the summer of 1993 were incarcerated in grain silos - to my mind that was the difference between the two sides. For all the vitriol of the world's press these differences never came to light.

There is little doubt that the Croat-Bosnian war was bitter beyond belief, but Croats also acted with humanity - the main problem for our side was the slant of the media coverage. We invited camera crews to film some of the massacres perpetrated around Gornji Vakuf and Konjic to little avail - they didn't seem to be interested in balancing the arguments put forward by Muslim sources. We in the HVO and those in Croatia can hold our heads high at the way we fought in Mostar - I also think the Muslim role in some of the atrocities around Konjic should also be taken into consideration when and if a war crimes tribunal ever takes place. Some Muslim elements massacred, raped and murdered people from their own side as well as Croats and Serbs.

During one break from the fighting I visited UNHCR (United Nations High Commissioner for Refugees) headquarters in Zagreb and bumped into Peter Kessler, the head of the UNHCR, who, in a very threatening manner, told me 'You can tell your government here in Zagreb that we are monitoring the situation in Mostar very carefully', insinuating that somehow there was some guilt on the Croatian side of the war. To this I replied abruptly, 'Zagreb is not my government, it is not even my country - I am fighting for Herceg-Bosna. The badge on my arm is that of the HVO, the army of Herceg-Bosna, so do not insinuate wrongly as to the part played by the Croat government in Mostar'. Then I walked away from this man. He was highly paid and motivated but too far removed from the conflict to really understand it.

One of his men on the ground, UNHCR aid worker Gary Milne, was much closer to the action and understood the difficulties - he was a man I totally respected. Such was the case with many of the other aid workers who did the job not for money or prestige but for the love of humanity. Peter Kessler's wife was another who acted in accordance with decency and respected all sides in the conflict. I would also like to mention Direct Aid from Edinburgh who helped me out with medical supplies and gave their time freely in Scotland and Bosnia.

I have visited Mostar since the end of the conflict and it is a strange place. It was eerily quiet while I wandered the streets in peace, the sun glinting on semi-destroyed avenues and rebuilt cafe bars - but the whole place lacked vitality. Mostar took such a heavy toll during the conflict that it was estimated that 90% of its buildings had suffered damage of one kind or another; as a result the city seems to have emerged from the conflict without a soul. Divided still by the Neretva River the Croat and Muslim population on both sides seem afraid to embrace peace - so I left, I couldn't stomach it.

SPRING 1993 - TO MOSTAR

Following a period of intense fighting in central Bosnia I moved down to Mostar. As has been explained the underlying tensions were different here and initially the HVO aim was to make Mostar the capital of the independent Bosnian-Croatian state of Herceg-Bosna. But as the battle for the city developed the two rival forces became deadlocked...

Many a day I would sit up on the rocky hill above the house in the village where I lived when the war was quiet. Peace of mind was to be had up there as the breeze cooled my face at the height of the Bosnian summer. Lizards ran about on the rocks and grass, small bees visited flowers and the afternoon sang with the joys of summer.

Six or seven kilometres away toward the Serb lines smoke billowed above the hills, interrupting the peaceful scene - a reminder that we were at war. There had been many such fires throughout Bosnia and Herzegovina, the blame being placed firmly on the Chetniks - regardless of summer the Serbs continued their war unhindered. A small scorpion scuttled away beneath a mass of boulders a few feet from where I sunbathed - thoughts similarly scuttled about my mind, nothing serious - just floating thoughts.

Insects continued to buzz about, they annoyed me but this was solitude - the trivia of nature for company. The insects carried on their battle for survival regardless - a futility and ruthlessness furthering their microscopic fight for life. Like our little battle in Bosnia, all would eventually be forgotten, mankind a speck on the massive journey of space and dimension. A few soldiers came and went at the house below; some lay sunbathing, others lay virtually naked, their kit and uniform drying on a washing line.

For the second time I checked out the explosives we had captured up near Prozor. They were Russian and had travelled via Libya and the Dalmatian coast before we had discovered them in a massive cellar. Windowless and damp the 'dungeon' had also contained much more ammunition; Chinese heavy machine-guns and thousands of cases of bullets. All of these were supplemented by a plentiful supply of pullout rocket launchers and other heavier East German made versions. My thoughts returned to the television cameras of HTV (Croatian TV) - they had filmed me victoriously standing upon cases of rockets and launchers, brand new in their crates.

Where was the UN when these arms landed? There was supposed to be an embargo on the whole region, including a blockade by US and

96

British navy ships in the Adriatic - but these had got through unscathed. Perhaps the Serbians had supplied it all? But this was unlikely, despite their Eastern Bloc origin. The explosives had definitely been intended for the Muslims as they had travelled via Libya. In the end I couldn't figure out all the political games taking place - there were so many international fingers in the Bosnian pie that it was difficult to ascertain who was allied to who in the end - I was just grateful that we had captured the consignment before our enemies.

I tried to return to happier thoughts but this was difficult - staring at the blue sky, watching the odd cloud wend its way across the stratosphere I drifted off to sleep. When I awoke I was sunburned - my face and arms red up to the T-shirt sleeves. I'd forgotten my Factor 15! I returned the explosives to our wine cellar and the plastic explosives to the back-room - to think that if the box I held went off then the house, the surrounding buildings and countryside would end up a mile or so away, halfway to Mostar. I summoned a jeep and left the other soldiers wondering what I was up to.

Two doctor friends of mine duly arrived. Everyone claimed they were fascists. In my mind they did their jobs perfectly well, saw the result of carnage more than most and, after a few days in their company, I came to understand their personal logic. I agreed, for instance, that Croats could be too soft in their approach to the war. It was a mark in favour of the Croat people, for instance, that they took in Muslims during the conflict and allowed them to pass through the country. But while we were at war with them? While their forces were killing our innocent men and women? I don't think many western powers would have responded so amicably. It was the kind of policy detrimental to the war-effort, we made friends at the expense of ultimate victory - I think it had something to do with Croatia's attempt to ingratiate itself with Western Europe and perhaps their wish to join Nato and the EC which made them less ruthless.

We talked like this on our way to Mostar but allowing the younger doctor to drive toward the hospital was a big mistake. He was an out and out maniac on the road. I tried to put aside the sheer cliff-faces on the mountain drops, ignore the mental picture of our vehicle dropping over the precipice corner after corner. It was unbelievable how quickly and dangerously people drove in Bosnia. I once asked a guy if it was just because it was war, trying to keep one step ahead of the mortars and snipers, but apparently they drove like that before the war - it was their way.

With some relief we arrived in Mostar; when you travel 2,000 miles to fight for freedom and had spent the last twelve months dodging bullets and shells, to die in a car crash would have been a real dog's death - a nonsense and total waste - but you wasted your breath as the drivers loved to frighten a soldier.

We had driven to a dental surgery that had been turned into a telephone exchange. It was the main communications centre linking Mostar, Split on the Dalmatian coast (which at the time was cut off from Croatia) and the rest of Croat held territory. The centre had been hit the day before we arrived and the girls who ran the offices had gone to be replaced by uniformed personnel - their faces pale for the time of year, the atmosphere serious and stressed. There had been considerable street fighting throughout Mostar in the days previously and the atmosphere had not been helped by the recent massacre of 36 HVO soldiers in the Tihomic barracks in the East of the city. Even I, a natural joker at times, took the strained effect from all those present - the jokes and trivialities were in the past - war in the fullest sense had come to Mostar.

AN ASPECT OF INHUMANITY ON THE STREETS OF MOSTAR

Bullet after bullet ripped into the dead body as it lay in the street, making it shake about as it absorbed blow after blow. This was the mentality of our enemy; they would play games with the dead and appeared to have little or no conscience about doing it, they exhibited hatred beyond most people's capability. As the seventh or eighth bullet tore at the cold flesh of the Croatian woman we decided it was time to exact a little revenge of our own.

My comrade Tomis nodded in my direction and a moment later we were moving quickly through the nearest wrecked and ruined building toward the Bosnian enemy. We reached a flooded cellar that looked beyond repair. By mid-1993 Mostar was well and truly destroyed - few buildings had escaped shell, artillery or gunfire. Initially, Croatian forces had driven the Serbs out into the surrounding mountains above the city to the East and North. The Serbian Army had certainly received a shock when they found themselves in retreat as up until then they had thought themselves invincible.

For the moment the City was locked in a stalemate - small but regular skirmishes taking place between the Bosnian Army and us. Again and again we fought each other tooth and nail before we finally drove the Bosnians across the river to the East, holding their forces there. Now we planned another skirmish. As stealthily as possible, we edged closer to the sniper who was taking sick pot shots at the corpse. We worked our way along the side of a building to where several Bosnian soldiers sat lazing in the afternoon sun.

Then we spotted our target - we were twenty metres or so from the blown-out window of a roofless building where the sniper lay. It was no matter of luck that we had got so close to them but more by their stupidity - they had failed to have two soldiers in the empty building where we now took up a vantage point. One of their number looked like a foreigner. Mostar had its share of foreign nationals - the night before an English volunteer in the Bosnian army had been shot dead, a bullet tearing through his face and head. We buried him in an unmarked grave like so many in this war.

Our position had a slight blind spot. We had an almost clear view of the building below but we couldn't see a few of their men because of a wall which they sensibly used for shelter - higher up this wall was a large window. As quietly as possible we took up firing positions - Tomis crouched a metre or so away and then nodded in the direction of three Bosnians, two of whom were stripped to the waist while the other, a mere youth of 16 or 17, was dozing quietly.

One of the other two was the sniper who had shot the dead body in the road - he was lying on his belly next to his partner as they scanned the buildings opposite from which we had come. Our AKs aimed, we instinctively fired at the same moment - it was now the enemies turn to have bullets rip across their flesh. As expected all three didn't stand a chance - then with synchronised precision Tomis and I swung our rifles over to two separate windows - waiting, not wasting ammunition - with us bullets counted and more or less always killed, we only wounded if we wanted to take prisoners. In unison we primed then lobbed a grenade each through the windows. Not waiting for the explosions, we ran back the way we had come, down the stairs until we came to a dark entry that led to the street. We laid three small mines across the entry before Tomis ran across the street into a shell hole, I quickly followed him.

A machine-gun clattered into action, how many Chinese guns there were in Bosnia was anyone's guess, but they seemed to be the weapon of choice. But the gunner could not get the right angle, as we lay sweating and panting close to the ground - stones digging into our bodies and legs. As expected our snipers pinned down the machine-gun position, preventing the gunner from being over-adventurous as he continued to shoot just above the hole where we lay. The whack of rifle bullets came into the shell-hole, it appeared that they were coming from near where their dead were lying.

Then mortar shells started to come in on top of us - it was time to get up and out - and, as our comrade Ivan started firing from the roof, we

The Silent Cry

fled the hole, knowing that the possibility of death was very close in these types of circumstances. Both of us landed in a heap just inside a doorway - bullets whacking into it inches above our heads.

'Shit Tomis, move, move' I called.

'Out the back - out the back' he breathlessly replied.

Tomis propelled himself toward the opening - a cry went out from him but he kept going then turned a corner as I followed quickly behind. Stone splinters and bullets flew everywhere as the machine-gun tore the entry to the building apart, fire coming right through the straight corridor within inches of where we took cover. Ripping Tomis's shirt I could see a bullet wound that had seared a rib on his lower left side.

'You lucky bastard Tomis, you never got it good and proper - the way you deserve'

His reply was swift even though he was still recovering from his fresh wound; 'you Scottish bastard, you should take one in the head!'

'Thank-you Tomis, thank-you'

'Well Tomis, no medics so I'll have to sew you up!'

'You will sew only your socks - not me you fuckin' barbarian!'

'Ok, ok Tomis, calm down'. He winced as I poured an alcohol solution and applied a dressing to his wound. A stone splinter whacked me on the forehead, I cursed over and over at the sting but then felt relieved that it hadn't been a bullet.

Some of our men made a racket as they came toward us - checking that we were still in one piece, there were looks of concern as they spotted Tomis's blood-soaked shirt and dressing. 'Nehme Problema... ok! Malo Problem!' I immediately assured them in broken Serbo-Croat - 'he's OK, just a flesh wound' I reiterated.

Tomis translated for them and they smiled at first and then broke into laughter - Tomis wasn't laughing, then I take it he realised that he was still alive and felt that that was something to laugh about, so he burst out with laughter but then abruptly stopped as it made his side hurt.. Shots were still being fired all about, the Muslims must have thought that we were making a concerted attack on their positions. It all died down quickly. We were pleased with ourselves; having left five of them dead and possibly more after we had thrown the grenades - it was a crazy war, then aren't they all? Tomis was taken to the hospital on the hill while I reported our little operation to the local commander, more out of respect for him than out of necessity. He was happy enough - as long as the killing continued.

Revenge was still an important factor in Mostar. When the initial fighting had begun between the Muslims and ourselves we had lost 36 men while they slept at a local barracks over the river. It was all part and parcel of war - one minute we defended Muslim families and shared our food, medicine and arms with them - the next they repaid us with death as our men lay asleep, exhausted from two months guard duty at the front.

Time after time it saddened me to think of Muslims and Croatians fighting each other. The only benefactor of this enmity could be the Serbs and it was they who were the real bad guys in this war - as a result Mostar was the main focus for fighting between Muslims and Croats while the Serb forces in the hills took a back seat, lobbing occasional artillery and shell fire in on the city from above. Later I was told that the dead woman's body which had been shot up had been recovered and returned to her family for burial - it was little consolation.

Fighting between Bosnian Muslims and Croatians intensified as the days went by. The horrors increased and to say that the war was brutal would be an understatement. It was at that time - just after the Konjic massacres of Croatian men, women and children - that the only rule of war seemed to be that there were no rules. The Bosnians could and did commit acts that made the Nazi pogroms of the Second World War look amateurish. Imprisoned Croat soldiers and civilians were forced at gunpoint to give blood beyond safe amounts - person-to-person transfusions were forced. Even the Nazis never did such as far as I know, other than perhaps in the experiments performed by Dr. Mengele at Auschwitz.

That evening I sat smoking a cigarette, easing my back against an uneven but cool wall - looking up at the stars, the heavens seemed serene, a place of peace looking down upon human war. Then I realised that I didn't smoke, had never smoked. So why? I threw the cigarette into the air and it sparked for a moment against the night and inevitably some enemy fired at it, raining machine-gun fire on us as we ducked for cover. Taking cover I looked back at the wall, a pattern of holed plaster and brick emerging with the fire - it felt good, really good that I hadn't been standing up. Of course, when I had sat down I had taken the precaution of checking that there was a wall opposite, which covered me from any direct fire. It was natural to survey one's surroundings or to look at the places other soldiers left unattended. Everything became second nature in war - if not your death would be quick through carelessness.

Immediately two small explosions could be heard in quick succession. I crawled over to a small man-made aperture in the wall. There was a commotion in the doorway, the same one earlier in the day where Tomis and I had taken cover - it seemed as if our hated enemy had come through the corridor and the two mines had gone off! Above all the machine-gun and rifle fire I could make out the cries of a badly wounded man, it was obviously one of their soldiers who had intended to get near our position - perhaps he had been hoping for revenge following the death of his comrades earlier in the day.

I suddenly considered firing an RPG round into the entrance as the enemy soldiers came back for their wounded - that thought appealed to me so I held back from firing my rifle. I signalled to one of our soldiers to get me a primed RPG - speaking the letters in a Croat accent - he made no mistake. Only a few metres away I aimed and fired, immediately pulling away from the hole in the wall - an explosion shook the air before silence came from across the way - smoke and dust billowed from the building. Everything was silent now - it was so eerie; seldom if ever did I experience such a sense or feeling, it stopped me dead in my tracks.

Mortars fired from the enemy lines interrupted the temporary pause. One was blasted at us from less than a quarter of a kilometre away, exploding on the top of a wall on the room next to us - only the dividing wall saving our group. The cries of the dead could be heard again, it was all I could hear above the force of the explosion. It was a sound I had known almost everyday since my first hours up in the mountain frontline of Babice.

We shouted for medics - a doctor sectioned to us looked at me pleadingly for he was under orders that under no circumstances should he ever help any unit other than Special Forces - it was an understandable order but this time I decided that as we had not been hit his priority should be to tend to the other unit. I nodded my approval. He crawled through a hole in the wall toward our wounded. Minutes later I was told that one had died and three others had been wounded but not life-threateningly so. Almost immediately a giant of a figure emerged from the empty doorway - it was Tomis. I was amazed to see him back so quickly, he was trying to copy me; a few hours in hospital and then back to the action. Of course all soldiers develop this kind of suicidal tendency, the tendency being even more prevalent in those who volunteer for action.

'Tomis you are a bigger fool than I', I said as I greeted him.

'Scot!' he replied before giving me a big bear hug - this was the common way to show brotherhood and it was the most emotion you could probably ever get out of Tomis, especially when it was directed at a foreigner. But then Croats showed me more feeling in 3 years than I had received in the previous 43 in Britain.

As he released me he spoke with concern, 'Scot we have a problem, No?'

'Yes, Tomis' I replied, 'four it seems dead or dying, another three wounded and out of immediate action. All of them from the Mostar brigade - their morale will be shattered regardless of how many enemies we kill.

My voice petered out as I thought of our dead, dying and wounded - had I really brought it all about by firing that RPG round or was it just another aspect of war, that business of cause and effect?

Life was shit for me and for all of us involved in taking the lives of others. Conscience played no part; that was for saints and angels and perhaps the UN to discuss in their meetings and debates but still I felt, as I lowered myself on to the gravel, that I had killed my own by launching that last attack.

'Scot, snap out of it - war is war. You are no more to blame than I, or him or him' he said pointing to a few more of our number.

Their faces said it all. They were waiting eagerly to go into action, to prove themselves again and risk their lives by the second - it made them feel worthy; it certainly was no matter of honour or heroism, too many heroes lay dead or crippled now to aspire to those ideals. All I wanted to do was see these great people live and survive through to freedom - to regain the rights taken from them - taken by a Serbian onslaught inspired by jealousy, irrational hatred and the powerful forces at Serbia's disposal, the Yugoslav Federal Army.

'Tell them Tomis. You're back in command now - tell them what they should do, give them your orders', my voice wavered and I felt like turning away.

'No Scot, I only came to see you shake in your overpriced boots. You're getting too old for war - it's a young man's game but I'll let you command one last time!' Tomis jeered, ducking as I tried to slap him.

'Right then, Tomis, who's coming with me' I demanded.

He pointed to 8 men with absolutely no hesitation - 'those other 9 will act as back-up if and when you run into serious problems, as you always do Scot. The Muslims have many fanatics, like yourself, they have many fundamentalists fighting on their side'.

'Yes, I experienced them up in Gornji Vakuf but they die just as any other soldier - for some reason the blood flows a little faster'.

'Go before I take over' Tomis chimed in, 'if not I'll have you clean my boots British Army style...' It was the old Tomis, a born humorist. In any situation, life or death, the 'bear' would always be joking, I didn't doubt that he'd laugh at my funeral.

A 49 year-old old Croatian guy was to act as our guide. He had lived in Mostar all his life and even amid the wrecked and ruined city of his birth we believed he knew every nook, cranny, bullet and shell-hole in the city. We followed him without hesitation. He couldn't speak a word - a result of him having been captured by the Serbs at the start of the war, his tongue had been ripped out while he was detained at a

The Silent Cry

Concentration Camp. This man was a personification of the Croatian struggle - one part of his ear had been sliced off, whether he thought himself lucky to be alive or not remained, like him, a mute question.

Instead he communicated by sign language, a useful thing during a raid, it was also useful that a couple of our number could read sign language, as I hadn't a clue. On we went - the guy traversing the rubble silently and wherever he would move I tried desperately to follow, but I was a little clumsier, moving the odd stone, he on the other hand was stealth itself. A number of times he crouched down and reached back his arm to check that I was keeping close by, it was essential that we grouped closely together, all of us would repeat this movement down the line to make sure we kept in tight formation; crouched, our guns low but at the ready. We were not spotted in those moments, as we finally made it to within 10 metres or so of one of the enemy's makeshift barracks. It had taken us about an hour to cover a kilometre distance, but we had penetrated their frontline.

Mostar was all about tit-for-tat fighting. The Bosnians and Serbs outnumbered Croatian forces by an average of 6 to 1 in Mostar so our forces were reduced to these sneak missions, a full frontal attack would leave us at a considerable disadvantage. But then only mad men would venture into enemy territory while the moon shone brightly, there was no wind to cover any noises we might make either - this mission certainly had the odds stacked against it. The moon flitted in front of and behind the clouds, to a man we were eager to make the final move. The soldier immediately behind me tried to attract the attention of the guide. Communicating in silence it was established that the entrance to the barracks had been changed - sandbags and heavy beams of wood now fortified it, whereas before it had been a normal double-door.

We stopped to check our weapons. This was it - the do or die stuff was here and now. This was one of the rare times when I felt a little trepidation before going in for the kill - I'd nervelessly killed so many times that it felt strange, it might have been the moon or the fact that we were in a city that made me nervous, whatever I quickly shook the feeling and replaced fear with a cold, professional resolve.

Before I had time to think again it was on - we vaulted a wall and then heard the sound of footsteps followed by a gurgle, our guide had ambushed a Muslim in the street that ran at the back of the building - I could see him withdrawing his blade from the victim's brain and neck. He lifted the body into the alleyway we had just left and placed it quietly on the floor. Back to the business in hand. It was 2 am now as the three of us removed the sandbags and crouched in the back door entrance - two of our men had positioned themselves in good sniper vantage points in the upper floor of an adjacent burnt out building behind the barracks overlooking the back entrance.

Meanwhile another two men waited eagerly by the dead body in the alleyway over the wall. We could hear light laughter coming from the front of the building as I drilled out the wooden surrounds of the lock before easing it from the door, laying it silently on a sandbag next to our guide. Ivan had joined us in this mission, sacrificing his preferred option of sitting behind a machine-gun, he was keen and, at only 24 years old, young, fit and fearless enough for this task. Once we had prised the door open we got inside. Our 4 soldiers outside had the doorway and windows well covered for our retreat, hasty or otherwise.

A truck could be heard as it drove nearer the barracks' entrance - it was probably returning from the frontline - the soldiers would be tired and drained, this was not so good however as they would also be hardened to battle with quicksilver reactions.

The next double door was opened with ease - there were no locks or bolts on it - and then we could see a dim light at the far end of the lounge room. The building was once a warehouse; all the windows were covered with cloth and blankets. The guide went about his business swiftly and murderously, shooting the sleeping men with his Skorpion silencer - he was efficient and with good reason, killing was now our first nature. Nodding to Ivan, who would act as a guard on the lower floor, the guide led me up a stairway and onto a corridor which had a dozen or so rooms off it. There was the stench of blocked toilets and our guide grimaced as he turned the handle of the first door that led to a massive main office. All the windows were blacked out as our Maglite torches scanned the desks for a sign of life.

Suddenly we spotted a soldier asleep at a desk, our guide stole over and plunged his knife into the enemies neck, ripping it deep into his brain and out again. My heart began to beat a little faster as I strained to contain my desire to fly into action. The guard returned with a sinister smile on his face, sheathed his knife and took his silencer pistol out again. He was temporarily in charge of the killing while I had an AK which, if used, would make a real racket and alert the whole building.

We crept to the next room which was empty and on to a third - a shout from the far end of the corridor made us turn and I fired a short burst toward the soldier at the far end - he was wearing a camouflage uniform but had bare feet and, as I caught him, he fell to the floor. Unfortunately the noise of my AK alerted everyone in the building, lights coming on in all the other rooms off the corridor. Our cover blown, it was AK time as we raked along the rooms while running down the corridor, blasting until we reached the dead soldier at the other end of the corridor.

The Silent Cry

I stumbled over him and flew through a swing door...

On we ran, to a landing and then down a flight of stairs. There was firing from both above and below. Realising that some enemy had survived our onslaught I backtracked up the stairs once more. Ivan would be covering the lower floor with no problem, they wouldn't be able to get near him as he sprayed his fire behind a barricade of beds, doors or whatever he could find, aware that a grenade could blow him to bits.

Outside firing could be heard left, right and centre. This was the reason for my trepidation - caught in the crossfire, escape might prove beyond us. I made my way back up the stairs and found the guide lying flat on his stomach in the small gap between the swing doors. This made it difficult for us both to fire as the angle was working against us, the return fire blasting just above where we lay. My guide intimated that some of the fire was coming from a room halfway along the corridor, from the direction of the first office.

There had to be another stairway - then I remembered that I hadn't checked a door to my right further down the hall. Pulling the guide back I rolled a grenade along the smooth corridor floor - it exploded killing the opposition in the far office. Quickly the guide was up, pelting toward the far office firing from the hip as he went, the guy was certainly something to see - an automaton with a heart like a lion. I figured that they couldn't have any grenades otherwise they would have used them on us by now, we really stood out as we pounded down the hall towards the stairway that we had overlooked.

Then an office door was ripped apart by enemy fire and we hit the deck, bullets whizzing above our heads as the door came off, its hinges toward us. I hurled another grenade in the doorway, it exploded and the return fire ceased for several seconds before a scream went up and the firing started up again. I threw yet another grenade in and heard a shout from that general direction before an almighty explosion deafened my ears and silenced the enemy. But just as quickly machine-gun fire could be heard outside. Blood pouring from his head, the guide led me back down the corridor toward the stairway by the back entrance.

With a crash a trap door opened from the corridor roof, the guide shot up the space and my hearing returned just as another dead Muslim dropped to the floor. We jumped down the stairs, Ivan shouting up to me while he covered us, shooting deep into the lower floor corridor.

'Scot, both of you go, go out the back way - All dead? All dead?' shouted Ivan.

'Yeah, all dead - good work but were fucked now - they're everywhere', I said pushing the guide out of the doorway and insisting he join the others over the wall - they had held their positions well, suffering only a hand injury to one sniper.

'Trip-wire Ivan, trip wire' I called but he needed no advice. An expertise gleaned from the many hasty retreats we'd made to save our skins in the past, as the guide and I ran from the building, over the small wall in the back and through an empty building nearby. Within seconds the tripwire had gone off, a huge explosion ripping the back entrance apart as the guide and I turned and trained our weapons on the falling debris - there was a figure and in seconds Ivan identified himself shouting at us not to shoot.

Immediately, as the Muslims recovered from the blast, machine-guns opened up all around us - by now the three of us were grateful still to be alive and were planning, privately at least, for a coward's retreat across the Neretva to our own lines. The firing finally stopped and we listened intently, trying to distinguish local movements from the rattle of machine-guns all around the city. There were running footsteps and shouts, as I reflected again on the nightmare possibility that they might chase us down and take us prisoner. We were in the shit now alright.

We had two options. To sit tight and ambush our potential captors, or make for our own lines and be forced to fight our way through, risking the chance that we might be discovered, killed or worse taken prisoner. The enemy surrounded us. On the way in it had taken us an hour to silently traverse the distance between our base and their barracks but on the way back we had reached the halfway point in a fraction of the time.

The Muslims were alert alright and were trying to cut us off from our own lines, this gave me a terrible feeling in my guts - knowing that my best laid plans had come to this, a feverish retreat with every chance of failure.

'Scot, Scot', Ivan finally spoke, 'where are all the others'.

'In and around', I replied, 'but what next?'

'It's best we keep together' he assured me before conferring in Croat with the rest of the squad. Quickly he and the old guide had co-opted 6 of the patrol while Franjo (an 18 year old volunteer), myself and a couple of others protected the rear.

All of this time there were the nearing sounds of footsteps - the Bosnians didn't need to think about noise now as they clearly held the upper hand and were organising themselves swiftly to eliminate us. To the left and right we could hear voices as we waited in an alley between two derelict buildings, they were working in unison, I sensed, as Franjo and I kept down in the near total darkness at the end of the alley waiting for the slightest movement up ahead. There was now no time to spare, my adrenaline singing, drying my throat, making me swig again from my water bottle.

The Silent Cry

Suddenly bullets lashed out in our general direction, belting into stone walls and doorways as we lay cowering for a few seconds before Franjo and I returned fire, lashing our bullets towards them less than twenty metres away - but the bastards were clever and had retreated back around the corner at the far end of the alley. They attacked again, taking advantage of the empty buildings on either side of us, hugging the walls for cover, there were six or seven of them.

Immediately I nodded to Ivan and we sprang our surprise counterattack, the six in front and our four in the rear gunning up the alley as one of my number hurled a grenade toward the far end of the alley while bullets ripped back at us, there was a scream at our end and someone next to Ivan was hit; the grenade exploded back towards us but we were safe from it while Ivan turned to his right to inspect the damage to our man - he was dead.

The blast had silenced the enemy, for now. We had lost one man for sure; another had had his knee shattered. Meanwhile the rest of us trained our sights on the alley ahead, there were moans and I could tell that they were weary; a Muslim cried out for assistance, we shot him dead. Still, we had a few hundred metres to go to reach relative safety. But as soon as this optimistic thought entered my head shots came towards us - so we moved on, carrying our dead and wounded through empty buildings nearby until we came in sight of the building opposite the hotel which backed onto the river - the main bridge beside it had long since been blown to pieces.

Ivan let off a small flare in an attempt to signal to our side which part of the river we would be crossing and within minutes our forces began firing at their frontline nearby, attempting to keep them occupied. We continued, trying not to think of the consequences of capture, one more street and we'd be upon the hotel - clearly there would be a huge number of Muslims nearby, this was their frontline.

Heavy gunfire reached out to us again as we made the twenty metres or so to the building over from the hotel. I laughed as I thought about the need for some John Wayne type character to rescue us, my laughter prompting a deluge of bullets to be fired in our direction. A couple of enemy soldiers were cut down by Ivan as we finally took shelter in the building - regardless of Ivan being encumbered by having to carry his dead comrade over his shoulder he was still capable of punching his weight.

Almost immediately a fusillade of bullets came upon us - our movements had been seen but none of us cared about that now, as four of us guarded the back of the building while the others went up front to try and figure out a way forward toward the hotel and eventually over the river. A Muslim gunman had been positioned a little down the street to our left and was firing into the road, almost as if he were warning of the consequences of attempting to reach the river. Down we went, hiding among the debris of war; the spent cartridges and empty mine boxes lying about in the derelict building.

I knelt before a window at the back of the building, blasting shots into the night, aiming at anyone in the vicinity - it was surreal, my head spinning with vague memories of Westerns I had watched as a child - this was The Alamo alright. Stone splinters whacked at my head and reality came back - in full Technicolor. Ivan returned with the news that all hell had broken out in the riverside hotel. Bosnian snipers had been seen jumping from first and ground floor windows - but still we at the back had to fight off the enemy.

Then there were shots from those up ahead as the Muslim gunman to our left started up again - it was becoming clear that our forces over the river had come across to the hotel and occupied it, that was the reason the Muslims had hastily evacuated it and landed slap bang in the sights of our men at the front of the building. Bodies lay in the street now - some still moving, calling out in agony as heavier fire came from behind us. We had to get out now.

Just then a grenade exploded right outside the back of the building, pieces of shrapnel hitting the wall I hid behind as the heavy machine-gun continued to train itself on my window. This attack meant that the Muslims knew that their men had been ousted from the hotel - they were desperate to make sure we left their side of the river. There's no doubt this time, I thought, I am definitely getting out of Bosnia after this - it's all too much for my nerves.

Ivan ordered us to get out and over to the hotel. Immediately the HVO forces in the hotel started bombarding the gunner down the street to the left, covering us as we emerged from the building. But no sooner had we reached the street than their forces began attacking from the rear, coming through the window I had just vacated, bullets flying past us, making us run faster and when we reached the hotel we flung ourselves gratefully at the feet of our men - they were the cavalry, I thought, the real life John Waynes. In minutes the Muslims had overrun our little hideout opposite the hotel, they were desperate not to offer the HVO a foothold and began firing at us in the hotel.

Mortar shells then came from our own lines giving us a little hope as they smashed into the building opposite. Immediately we recognised the opportunity to escape and sped through the lower floor of the gutted building towards the river at the rear. The Neretva was cold and in the dark fairly uninviting, but our men had brought over a couple of rubber

The Silent Cry

dinghies and a rope had been erected so that we could pull ourselves across.

Ivan took the dead Croatian in one boat while a number of us took the other, fire erupting all around us as we floated across, the water spitting up as the bullets thankfully missed their targets. Finally we reached the other side and sent the boat back to evacuate the others - grenades exploding from the building opposite the hotel as our own men made a dash for it, tumbling down the bank and into the little boats as our forces on the West bank let forth some of the heaviest firing I have ever seen. Nevertheless one dinghy was holed, a soldier screaming before falling into the grey Neretva, his stranded comrades swimming the final few metres to safety.

Jeeps were waiting as we witnessed the final evacuation of our forces from the Muslim held East bank of Mostar and, as we were taken up the hill to the hospital the night came alight with explosions and gunfire, the city shaking after another bloody night as I pondered once more the wisdom of the whole operation.

Throughout the summer of 1993 the situation in Mostar remained tense. The action on the ground remained intense to the extent that soldiers would come and go from the conflict, leaving to rest their shattered nerves. I left Mostar in spring and returned in midsummer. Little had changed, but the need to maintain decent intelligence on the enemy occupying the opposite bank remained...

A Croatian crept ahead of me. Fearless, calm and controlled the teenage soldier was well versed in the rules and tactics of the war in this city. He had high cheekbones, a big forehead below which his furry Brezhnev style eyebrows rested. He was hewn from Balkan rock. His spirit was as his face, large and daunting and while I often feared action in the immediate moments before a shot had been fired allowing doubts to creep in, this guy was raring to go - for me it was a matter of survival, for him war seemed like oxygen, each skirmish and battle making him stronger.

The young soldier crawled forward and scanned the area in front of him. We were on the west bank opposite the back of the main hotel in Mostar. It was already gutted and burnt but its rear offered a secluded spot from which we could negotiate the river, moving from the Croat controlled west to the Muslim east by floating on car inner tubes. The river was as cold as any I had experienced, the moon, well hidden behind dark, slow moving clouds, offered another cloak behind which we could stealthily negotiate the dividing line of Mostar.

110

Nerves racked both of us, however, as we paddled with our hands across the short stretch to the Muslim side where nervous trigger fingers waited, itching for a shot at real instead of imagined targets. Finally we reached the east bank. As we climbed off our makeshift boats the moon seemed to target us for what seemed like an eternity, focusing on our surreptitious movements before more clouds hid it from view. In my brief panic I tripped over a piece of rubble from one of the destroyed bridges of Mostar, sending it into the Neretva, the splash it made was a little loud.

Immediately, machine-gun and rifle fire split the air as down my comrade and I went, hugging the damp debris on the bank - there was no return fire from our side, our few men under the commander were under strict orders to hold fire. What an idiot I was; this was no game of weighing up some criminal enterprise - sure my criminal past had been essential to my survival so far in Bosnia; the waiting, watching and reccying for potential robberies - knowing that if it didn't go as planned another piece of work could be done and no big deal.

All that is second nature to me but this time failure meant certain death or capture - the latter would probably mean castration as I was a mercenary; no one cared that foreign volunteers were underpaid by the Croats - the Muslims had Arab money, the Serbians the backing of Russian arms, intelligence and 'wherewithal'. No, the Croats were on their own in 1993. But there was no more time for a wandering mind; voices were echoing, they were close, too bloody close - I remembered our mission; there was to be no contact with the enemy, we were to check out all their set-positions; machine-gun, mortar etc. - this information was due to be used as part of a planned assault across the river to take the whole city. Failing that we would try and shell our way across, but in a built-up area that would require pinpoint accuracy and reliable information.

Foot after foot we crawled in the dirt and puddles. The smell of shit everywhere about, the Neretva was a massive toilet now, and the stench hurt my nose it was that bad, but as good soldiers we carried on. The kid knew every part of this building and its surrounds - I passed him the night-sight glasses and he whispered in good English that there seemed to be a frontline command centre 30 metres up the street opposite at the hotel - this would probably house stocks of ammo for the rest of the frontline.

'Dobra, dobra', he whispered, a tinge of glee in his voice as I handed him a timer charge with a pound of plastic explosive attached - we were about to break our orders but it would be worth it. I had disappeared from my normal unit again, only three Croatians knew I was here - this was a revenge mission for the soldiers killed in barracks on the east side of the river while they slept.

The Silent Cry

At 11pm our side finally opened up - lighting the night with explosions - we could get about without so much fear now; we'd seen all we had to through our night-sights. The vibrations came through the rubble and concrete as my guide led the way; he was made for all this - after the war, I thought, he'd make a good ally on raids on the banks of Europe. (Once a criminal...)

We took cover behind some more ruins, the dank smells reminded me of my early years as a child playing in the bombed out, derelict buildings by the Plantation docks in Glasgow. But I was becoming distracted. I had to concentrate on the job in hand. Just then a Muslim soldier came over to investigate our slight noise and paid with his life as the teenager plunged the blade time and again into his heart while he punched the inquisitive guy's face with his free hand. He was quickly dragged away.

Over the street I saw a head and rifle protruding from a lower window. One, two - I hurled a grenade into the window as we ran across the few metres, another explosion hit the street 10 metres away, while the blast from my grenade came down on us sending chunks of masonry and bricks into the air. We tumbled into the building where I had seen the 'rifleman', my torch lighting the back wall where he was slumped - wounded or dead I made sure with a kick to his windpipe, a gurgle and he finally fell to his side.

Bullets tore into the gaping window; the wall plaster disintegrating - a scream from my comrade, a piece of stone had hit him on the side of the face, fracturing his cheekbone. I crashed through a broken door, taking it from its hinges as more bullets flew toward us - there was a back yard, an alleyway and some stairs leading on to the next floor.

'Go', I shouted to my buddy. He went as I waited - the first one came into the darkness, a bullet from my Skorpion silencer hitting his face - it was instinctive now, down he went. Then the next received a burst to the chest, yet another started firing at me from a window near the door - I fired blindly and quickly ran out into the yard trying to find cover - crouching then, hand in pocket, I threw down a few plastic mines. I pounded out of the yard and into the alleyway as wild shots flew about, I figured the guy after me was enraged yet fearful after the death of his comrades - it seemed as if he was firing blindly, his gun angled around the corner of the back door.

My luck was in as I teamed up with my comrade once more, as we crashed down another entry into another derelict building. Everything was on top now. We reached within vision of the frontline command - so close we could hear running feet as the Muslim forces tried, in vain, to retain their cool.

Slowly but surely we reached the back of the command centre and laid the first charge - five minutes for this one, the detonator facing through the charge to increase the impact of the explosion - it was of Russian origin - the explosives were pink in colour and smelled quite pleasant. A set of stairs led down to a basement - I checked the door that led to the rest of the building - it was locked up tight, there was no reason to think anyone would spot the device before it went off, to make sure I covered it with a piece of plywood and handed my buddy another explosive. He timed this one at four minutes, we were pushing our luck! He forced it between sandbags at the side of a window – detonator facing inwards again.

Off we went as shouts and bawling could be heard - we fired but there was no reply, we were nervous as on we ran two abreast toward the hospital. A light support weapon ripped at us from nearby, followed by an almighty explosion as we were leaving Mostar - Bullseye. Just above in the hospital car park there were a few wrecked but drivable ambulances and we jumped in. It would be a straightforward escape, I was well known to the checkpoint staff there. We were home free now, at the top checkpoint I was greeted with smiles and a wave on, they knew me as a friend of their doctors and must have wondered who the other guy in the car was, it didn't matter, I was enough.

Another nightmare drive back to Tomislavgrad in the dark as we came under the hated shellfire. I stayed at Tomislavgrad hospital that night and talked to a German guy who had been beaten up for 'talking out of school'. He was alleged to have given away military secrets but claimed that someone had got him drunk - a harsh punishment but a transgression nevertheless. I advised him to leave before something more serious happened. Days later he left and was never seen again. German police believed that he had been killed; enquiries as to his whereabouts are still continuing but truth is often difficult to find amid the fog of war - it's best to let sleeping dogs lie.

Morning came and I left the hospital and headed for Zagreb. I had an appointment with Professor Culo who could tolerate my craziness - it was enjoyable to converse with him on our walk up to the mountains overlooking Zagreb.

Within weeks I returned to Mostar and the harsh realities of the battle in the city returned once more as a squad of us hid in a bunker near the frontline.

The soldier beside me dropped - dead before he hit the ground. A sniper's bullet hit my 24 year-old friend in the left side of his forehead. Down he went, sprawled out to my left - the morning sun glinting blood coming from his head. A sniper was at work with a silenced weapon and subsonic ammunition. He would be relatively close to where we lay. There was movement among us as just about everyone was up and about attempting to ascertain the exact position of the killer.

A serious problem we faced in Special Forces was that we were normally ahead of our well-protected frontlines, reccying forward of them, this often left us exposed and was the reason that we had lost a good man. No matter how good or professional we were, death came to us with the swiftness of any human. It might not be so easy to kill us but it did happen, and one momentary lapse had caused the death of my colleague.

Several minutes passed before we worked out 'our man's' whereabouts. He was firing from the broken-up minaret. The angle of the bullet and the position of our dead soldier meant it had to come from the Mosque. A Barret .50 calibre sniper rifle was handed to our best shot - we then set-up the enemy soldier, he was only three hundred metres away.

'Whack,' the bullet ripped through the neck and windpipe of our enemy. He had only shown our sniper a couple of inches of his neck but that was enough, the bullet smashing into, through him and then into the wall behind. There were no smiles among us, regardless of our kill, as it was a one-for-one game. At least he was dead, as of course was our man, and he had been no fool, well experienced in war and up to date with the position of snipers and aware of their ability to hit the smallest target.

His death woke us all up because we knew he was experienced - if he could be caught out then any of us could suffer a similar lapse in concentration and expose ourselves to enemy fire. An order was given and within seconds a shell hit the broken top of the minaret, it toppled down to the ground; making it easily exposed to our position. It might have been a little late in the day for our dead comrade but at least it was done, it would not offer such an easy hiding place next time.

Medics took the body of our man away. Each dead soldier was a loss both as a human being as well as depleting our fighting numbers. We were low on numbers in Mostar and often tried to even the score by taking out four or five of theirs to one of ours, we knew that another five Muslim snipers would be waiting to substitute for the dead enemy. Mortar fire came from our lines toward the Muslims. In and around the old Mosque they landed sending smoke, debris and shrapnel through the air. Four, five, six - the 120mm shells exploded in quick succession leaving no doubt in my mind that they would cause more death and destruction - their soldiers would be out to check on the sniper in the minaret, it was a regular tactic to catch them on the hop like this.

Heavy machine guns subsequently opened up on us from the mosque - the bullets ripping toward a wall that protected us, no problem, as it was thick enough to withstand that onslaught. Yet still it unnerved us to know that they knew exactly where we were and made us wonder why they hadn't shelled us as we hid in the roofless building. The only possible explanation was their reluctance to reveal their mortar positions - our mortar squads were as accurate and as swift as any in the world, fear had taken the Muslims again.

Tit for tat fighting continued unabated in the divided city for 6 months. During this period I made occasional visits to deliver aid and supervise other aspects of the HVO struggle.

Tracer fire scored the night sky as the city of Mostar blazed. Fire and smoke painted the heavens, licking the darkness, creating silhouettes against the background of war. There was an unfair artillery exchange going on between the west and east of the city; such was war and whichever side you were on the fighting was intense - over a building, a street, a life.

As men died in their pain and agony the world at large sat at home in comfort, ate in fancy restaurants and counted their wealth. Our evening out was of an entirely different nature. We counted bodies, the bodies of those the world no longer cared for. A malaise sometimes crept over both the enemy and us. The rats still scurried about their business, thriving on the bodies, gnawing at the flesh; the same bodies lay for days when the fighting became so intense.

As usual the almost incessant chatter of machine-gun fire stole more airtime, each bullet had the breath of death upon it. Tonight was a little different - it had started with a series of explosions that became more intense rather than dying down. More than a thousand had gone off by now according to my old friend crouched beside me. The old bastard had tried to calculate how many people had died per explosion, taking into consideration the power of the explosion, its location and his knowledge of the population in Mostar - he was still trying to work it all out.

Masonry fell on us from a burning apartment block, showering us in our roofless, burning building. One minute it was shells, then rain and now the indignity of being showered by pieces of plaster and stone. This Godforsaken war! Cigarettes went flying as soldiers ducked for cover - there was nothing Special about us in these moments as we clambered and tried to get under or behind one another to ward off the crap that fell on top of us - a few cuts and bruises later we returned to our role as spectators.

Suddenly an anti-aircraft gun opened up on us and our surroundings - the son of a bitch was too near the mark for my liking as holes opened up in the upper parts of the building's walls - we were too exposed where we lay, hugging the ground as any sensible snake would do.

We couldn't be seen unless, I thought, this was the point at which they were attempting to attack. Every bridge was blown up apart from the old Ottoman one (although that was soon to change!). That bridge was to my left, up the river - it had already taken a pounding and offered the enemy a foothold on our side of the city.

All of this led to more than a little consternation; unless of course it was as I had originally suspected - that they were aiming at our small group. Their little sortie was trying, as my commander had pointed out, to breach the river where the numbers appeared to be thinnest. Proof of this came soon enough. One of our number had made his way out of our little hideout as the heavy anti-aircraft reached out towards us again. He returned with two others from the observation post and one of them climbed a little higher to overcome the blind spot that blocked our view of the river.

I passed an instruction to them to try and take a prisoner - we needed some information and it was the easiest way. Unless of course the man captured was a fundamentalist, in which case he would probably have died before telling us a thing - if we could understand him. A lot of Mujahadeen volunteers had joined the Muslim cause. We found papers on many dead enemy soldiers including Middle East passports and identification papers. They were determined fighters and would die before breathing a word of any plan - so we needed a Bosnian Muslim, who we could grill and then release.

Our breed, myself apart, were the sons and grandsons of Ustashe. They were the relatives of many of those slaughtered after the war when Tito rounded up the puppet Fascist government and military on the borders of Austria (with Allied help) and returned them to Bleiburg Concentration Camp. There they had been shot and buried - this was the reason that their grandsons fought so fiercely - many in Special Forces had cause to feel aggrieved.

Like the Chechens who I helped fight the Russians, these men were elite. HOS was another group of fighters who I respected. They were said to be fascists in the worst sense of the word, but if they appeared extreme it was because they were engaged in a war against a long-time Serb enemy that had taken every opportunity over the years to subdue the right of Croatians for independence. Elite forces in all countries need to be ruthless - it is just that these guys seemed more determined than the SAS or US Special Forces for all their fancy weaponry and gadgets. Their homes were at stake after all.

Just then, an explosion ripped through the city to my left - it made one hell of a racket, it was as if an earthquake had ripped through the place. A cry was heard as at least two bodies splashed into the river. Soon our man dragged a government soldier over the rubble; he was unconscious. Before I could say a thing, our other men ran past the first one who had the prisoner. They had been responsible for the deaths of two of the enemy - the ones now floating down the Neretva River. Shots had been fired but it was the explosion that had killed them. Laughing faces appeared over the wall into our little shelter, a rope was quickly found to tie up our new addition; never could a soldier be more unfortunate than the one whose arms and feet were now being secured. Two of our soldiers then dragged him by the feet into a nearby Land Rover and off they went.

Such matters at times may seem cruel to civilians but to us it was part and parcel of our ways and these were abnormal circumstances. We settled back down again - cigarettes lit once more as talk broke out among the Croatians. It seemed incredible that they could return calmly to everyday discussion - but that's war and killing, it brings an easy acceptance among really hardened soldiers - a willingness to forego civilian rules in exchange for the sole rule in this war - that there were no rules.

Several hours passed by as we dozed to the sound of the odd bullet zinging the air which was OK. The staccato sound of machine-guns continuing to break the stillness of the night as my mind wandered back to my years in prison, the solitary years and the incessant mind-games played by the prison warders whom I had wished to kill. They can be thankful now. I once thought that there were no brakes on my criminal life. But I reasoned that my life had changed these 12 months or so in Bosnia. If I was to die right here and now in the ruins of a once terrific city then I would have perished for a purpose.

When all was said and done, my life had a value to these Croatian people. In turn I valued their land and people. Their history is long and tortuous, intertwined with the too-ing and fro-ing of power in the Balkans as the East and then the West gained ascendancy. As a result they had never really had their own nation. They had always remained accountable to an external force, be it the Serbs, the Ottomans, the Italians or Germans - this war was their chance and I was here to make sure they took it - they are a people of great worth and stature.

Croatia and Bosnia-Herzegovina offered me the chance to be something in life. To show that I could conform to law and order, move in both the higher and lower circles in Croatia and be respected by people regardless of their circumstances. When given work to do and not ostracised by society and flung in a prison cell, I had proved that I was a

The Silent Cry

decent bloke not an animal.

I smiled quietly and kicked one of our dozing men before we headed off to our barracks to check out the condition of the prisoner. Yes he was in a reasonable condition and had given what appeared to be reliable information. We moved the prisoner out of the barracks and took him to the prison camp behind our lines in the mountains beyond Mostar. Along the way we passed a UNHCR convoy heading for the east of the city. I couldn't and still can't believe that we let them through to re-supply our opponents, but it was the Croatian way, I always felt they were too soft in war.

5 - A PERSONAL LOSS

Following six straight months in Bosnia I went on a working holiday for a few weeks to help out a friend. Ante was one of life's best, a great soldier and former Legionnaire who had deserted the French to fight for his country. Thin, blond and wiry he didn't look like a great fighter, but he had the courage and strength of a lion. He was a commander in HOS, a fighting unit termed 'extreme' in Western newspapers. That may have been the case, but the simple fact remains that they fought with Croatian freedom in mind - to my mind they were a true brotherhood, representing an adequate response to the many Serb paramilitaries who had butchered their way through Croatia and Bosnia during the first two years of the war.

Ante and I had arrived in Montenegro, then as now part of rump Yugoslavia, to carry out a 'rogue' mission - this was most definitely an unordered kidnapping. On a veranda lay a Serbian soldier. I take it he was supposed to be a guard, but he appeared to be oblivious to his surroundings as we approached the larger than usual type of house known to Montenegro. Since the fall of Vukovar the soldier accompanying me had burned with what I would term a controlled hatred. At the time of the siege of the town I had been a prisoner in Strangeways Prison in Manchester. I knew of the general struggle taking place but knew little of the 'Butcher of Vukovar', one Colonel Sljivancanin.

Day by day I heard the radio bulletins while in prison. They related the continued bombardment of the town, the relentless shelling by T-55 tanks. Upward of 500 artillery pieces, from the smallest mortar to the more lethal 120mm, were used to bludgeon the civilians of the border town into submission. Following Vukovar's fall its people were slaughtered like cattle while the International community continued to take a neutral attitude to the siege.

As a result the slaughter in Vukovar was, in many ways, a defeat for the Serbs. They might have overrun the town and had their wicked way with the Croat population but in the minds of all Croats the news of defiant civilians holding off the mighty Yugoslav Federal Army was a battle-cry for independence - the town becoming known as the Phoenix of Croatia. It also belatedly alerted Nato and the UN to the Croat cause and played a large part in persuading the Germans to recognise Croatia as an independent nation a few months later.

The role in the siege of Colonel Sljivancanin became infamous. He was the Yugoslav army commander who expelled the Red Cross from the town on October 19th when Vukovar hospital finally fell. All but 60 of the remaining 420 patients were removed from the hospital, the rest were killed and their bodies dumped in a mass grave on a sheep farm near the town. There was no doubt that Colonel Sljivancanin held the burden of blame for slaughtering patients at the hospital and that was why Ante and I were in Montenegro. We were attempting to take the Colonel prisoner, but it didn't quite turn out as intended...

It was summer up in the hills, on the outskirts of a small village in Montenegro, as the Colonel slept off another night's heavy drinking, surrounded by assorted guards and military flunkies. This was the complacent nature of these people, a weird aspect of the Balkan mentality, an attitude that was going to cost them. It was as dark as possible, there was no moon and, as we crept closer to the villa, some dogs could be heard barking in nearby houses. I stopped, they could easily give us away, but I needn't have worried, the occupants of the house were well away. Ante and I continued into the night, nearing the house and closing in on the drunken guard on the veranda.

Lights were shining through the shutters of the lower windows. Meanwhile the human pig was snoring away into a clear night sky, the stars twinkling, acknowledging our desire to wreak carnage on the occupants of the house. Montenegro is a puppet satellite of Serbia (their forces were involved in the shelling of Dubrovnik) and they remained a vital strategic ally as they represented Serbia's only access to the Adriatic coast.

Ante crept ahead of me, my comrade-in-arms stealthily covering the few remaining metres to the sprawled out Serbian. He quickly advanced and speared the guard near the solar plexus before flicking his blade free, his left hand covering the Serb's mouth before bringing it away, the stale smell of Rakija upon it.

Slowly, Ante turned the front door handle as I turned the Serb over - slipping a pillow under his head to give a passer-by the impression that he was asleep. I felt he had got away a little too easily for my liking, his death too instant. A second later I followed Ante into the garlic infested hallway; there were rooms to the left and right and stairs immediately ahead against the right wall, beyond which was a kitchen door.

The hallway light was switched off as we entered. Ante nodded to my right as we took a door each. I quickly turned the handle, it opened in silence, not a creak; before me two soldiers lay asleep, one on a large sofa the other on the floor, a woman occupied another sofa. My Skorpion silencer spat twice into the half-dressed woman on the sofa, the fact that she was a woman gave me no second thought; she was a soldiers' whore and died like a dog. I shot her prone lover in the brain, always and without reserve I regret the swiftness of their deaths. Never did I tire of giving death to the enemy. Yes, I was callous and brutal, the changes in me made by the daily events and mentality of our enemy in Bosnia as they wore down my humanity, seeking the animal in me with pinpoint accuracy.

I returned to the hallway, light out, door closed. Ante triumphantly raised his bloody knife before he led the way to the kitchen and diner. In we went, each to a separate door. A shot barked out behind me and I smashed my door wide open and instinctively opened fire - hitting a head, back and shoulders as they began to rise from a slumped position at a large wooden table. One bullet smashed through an ear, the others I fired into a spine near the neck. Both shots were reactive.

I turned and automatic fire could be heard before I saw Ante crashing out of the room he had entered - his hand throwing a grenade back into the room - Whack! - the explosion deafened me and before I knew it we were running up the stairs.

A door flew open and a figure in green underwear appeared on the landing. I grabbed a Kalashnikov standing at the bottom of the stairs as Ante's Skorpion spat out in silence, hitting the soldier in his chest and stomach - the unfortunate tumbled down the stairs, his pistol falling from his dead hand. We caught him and toppled him over the railings. On we went smashing our way into an upstairs bedroom - the 'Colonel' attempting to free his drunken mind and body from another whore who had, it seemed, collapsed asleep on top of him. Less than 60 seconds had elapsed since the shots in the kitchen.

Through a drunken fog the Colonel struggled to push the woman aside, both were naked - fit for death. 'Vermin', I screamed, crunching my boot into the woman's neck, forcing it to break and snap, the same foot then came down on the commander's face, shattering his teeth, snapping his jaw and cheekbone. Quickly, Ante grabbed the dead body of the naked woman and removed it, the Colonel was unconscious.

As a 'field mattress' she was finished. Although not more than sixteen or seventeen years of age there was an appearance of beauty to her in death, her features were perfect; but these afterthoughts felt out of place to me - I was slipping by seeing them as human beings. Nevertheless it disturbed me for days knowing that I had seen her as a human victim rather than merely an obstacle to be eliminated - I considered retirement! I dragged our prisoner by the legs. His head hitting every stair as we made our way down. My good friend Ante led the way, carrying the Kalashnikov I had found.

Out the back and through the kitchen. We stepped over the dead bodies, dragging the Colonel over the concrete slabs at the back of the house. Then we heard it all; screaming and shouting, lights coming on all over the place. 'Live and let live', I said as Ante wrenched open the door on the Land Rover. Keys in hand - Ante had been sharp in spotting them on the bedside table in the Colonel's bedroom - we prepared for our getaway.

The Colonel was well out of it as I dumped him into the back - local people were running toward the house and the jeep; Ante drove away from the scene as I urged him to knock as many of the locals down as possible. He later took a swing at me when he recalled me saying this, especially as I came out with the clichéd 'all's fair in love and war' nonsense - still it can't all be about squirrels and picnics can it.

Through the hills we rattled and for once I wasn't nervous about the speed at which Ante was driving as we swung dangerously close to the sheer drops, my Croat friend a maniac behind the wheel. After ten minutes of his driving and a few near misses with the cliff-side I had had about enough. I would rather face a mortar shell attack (which I loathed) than Ante's crazy type of driving. He laughed; then I spotted his arm, it had been cut wide open and I asked why he hadn't mentioned it, but then there was little time to tend to light wounds.

All our plans had flown out of the window - it was not a matter of being thwarted but more an expectation that something had to go wrong, it had all gone far too easily to this point. It had been far too simple as we had approached the house and before that when we had stolen a car from the coastal area. It had all gone too smoothly for a pessimist like myself.

Still, what mattered was that we had 'the Butcher of Vukovar' in the boot, the same man who had ordered the deaths of doctors and dragged the wounded from their beds, kicked, punched and then killed them, while their forces raped nurses at gun-point. Kidnapping Colonel Sljivancanin was a coup by any standard - to capture and take him back to Croatia would be a morale boost for our side, even though there could be no official backing or publicity about his kidnap. The Serbian and Montenegrin governments would hate to admit that one of their most decorated and high profile officers had been captured on their own turf.

The day was slowly dawning as we sped further into the hills,

John
MacPhee
aged 3 years..

..and at 49
years, below.

Above:HVO Special
Forces with
MacPhee, centre,
complete with
Glengarry.

Right:A Building in
Proznor shelled
following an attack
by Croatian Forces

Above:John standing beside an HVO Patten 1947 Tank.
Below:On the front line in Babice after a hard days work.

sunday mail

May 3, 1998

Truth about Royal psychic Rita

CENTRE PAGES

SHE SAW INSIDE DIANA'S MIND

WIN A DREAM HOLIDAY FOR LIFE — PAGE 37

MONSTER

He killed dozens of innocent women .. and he calls himself Superscot.. who will bring him to justice?

sunday mail SHOCK REPORT

THIS evil mercenary has the blood of dozens of innocent women on his hands...

John MacPhee has butchered unarmed men in the bloody Bosnian war.

Now the Sunday Mail can reveal that he has written a detailed account of his grisly role.

He is touting it around publishers to cash in on his terrible deeds.

We here refused to pay a penny to see his gory confessions.

They may instead be used to bring him to justice.

Last night, Defence Secretary George Robertson pledged to present our dossier to war crimes investigators in The Hague.

Foreign Secretary Robin Cook also promised to examine his confessions.

MacPhee spent three years fighting for an ultra-violent wing of the Croatian army.

He boasts: "I did my job killing all who came before me. Enemy after enemy we killed. I never looked for a uniform."

Colonel "Bomber" Bob Stewart branded MacPhee "scum".

UN work of Larry Hollingsworth said: "The people he associated with were cowboys. They were butcher-type soldiers."

Lifelong criminal

JOHN MacPHEE ... 2,000-mile trip to audition

2,000-mile hike to get nowhere!

A SCOTS volunteer fighting in Bosnia hitch-hiked 2,000 miles to audition for the part of Robert the Bruce in a new film.

But when John MacPhee finally arrived home he was told: "Sorry, but the part is **NOT** open to offer any more."

By RUSSELL FINDLAY

John, 44, a soldier in the war-zone of the former Yugoslavia, headed home the moment he read about the film in the Mail a pal had sent him.

It said the producers wanted unknown actors to audition for the leading part.

VICTORY

John, who is from Bridgeton, arrived penniless at a meeting in Glasgow last week after thumbing lifts all the way from central Europe.

But Bob Carruthers, who will direct the £500,000 movie, already had a shortlist of six actors for the lead role in The Bruce.

John said: "I was sad I

had travelled so far only for the decision to have been taken already.

"I made the journey because I love my country and I wanted the chance to play Bruce."

John will return to Bosnia next week.

Production chief Pete Ross said: "We were looking for an unknown Scots actor but one with a reasonable track record.

"I was surprised to hear John had come all the way from Bosnia."

Starring in the publicly-funded film that tells the story of Bruce's victory over the English at Bannockburn are Oliver Reed, Brian Blessed and Wolf from TV's Gladiators.

BLOOD LUST

Scots war criminal is the brutal beast of Bosnia

EXCLUSIVE

By RUSSELL FINDLAY

HE'S the evil beast of Bosnia ... the Scots mercenary with the blood of innocents on his hands.

Convicted criminal John MacPhee has admitted slaughtering unarmed men and women during the hellish Bosnian war.

As part of a ruthless unit of the Croatian army, MacPhee took part in atrocities which will shock the world.

Now the evil Scot's killings are to be reported to the war crimes tribunal in The Hague.

In an exclusive interview with the Sunday Mail, retired MacPhee boasted of his three months' work for the Croatian army.

HRVATSKA ZAJEDNICA HERCEG-BOSNA
HRVATSKO VIJEĆE OBRANE

VOJNA ISKAZNICA

JOHN MACPHEE

Croatian army identity card

BOB STEWART
'They were scum'

HOLLINGWORTH
'Cowboys'

Contrasting stories in the Sunday Mail from April 1998

The Old Bridge in Mostar before the War. It was destroyed on November 9th 1993 as HVO soldiers attempted to hold back a Muslim assault.

Below:John's' I.D.from his time in Bosnia

HRVATSKA ZAJEDNICA
HERCEG-BOSNA

HRVATSKO VIJEĆE OBRANE

VOJNA ISKAZNICA

JOHN
(Ime)

MACPHEE
(Prezime)

Nº 56123

Above:"Car I accidentally ran over in the tank"
Below: Using a Grenade Launcher at Tomislavgrad.

Above: John three months before going to Bosnia
Below: the town of Tomislavgrad

Above and Below:Whilst inTomislavgrad

approaching the sun as we headed east, the opposite direction to our original intention. What we were doing was against all orders, Croatian or otherwise. We stopped and I trussed up the Colonel with a little flexi-wire, winding it round his neck and down his back to his hands which were forced behind him, tying his legs to his wrists to make sure he couldn't escape.

That done our friend began to come round with a moan. Each time he moved a limb the wire tightened on his wrist, every movement of the head making the wire around his neck tighten a little more. I re-checked to make sure it was tight enough, just so it choked him a bit.

He spat pieces of teeth and blood from his swollen face - then I thought, if news of this ever came out and we were captured they'd shunt Ante and I around every punishment cell and torture chamber in Serbia for years. A gruesome thought. We moved off again, the gears crunching as we went flying into a fence at the side of the road, two wheels dangling precariously in the air. Cursing I got out, leaning on the upended side, forcing it to the ground and, as soon as I had righted it, Ante shot out onto the road again.

He took the road with care this time, which meant relative comfort for our Colonel. He was feeling the mountain cold now, so I stabbed a Morphine Syrette into his thigh to relax him. We continued in a Southeasterly direction toward the coast - it was a strong possibility that an inquest was already in progress back at the command house we'd wrecked and it was vital that the enemy believed we would head northwest to the border with Croatia or Bosnia.

We had gone in this direction accidentally, but we had turned that cock-up to our advantage as we sped toward the rising sun. Round another bend a goatherd was walking toward us - Ante swerved to avoid him, scattering his flock. The old, bedraggled man turned and attacked our Land Rover with his staff, his funny little hat and bearded face appearing at Ante's window. My Croatian friend told the goat-herder to do something unspeakable to his mother (in the grave I thought, judging by the age of this guy) as I readied my silencer again.

'No, no,' shouted Ante, as he handed the guy fifty Deutschmarks.

'We should kill him, kill the motherfucker, Ante. I'll do it, smash his head in - I've seen his type before, good men die because of shits like him, he'll go straight to the police'.

My breath was wasted, Ante was too good a soldier and Croatian to do the necessary but ruthless thing. Then again the old codger seemed pleased with the money as I snarled at him and made faces, trying to make sure that he didn't look into the back of the Land Rover. He was only an imp of a character, his head barely coming to the top of the window. A transfer of positions was finally made, the goats to the direction we'd come from, us the way they'd come. But as we passed the herder Ante stopped the truck. The guy was stood in the middle of the road holding the Deutschmarks to the sun to check if they were forgeries.

This was a trick I had pulled in Bosnia on the Muslims when we were allies; I'd haggled them down to a fair price for some ammunition, mainly launchers and explosives, and paid them with hooky Deutschmarks - for weeks there were bitter recriminations as allegations and threats were bandied about.

Now Ante returned laughing. 'He won't know the difference Ante', I said, 'they're all good!', as he laughed again and jumped back in. A short time later we were steaming past civilian homes, passing village after village as we descended from the mountains toward the coast. By now our fuel was low. I pointed to a garage and we stopped, hidden from the road below by some tall rocks that provided more than adequate cover from the eyes of prying goat-herders.

Ante checked the prisoner to see that he was still breathing - it was now after 11 am. The sun was high, roasting everything around as we drank from our water bottles - prisoner included. We wanted him in tiptop shape for later interrogation about Serb positions; it was pointless making him suffer any more than he would do behind our lines.

There was now the definite possibility that certain Serbian military matters would be altered by the Colonel's capture, but we knew that certain things couldn't be altered and that knowledge would be vital in the weeks ahead. Regardless of the Colonel being out here in Montenegro he still would still have relevant information about matters further north - he would be in touch with senior politicians and Generals and would hear the rumours about possible offensives.

He would also know a lot about Vukovar and its frontline surrounds, it had been rumoured that he had recently been promoted to General. For such reasons Ante and I had to keep him alive and slowly my senses returned to normal. Killing did not affect me when in these types of 'criminal' circumstances, I always wanted to continue in order to leave no witnesses. We approached a main coastal town and decided to backtrack a kilometre or so up the hill. We opened a gate and drove into a small wooded area to hide the jeep - Ante handed me a Kalashnikov and a couple of spare magazines that had been in the Land Rover.

He watered the prisoner and covered him with a tarpaulin found in the back, then took out his spare Morphine Syrette and pumped it into the Colonel's leg, he was already unconscious, but this was to make sure he remained silent. Ante asked me for all the money I had, so I gave him more than 5,000 DMs and off he went - no words were needed.

An hour later he returned. I was hiding behind a tree near to the jeep facing the track that led to the gate. I zeroed in then realised by the beeping sound that it was Ante. Well there it was, an old Mercedes Benz in reasonable condition and in excellent working order. He had a bundle of clothes - we had left our civilian ones back in the stolen car further north.

We put on our new clothes and undid the flexi-wire on the prisoner - Ante dressed him as he mumbled, doped to the eyeballs, morphed-up. I turned round. Ante was staring intently at the Colonel. He carefully cleaned up his face - the morphine was wearing off fast. Suddenly Ante looked up at me, 'John, John - this is not him, this man is not him'. Dumbstruck, I replied with a few expletives and a half-hearted 'Are you sure'. This was beyond a joke, but had to be true. As we had rushed into the room where the 'Colonel' lay I had crashed my boot in his face so quickly that accurate identification of him was impossible. He was a mess - all I knew was that this guy had a build and moustache similar to the newspaper picture I had seen of the Colonel, unfortunately this was not the butcher of Vukovar.

Fuck it all. We deserved this as this mission hadn't been sanctioned. It had been our personal desire to grab the bastard that had led to us being unprofessional and failing to notice the mistake. I turned to my friend. 'What now Ante, aren't we a pair of clowns'.We sat forlornly by the car and jeep for a few minutes. We stared at the ground and then began laughing - Ante got up and opened the passenger door of the Mercedes, taking out a bag containing a bottle of wine, some water, a tin of sardines, a large loaf, a kilo of cheese and some Paradiso (tomatoes).

As soon as we ate our frontline rations (this was our daily breakfast) Ante began talking to the Colonel. Apparently the prisoner was a Major, he swore blind that he had never seen frontline action, let alone Vukovar and Bosnia. Our target had apparently left the house we had raided four days before. I continued to press the guy on certain points, trying to make sure that he wasn't fibbing his way out of punishment. I measured every word as Ante translated - exchanging quick-fire questions and answers between the prisoner and I.

By this time Ante had removed the 'tie-up' job on the prisoner's hands and the guy looked a little more comfortable with just his feet and hands tied. Weighing up all the options I decided to kill our man. We would be carrying dead weight and he would create a sure-fire problem if we took him with us. So often in my criminal career have I had problems kidnapping other crooks, attempting to move them from place to place.

The Silent Cry

This was a different kettle-of-fish however with no possible benefits now that we knew who our man really wasn't. Swiftly, Ante tied our man to a tree in a sitting position - it was after 6pm now and it would be light for hours to come.

Further talks took place between us old comrades as to the future of our victim. True, I'd already decided, but respect had to be given to Ante, he was a good man who I always met up with for special occasions - as this was supposed to be. Never before in my life had I been at a loss to execute one of my own decisions - then again, never had I been in quite a predicament as this before.

'Give me a few minutes to think it out Ante. If we leave him alive the chances are that we will come unstuck. Who knows, it happened to me on a sting with a jeweller in Amsterdam way back'. Ante lifted his hands into the air and asked God to help him (he knew I was a devout non-believer). He pleaded for the guy's life again and finished with, 'if we kill him then it is us who will be the butchers'.He had me in a spot there. I thought it through again before finally caving in; 'OK Ante, you skinny piece of shit, we'll do it your way'.

He smiled! But I knew he was right - the guy was the wrong one and we'd already killed all in the house - I hated getting the wrong ones. But then a part of me remembered all the years the English police had planted evidence and 'verballed me up' when they really knew I was innocent. So I had a kind of sympathy with the guy, that is why I had a little rethink as to my original decision to eliminate him. Ante made sure that I was convinced that to kill a prisoner was beyond justification and that my past life was gone and lost to the prison cells I'd inhabited for 21 years of my life. He was right again, of course.

Our problem now was how to escape. Montenegro was as Serbian as Belgrade and to be caught here would be to consign ourselves to a prolonged spell of torture with death as our only possible escape. It was this thought that played on my mind. It was now ten o'clock (almost 24 hours had passed since our initial storming of the villa) and, as we relaxed a little against the trees out of sight of the road or any passing traffic, I reflected on the 40 kilometres we had travelled and the length of time it might take the Montenegrins/Serbians to muster a search party for us.

Our man smiled through broken teeth and swollen jaw. He related to Ante that the women were whores and therefore dispensable. Ante cringed at the memory. He would not kill women under any circumstances unless by pure accident, fortunately for him it was I who had done the dirty deed.

Darkness came silently as we chatted away, the Serb or whoever he was, joining in like an old friend, relieved that he would survive a day of kidnap. All of a sudden Ante and I decided enough was enough. My friend covered the 'prisoner' with a white sheet to keep him warm in the chilly night air (a drop in temperature had made Ante considerate) as I pulled out a Morphine Syrette and looked into the eyes of the guy who, just a few hours ago, would have been dead if I had had my way. 'Dobra, dobra', he said - so I handed the morphine to Ante (this was good cop, bad cop alright) to do the business. Ante told the Major that we would try and get word to someone as soon as we believed ourselves safe. Then we set off. Half an hour later we were driving down the coast road and Ante stopped at a phone-box. He returned saying that he had alerted the police to our man.

'Are you sure he never saw the Mercedes or anything Ante?'

'Steady John, steady. It's good, really good. We are safe' his voice not inspiring any confidence in me at all.

'Hope you're right my friend' I replied sceptically.

A little further on we parked up in a side street by some derelict garages and took with us our trusty AK 47 nicked from the 'Colonel's' house. We walked down the street to the beach front then over to a small harbour. Before we had set out on this ill-fated mission we had checked out all the likely looking harbours and the availability of boats along this stretch of coast so this was not pure luck. There was no security or military presence to be seen, so we cautiously continued.

Glancing at either end of the small jetty we happened upon a likely looking craft. My head was banging at the thought of it all, what was all this about anyway? I'd rather rob a bank or 'have over' some drug dealers for their cash than this kind of life or death escape palaver. At the end of the day I loved the work, that's why I always volunteered for the most daring and ridiculous ventures. I also knew that I was at my best when up against the greatest odds. Still this was a crazy end to a crazy mission.

Along the coastal road flashing lights could be seen nearing the little town where we had left our man. Even Ante looked apprehensive at this sight as police cars zoomed along the road we'd just travelled down. It could have been coincidence but I just knew that it wasn't - our problems were mounting by the second.

The one saving grace was the total lack of any coastguard or naval presence in the bay, although out there in the Adriatic there were bound to be British and American ships scanning the radar. Capture by them would be pleasant, by the Serbs it would mean a long, drawn out death.

We boarded a fast looking cabin cruiser, the boat rocking to and fro as we lumbered about, Ante fumbling with the controls, cursing me and telling me (in not so many words) that I was perhaps the worst former Marine engineer he'd ever had the misfortune to meet - we were panicking now alright.

The Silent Cry

Truth was I couldn't get the boat started. I told Ante to check the fuel tanks and suddenly it came to life and we were away to sea. We managed a good 17-18 knots, no more. But time was against us and we had already been spotted by a bloke in the harbour who was busy trying to alert anyone who would listen. Fortunately the sea, unlike our nerves, was calm. We intended to head for Dubrovnik but the light on the shore made me nervous so I decided to take a less obvious route south toward Albania and, if our luck held, eventually Greece where we stood a greater chance of escape.

The light from the coast receded as we headed out into the pitch-black Adriatic. My heart quickened as we noticed that some lights several kilometres away seemed to be gaining on us, coming almost directly toward us even though we were running our vessel in darkness. Then, just as suddenly, some searchlights appeared in the distance scanning the sea, the intense beams bouncing off the water. Before long they drifted away and gradually we relaxed.

Many hours passed as we drifted along, down the coast before making our way onto Albanian soil. Fortunately we had enough cash and bits of jewellery to bribe our way onto a tourist ferry and by the following afternoon, with some relief, we reached Corfu for a well-deserved break. Luck or not, both Ante and I agreed not to attempt such a mission again.

JAKA

Some days later I sat outside Tomislavgrad hospital watching the doctors and nurses eat some of the supplies I had just delivered while I stripped and cleaned my AK 47. I went through this routine every three days when not in combat - I knew that it was the single most important item of kit I owned and didn't need a sergeant-major to tell me the importance of maintaining it. Seven and eight-year-olds could strip and clean rifles in Bosnia as quickly and as well as any hardened soldier - life was dependent on such, it was a must. Finishing this job I looked up and caught the eye of a camouflaged HVO soldier. She was so very beautiful. Her name, it turned out, meant 'strong', she was called Jaka. Immediately my vision held her as she approached with a driver friend of hers.

I vaguely remembered that she was from Livno and had been a combatant from the start of the Bosnian War; she was shot and wounded at Kupres as eight or nine Serb tanks entered the town 40 kilometres north of Tomislavgrad. Jaka was taken prisoner and moved to a Concentration Camp west of Kupres - my black heart went to her as she came over. Her friend, the driver, attempted to make conversation with me while I stared (or should I say drooled) over the girl.

Eventually I told her that I thought she looked Scottish, in some ways she reminded me of the young Croatian lass that had died in the village near Gornji Vakuf. Yes, the same fair hair, colouration of eyes and freckles, her silken blonde-red hair leading all the way down to a slim waist - it could have been an older incarnation of the dead child. In appearance no one would have dreamt that she was a soldier, especially not a HOS soldier, the most ruthless brigade of Croatians who were said to be fascist. Regardless of all that, this girl was a dream. Jaka played up to me, I believe. She sat on the drain cover beside me and I felt her presence - a warmth radiated from her, affecting me. Never can I remember having such a feeling before, my past-life is blighted by the bitter tangle of broken relationships.

Yes, Jaka moved me. We had a sign language of sorts and could make conversation with the assistance of the driver who brought her to the hospital for regular check-ups. The girl was 21 years old and had arthritic pains in her upper arm and shoulder as a result of a Serb bullet that had ripped through her arm before deflecting out of her upper back. As we sat there Jaka showed me her war wounds.

I marvelled at this girl - if ever it was possible for me to know love then I felt its beginnings towards her, she was a vision. My interest in her was obvious and she knew it. Jaka had been on television as to her story about being wounded and captured by the Serbs, I was also told that she was full of courage and would fight without hesitation.

After an hour or so of makeshift banter I was offered a lift and we drove around for hours, I was completely smitten by her and I hoped she felt the same way. At one point she took out some perfume and let the driver and I have a sniff, then she let a little of it spill on my uniform (it was nine days before I washed it off). The hours in her company gave me a touch of humanity in an otherwise savage existence.

For years after the war I attempted to find her, missing her here and there time and again. Even a female professor at Zagreb University of Law tried to track her down for me to no avail. The nurses were quite unhelpful on my subsequent visits to Tomislavgrad hospital. One of them told me that Jaka was a killer the day after that semi-romantic encounter. To which I replied that I was one also, as soldiers are supposed to be - I also told her that I would love to be killed in such a way by her!

'Not that way you fool' the nurse replied, 'I mean to kill you when you're asleep' at this she made a gesture of a throat being cut. I laughed. The nurses were a little jealous of Jaka and it often made sensible conversation about her impossible. I often think of her in moments of peace and tranquillity, but more often whenever I pass a hospital.

DEATH ON SLATINA RIDGE

Later that summer we were up in Slatina once more, the venue for more death and destruction. During the summer the Muslims successfully occupied the high ground overlooking the dam and tunnel, which led to Jablanica. And as further North the Muslim assault increased so had Croatian resolve to push them back. I had only recently arrived when a Shogun Jeep came to a halt and a lean, fair-haired figure emerged from the front passenger seat - my eyes searched for the face, it was him - that soldier of the damned, yet if ever there was a Christian soldier it was Ante.

'John, John... Scot' he said smiling, as I ran toward him.

'Ante', I finally realised, 'there is a God after all, you died in Gornji Vakuf. Six yes six bullets'. I couldn't work it out as he replied, 'John you old wolf - it takes more than bullets to kill me'.

Both of us, regardless of being hardened soldiers, wrapped our arms around each other - we hadn't scored a goal in a football match but had survived to meet again, living by the second, by the heartbeat. We still fought for freedom, for the love of our people.

Past mentions were made about our pledges to fight for each other's countries - Ante had committed himself to the Scottish cause as fervently as I had committed myself to the Croatian one - we were nationalists.

We finally held each other at arms length, struggling for the next words. It was morning and the tourist sights in the Slatina region were spectacular, but the only tourist here was I, a war hardened traveller with marks on my body where others would have them on their passports. Struggling to find something worthy of the occasion I came out with, 'Ante you old dog' (he was 26).

He smiled. He was a natural - I shuddered and became saddened. I knew his death was imminent, my dream that he had died in Gornji Vakuf was a premonition, I was convinced that this would be the last time I would see him. He was a man for the moment and I knew death would take my comrade-in-arms - seldom can Croatia have produced such a beautiful man.

Ante looked at me, questioning my saddened look, before he cleared his throat and said, 'You've got years on me Scotsman, you can load my guns and carry my ammunition.' A playful exchange of punches were made before we headed off to a disused and abandoned building converted into a mess hall for that morning's breakfast. One of the nurses wore an old American helmet that I had given her when her hospital came under shell attack.

Meanwhile, Ante continued to gather greetings from long lost comrades. The building was alive with the sounds of old friends greeting each other, the mood was good. New additions had come from Croatia to supplement Special Forces and most of these men had been at every major battle since the start of the war with Serbia. As we bantered another white jeep pulled up. It was our commander Glasnovic, a good friend of Ante's from his foreign legion days. Both of them had escaped to come and fight for their country and I had met them, for the first time, while they were together down in Tomislavgrad.

The greetings continued before breakfast was served and while we ate we listened to a briefing about an imminent attack on Jablanica to the east - a stronghold of our former Muslim allies. It seemed that the Croat President had ordered us not to attack as a Turkish delegate was trying to talk us back to the negotiating table. This order came a few days after I'd launched a number of Orkan missiles, firing part of the town and killing a few civilians - I took full responsibility for the attack.

There had been a lot of anger at the time of that attack and President Tudjman had publicly distanced himself from it because of possible action by the UN and UNHCR regarding aid to Croatia. So this latest attack was going to be a little more planned. Ante's group was to outflank the Muslims to the right and back while the men of our 1st Battalion Specials would go left as my own group took the full frontal position - we would have to be 'Storm Troopers' now.

Later that morning, at 10 am precisely, our anti-aircraft guns opened up from the back of a purpose built truck and hit the top of the main hill in the distance supported by another tank and mortar squads who aimed a little lower down the hill. All day long the explosions blasted the hill and, as night approached, we began to edge into position.

The trees and undergrowth burned to cause quite an effect but we trudged on regardless, anchoring ourselves briefly along the route behind tree stumps before continuing again. The fighting continued as we slowly ascended the hill, machine-gun and smaller rifle fire lashing us as we continued our journey - metre by metre.

Mortar fire then descended on us from the top of the hill - there were screams and cries but we continued, losing a few men to the mortars as we ascended. At the top of the smaller hill, savage hand-to-hand fighting took place - one of our men was blasted in the head - toppling and falling down the steep hill, his body coming to rest impaled on a broken tree stump.

The Silent Cry

Blood curdling screams could be heard as we used our bayonets, sticking it to them as they fought back. By this stage the hill was ablaze, grenades exploding all around us, dying soldiers calling out for their comrades to find medics, of which there were none. We carried on fighting regardless; any respite given to the enemy would only encourage the Muslims to reassert themselves on the higher ground. But their machine guns kept us pinned down; at 1200 rounds a minute I didn't want to argue for the moment.

Eventually we advanced - clearing the foxholes and a small bunker, searching the dead bodies of the enemy before throwing them down the hill for the enemy to collect, before we took toward the dam side of the small hill overlooking the road-tunnel to Jablanica. Screams could be heard as the trees and bushes flamed - machine gunfire aimed at us pinned us down and finally, having taken the smaller hill, we took cover securing it - we were due to be relieved the following day.

The final hours of our vigil were tough. As the Sun beat down that afternoon we were dehydrated, being roasted alive while occasional shots and exchanges of fire kept us hot, irritated and anxious. Then our tanks and anti-aircraft guns blasted the higher Muslim held hill - the Muslims held that position for a week longer before finally falling.

That afternoon, having been relieved of our positions, we walked slowly and silently through the hilly forest to the base of the newly taken position. We were a bedraggled lot, covered in cuts and bruises, two of us with slight wounds; I had blood on my forehead and face mixed with the usual grime and when I caught myself in the mirror once we reached camp my eyes stared back intently, I was still hyped.

As I approached the first of the village houses in the valley below a hand slapped me on the back - it was Ante. I hadn't even seen him, my senses had gone. 'John well done', he said, his words bringing me out of my trance-like state. 'Shit Ante, we only took the lower hill - just the small one and still we lost one man and a few wounded' I replied, disappointed that all had not quite gone to plan. 'You are wounded?' he asked, mistaking the blood on my forehead for something more serious. 'No Ante only a scratch'.

My head was pounding. It turned out that I had fractured my skull when a Muslim attacked me with a shovel - then again I had never got much sense out of the damn thing before, perhaps a crack might loosen some of my pig-headedness. 'Come John, all of you, you must eat - Rakija all round, sorry John there is no whisky', he smiled.

We tried to force a smile as we were guided to the food served by nurses who eyed us up - they were fresh in from Rumboci hospital but we didn't smile back like humans, just maintained our battle weary expressions. Ante joined us with a few other soldiers - apparently three men had been lost, not just the single casualty as I had initially told him. At this new information my head swam, I couldn't quite take it all in as Ante continued to tell me more about our battle - he seemed to know much more about it than I.

The other men were exhausted and dragged themselves off to bed, some lying outside the hastily erected mess-tent - it wasn't the Hilton but it was good enough after that night. Meanwhile Ante continued to tell me about his offensive. Apparently all hell had broken loose on the east side of the larger hill - Ante's group had lost 3 men and had five wounded plus another missing in action.

He was telling me all about it when a Croat ran in and spoke excitedly to Ante. There was a shocked shake of heads before Ante swore in his own language and translated the message to me. 'The bastards, Scot. They have crucified one of our men up there - this guy here', he said pointing to the excited soldier, 'got up to within 50 metres and saw that the Muslims had tied him up and then shot the hell out of him'.

There was little left to do but plan our revenge. But Ante wanted a little calm. 'We'll do it later, first you sleep, then we go out tonight'. So I rested for the moment and by evening a HOS unit had arrived after hearing of the Muslim atrocity. We went out to check. There had been rumours of tortures and deaths but this one was a fact - as I neared the site I grimaced at the guy strung up on the tree, shot to pieces.

I took out my binoculars. I recognised his face, he had been with Ante when he arrived the day before and I had spoken briefly with him - he was a man of few words but seemed capable in battle. I had only known him for a few hours but it is one of the strange aspects of battle that his death meant as much to me now as if I had known him all my life. I knew that he was a comrade-in-arms, that we fought for the same cause, and that he died in circumstances which none of us could have avoided.

The black uniformed HOS units arrived a little later. Jaka, the girl soldier I loved but could never have, was there - she spotted me and walked over to where I rested by a wall. I noticed that she still sported the Scottish knife that I had given to her as a present sometime ago. Her eyes stared at me as she steadily walked my way - her gaze fixed mine but no words were spoken as she took out a small medical pack and started to tend my head wound.

The eyes of the rest of the soldiers were fixed on us as I winced a little at an alcohol solution poured on the wound - her eyes smiling at my discomfort. Immediately the men surrounding us made lovebird noises and catcalls in Croatian.

The Silent Cry

'Smile', she said, 'smile for me John'.Trying not to I did. Laughter broke out; the tension was relieved for the previous hour's horror and hate. Jaka finally sat down beside me and we drifted into a kind of sleep.

When I awoke it was dark and Jaka and the rest of the HOS unit had gone. I adjusted my senses, listening out for sounds, my eyes adjusting to the darkness. I went out alone, passing a packet of cigs to the guard on duty so he would keep quiet and traversed the distance over the hill until I reached a ruined building that had a view of the eastern hillside.

In the near distance flames still covered the upper reaches of the hill - it was a sinister and eerie sight. I lay a booby-trap down by the stream and retreated a distance. I waited. Then an explosion. I had calculated that one of the Muslims would sneak down to the stream to check things out and I had caught him - he was screaming to Allah as I approached him.

He lay moaning, his torn shirt wrapped around the stump of his ankle, the moonlight glinting on his destroyed legs and bloody body. At the last second he saw me, it must have been a moment of eternity to him - I made sure I hesitated, to make him think that I would spare him before I moved forward and decapitated him. His head came away easily, my 18-inch killing blade slicing through the Muslim's neck, sparing him a few more moments of suffering. I retreated, placing the head in a polythene bag normally used for carrying stolen medical supplies and strode back to the camp.

I passed the guard again, winking at him as he thanked me for the earlier gift. The rest of them were in a cellar lit by several candles and they spoke in low tones that became absolute silence when I revealed the contents of the bag. Only one person shuddered, a nurse who was in the process of handing out mugs of coffee, she looked away in shock, but the others remained transfixed by the head in the bag - it was my good fortune that the commander had gone back to Tomislavgrad, he wouldn't have tolerated this kind of thing.

I looked to all eyes directly and felt Jaka's grip on my arm - she was with me through every hell and horror. 'Ok', I said presently, 'if they crucify then I shall behead. It's the Muslim way to put a head inside a pig and offer it to the enemy - it's said now'.

There was shock and disbelief as I stormed out of the cellar and up into the night air. Jaka followed me and then led the way up onto the lower captured hill, I realised then more than ever that I loved her with all my barbarous heart. Our men in the foxholes on the top of the hill approved of the action and were happy that revenge had taken place. I placed the head on the edge of the hill facing his comrades higher up on the next hill near where our man had been crucified - the source of this macabre game.

A Personal Loss

A Croatian joined us within minutes carrying a small dead pig under his arm. I sliced open its stomach and put the head inside, sewing it back up with string before throwing it down the hill towards the dam - cheers went up along our ridge positions as the dead animal and its human cargo thudded its way toward the Muslim position below. 10 or 15 minutes later there were screams, curses and shots - they seemed a little upset.

We had waited for this - Jaka readied the men, and as hell broke loose we machine-gunned those below. By this time all the HOS unit had come up to be with us while down below Ante and his men rushed to the east-side to attack hard and heavy. We continued our mortar assault on Slatina Ridge - barrage after barrage lighting up the night, setting bushes and trees on fire. We continued to press around the hill, past the crucified soldier, his body now rotting he was finally taken down, rats scurrying from their 'meal' as we continued. Jaka was first into the enemy's tunnel shelters a little further on - she killed, we all did - we took no prisoners as we decimated and bayoneted our enemy. For two days we continued like this, hardly stopping to rest or eat - living for the next kill, the bloodletting.

In effect our determined assault was the turning point in Croatian fortunes in Bosnia. It was a bloody battle, a fight to the death for which the Muslims seemed ill prepared. They believed themselves infallible on the hill - looking back I can see why. Orders had been made that under no circumstances should we blow-up Slatina Dam - the main source of power in the region. Our forces were tempted and it was only the standing of our commander that prevented us from taking this course of action. His career and reputation would have been in tatters if we had done such.

This made our task harder - rather than being able to blast through we had to fight them off the vantage point and force their remaining forces back through the tunnel toward Jablanica. I have since described the hill and the dam to military experts and they were amazed that we could have taken it within a week. But the resolve and skill of Croat forces during this period in the war was consistently underestimated and the taking of Slatina Ridge was just the start of the advance. An advance that pushed back the Muslims and then the Serbs until ultimate victory in 1995.

In the closing stages of the battle, one of our tanks positioned near a Muslim graveyard fired on an enemy tank a couple of kilometres away scoring a direct hit. I sent a bottle of Black Watch whisky to the tank crew, they in turn saluted me by firing again into the burning carcass of the Muslim tank. The victorious morning was upon us as we watched the remnants of the tank smouldering in the distance. The whole damn war was changing. We were going forward but it was the Serbians we really wanted, our war was with them not the Bosnian government's army.

The Silent Cry

That afternoon we returned to Slatina Village and swam in the lake. Cleaning two day's grime away, I was waist deep, the dirt from my face and body stubbornly refusing to remove itself. From the shore my commander shouted to me. At first I didn't understand, couldn't fathom what he was saying, I approached.

'Ante is dead John'.

I refused to believe him. Ante was my only friend out here, along with Jaka and the commander, the only people I knew well.

'No, he's out there I know he is, he's not dead', I remembered my earlier thoughts in Gornji Vakuf when he had gone missing and reassured myself that he would survive; 'it takes more than bullets to kill me' I remember him saying. I approached the shore in a daze.

'He's dead', the commander reiterated, 'I will show you his body. John it's war, we play the game but we also die', he emphasised.

'Ante. Why Ante? Why not me?' I thought aloud.

I was taken into a room in a makeshift hospital. A curtain was pulled back and there he was - Ante with a bullet in his head. The nurses told me he had been alive an hour after he was shot, he wasn't given morphine or anything but stayed alive for a whole hour with a bullet in his brain. I walked from the room refusing to believe that my friend had gone.

Looking at the faces in a large waiting room full of HVO soldiers I searched the features of each one trying to find him. I even called to him 'Ante, Ante please come out', hoping that the whole thing was a huge and intricate practical joke - it wasn't, it was war. Two nurses led me out. 'Ante's alive' I told them pointing to the sky, 'he's up there'.

Breaking free I ran up the hill (no weapons, nothing, just my knife) I was a man possessed as higher and higher I ran with little or no effort. Shots rang out as I came up, the Muslims hitting the trees and earth around me. I looked to the sky again, 'we made a deal that you take me before him. That was our deal', then I was tripped up and thudded to earth.

Jaka had spotted what would happen to me on hearing the news and, as her lithe body wrestled me to the floor, I tried to recover my breath. Mortar shells landed around us as Jaka picked me up and led me to a shell hole on the hillside. She was only a slender girl but her bravery both before and after her capture by the Serbs was legendary.

I loved her in my own ruthless way, ever since that meeting with her at Tomislavgrad hospital I'd held a flame for her, been electrified by her presence. And, as usual, she was there to bring me back to earth, make me see sense about war and control its continual onslaught on my senses. She held me in her arms as I stared at the blue summer's sky and wondered why my good friend had died.

6 - STREET FIGHTING

OCTOBER 1993

I returned to Gornji Vakuf along with the rest of Special Forces as a fresh counteroffensive was underway against the Muslims. Our Special Forces combat headquarters in the town was at a former Junior School. An old Croatian guy ran our kitchen - he was a marvel who had fought as an SS officer at the fall of Berlin. My heart went out to that 70 year-old guy, he was fit and lean for his age and as agile as any soldier I'd met in Bosnia. I knew that he would love to be fighting in the streets with us, he was a natural as well as being perhaps the most experienced soldier in Bosnia.

Gornji Vakuf had been the centre of conflict in Central Bosnia for the preceding 6 months and was the scene of some of the most vicious fighting. It was a Muslim stronghold and we knew that taking it was vital because the Muslims were fighting us with weapons that we had loaned them during our alliance.

Once again, as wars come and go, Bosnia had many aspects that were totally alien to normal conflict. Life was bitter and unchained in those days; soldiers came to and from whatever battle-zone - tired, weathered faces strained with the type of fighting taking place. Ethnic cleansing had side effects not just on the local population but on their relatives in the forces of all sides.

As a result so many of them must have thought as I did; what in the hell is there to life or humanity any more? Why should I continue to pretend to stick to the rules of war? Our enemy up here in Gornji Vakuf had changed. Initially we had fought against Marshal Tito's Yugoslav Federal Army - a force that had carried out man's inhumanity, which had plumbed the depths of man's bestiality and perversion - this perversion had advanced to a modern setting under Milosevic, where propaganda had given the enemy a psychological overkill.

The Silent Cry

Hyperbole had given the Serbs a reason to think they were somehow superior, that they deserved a 'Greater Serbia' at the expense of all other races and nationalities in the region - theirs was a Godless, greedy cause - its sole aim to inflict their will on the old and the young of Bosnia and Croatia and annexe as much of their land as possible. The Communists' camps bludgeoned the idea of revenge and slaughter into the minds of their Croat and Muslim detainees. In the process, the mass of deaths resulted in a loss of our last vestige of humanity. The age of lust for death was upon us.

Now our enemies were Bosnian Muslims. The loss of Jajce had triggered off a long-concealed mistrust of the Bosniaks, the recent massacres I had witnessed had strengthened my view that the Muslims were fighting out of revenge. My only hope was that the children of all three sides could live for a better tomorrow, that they would turn from the present-day atrocities and bring about the absolute right to live and walk free; that the soldiers already dead and those about to die would not suffer in vain, but that they fought bravely for the freedom of the children to right the wrongs of their parents - not through revenge but peace and freedom.

Yet still the soldiers came before me along the road that led to death and destruction. A jet soared high in the sky oblivious to all that went on below; who in all reality cared for our dead and dying? Did those high above see our burning houses - did they feel our pain as we walked upon the blood-soaked soil? We were on a road in Gornji Vakuf, walking toward the fighting. Street by street we fought against the Muslim enemy in a counteroffensive against our former ally. The road was chock-full, at points vehicles and foot soldiers ground to a halt - the UN were nowhere to be seen, as houses and factories were set ablaze.

Street fighting had become unbearable to most of us but we had to carry on - house by house - in moments of respite my mind was taken to the thought of Stalingrad in the Second World War - that city had resisted one of the biggest onslaughts known to mankind but at a terrible human price. Gornji Vakuf was on a far smaller scale, but no lesser for the fact that people died. We had done our best to pull out the women and children, the old and the infirm but many refused to move and they were often found dead a few days later.

Sometimes they succumbed to incidental explosions, other times their deaths had been deliberate - whichever the war made all of us animals. In the end I reasoned that we were all fuckin' frauds. Anyone who could understand right and wrong knew that; I could and still cannot kid myself about my part in the war. I stand as one who saw its death, its finality and tried to reason with it in my own mind before giving up and carrying on.

The wounded came by me again and again. Ambulances, most makeshift and ill equipped, carried the victims and I grimaced. On the other hand I sometimes saw soldiers with light injuries that would take them away from this place and understood that they had found a different kind of freedom, a release from hell. Shells flew by, their explosions echoing around the hills, forcing me to stay alive to the possibility of death and, as the night closed in, the sights became a little more macabre.

I remember the British soldiers in the foothills of Gornji Vakuf, they were all but useless and helpless amid the carnage - bored and restless they must have wondered what the hell was going on. We were on our way to clear out a factory close to the British base, with a proviso that under no circumstances should we fire at the base. Threats were made by our commanders as to the possible consequences of such an action. We were here to fight the Muslims - to give them a little payback for the massacres in Konjic and surrounding villages where Croatian civilians had been massacred and burned alive during the spring and summer.

Of course we didn't know how many Muslims had been involved in the massacres, or even whether it was official Bosnian policy or perhaps carried out by 'rogue' fundamentalist elements. But their tactics made us all the more eager to fight a cowardly enemy. I remember two Muslim prisoners I met in Tomislavgrad hospital. A Canadian TV company had interviewed me at that time and I had met an Arab representative for big money who were considering helping our hospital. He was there to investigate and help his bosses decide whether to sanction aid or not.

The two prisoners were very likeable characters, although understandably very nervous. Anyhow they were treated in accordance with typical Croat hospitality, just as all wounded were treated in Croatian hospitals regardless of ethnic background. Believe me, I'm not a nice bastard in any situation, war or otherwise, but I did try and respect prisoners - remember I've been one myself for 21 years or so and therefore I always remembered the way I had been tortured, beaten and degraded in custody - I'd also known what it was like to be captured as a prisoner of war by the Russians in Afghanistan.

Stories will always surround me claiming that I am a killer without conscience - even some Croatian intellectuals classed me as 'the bad side of the war'. These allegations tear at my heart and mind. For the rest of my life I can swear that I never killed a prisoner because I never took any to kill. That is also why I wasn't involved in the alleged 'Mostar massacres' when Bosnian army elements were said to have been taken from the football stadium up into the hills. Because of my experience as a former prisoner I was offered a chance to control these camps. Did I laugh? Of course I did - me as a camp commander! I will say no more but the offer had been a serious one, as I knew about security etc. I was honoured by the offer but I'd rather see prisoners die than be kept in camps under any circumstances.

I was far happier in Special Forces. Our aims were to target the enemy, kill and destroy; cause havoc behind enemy lines and take objectives not suitable for ordinary army units. This required a mental outlook that would not accept defeat. As a result certain aspects of reality had to be pushed to one side. We killed and occasionally some of our number were sacrificed for the purpose of victory. But death visited the enemy many more times than ourselves, as we jumped over rubble, debris and through broken windows while the fires burned reinforcing our determination. Street by street we pushed their fundamentalist elements back in Gornji Vakuf as passports and other ID was discovered showing many of the 'Bosnians' to be foreign nationals from the Middle East. This was no big deal, they could die as easily as I, another foreign national, might.

I ran into a burning house and immediately went into a bottom floor room. I could see one of our soldiers, a young German, pinning an enemy soldier to the wall with his bayonet. The guy was still alive, the bayonet embedded into his guts, blood pouring from his mouth.

'Shall I kill him, shall I kill him' the German threatened.

'Yes', I replied shooting the dying soldier in the head, the body slumping to the floor, his entrails oozing onto the bare concrete floor.

'Let's move, let's move', I shouted hurrying out and on into the next building, the German following right behind. Bullets screamed all about us, kicking up stones as they aimed at the building we had just left.

We blasted at the top floor of an opposite building, as the German and I covered each other. 'Grenade' I shouted, loud enough for even Boutrous-Boutrous Ghali to hear (I hope it didn't disturb his evening meal), and I hurled the explosive into the building. As the grenade exploded we bulldozed our way in; blood spattered the walls, pieces of flesh and brain lay on the floor - there were no further thoughts as my German sidekick and I shot another half-dead Muslim. Then, yes, I saw that some of them were in civilian clothes but it was too late. I had been squeezing the trigger of my Kalashnikov as I heard the moans, then realised too late that three of them were fatally wounded. War gives us more 'victims' than justifiable targets that is a fact with which no one will argue - it is undeniable and inevitable.

In and up we went, taking each room before the German and myself searched for the next door. Still the flames ate into the night; we stood out as we made our way steadily forward, hugging the walls of the ruined building to give off less of a target to those who were intent on sending us to hell.

Then a number of mortar shells began to land in our midst as more of our men began clearing buildings in the area - it was becoming hell on earth, but it was worse for the Bosniaks. Suddenly a heavy machine gun (possibly Chinese) opened up on us, sending the both of us to the floor behind a small three-foot wall. These Chinese guns are perfect for war; but when you are on the receiving end it is a nightmare - ricochet after ricochet glanced off the ruined building - a bullet hit my German friend's rifle, ripping it from his grasp.

Over and over the shells came - 'where the fuck did they get all this ammo from' I wondered. It seemed that they had stored it all up for use on our little group. For the time being we were fucked, so we laid low. We looked plaintively at one other - the building had no roof, like most in Gornji Vakuf at that time. Most buildings in the area had been destroyed or severely damaged and as the German and I took cover we started to despair of the incessant gunfire.

The German's name was Klaus - he had a handlebar moustache and out of combat was untrustworthy. He was light-fingered and would steal from the refugees if he thought there was something in it for him. As a result I didn't like him, but in combat he was a killing machine and I was grateful for his company now.

Looking again at my comrade I nodded towards the empty window overlooking the street - there was a machine-gun nest further down, to the right of the window - opposite to that was some open ground. The open ground made a full frontal attack on the gunner impossible. But neither could we bombard the nest with mortar fire as many of our men were near the gun in the buildings surrounding it. An RPG (Rocket Propelled Grenade launcher) would be perfect in this situation and we had radioed for RPGs on our way up here but our supply lines were stretched to the limit as it was, so we knew we would have to improvise.

By this time I'd made my mind up to go and told Klaus to follow. I ran into the street as the machine-gun was busy firing at our emplacements nearby - it proved a worthwhile distraction as I leapt into another ruined building, smashing my knee and forearm. Within seconds my comrade came tumbling through the broken window just as more Chinese bullets ripped into the tarmac of the street from further down the road.

We got up and I made for a doorway in the left of the room - there were gaping holes in the high ceiling; the German went to the far right window twenty metres or so along the ransacked building - the floor was swimming with water. I raced over to the door, attempting to secure it

The Silent Cry

while the gunfire intensified. It unnerved me somewhat as the sounds were louder than those normally associated with combat. Then 'whoosh, whack' a bullet struck into the wall behind me; it was a subsonic 'silenced' round of ammo probably from a Draganov sniper rifle. 'Klaus, Klaus', I yelled, 'get down, sniper'. He was already crouched beneath the windowsill at the far end; previous shelling and fighting had already smashed all the windows - the whole town was a wreck beyond the usual standard in Bosnia. There was not much light from the fires that raged elsewhere within the surrounding buildings and, peering into the near darkness, I could only make out the window frames on the two floors of the buildings opposite - all devoid of glass.

The Muslims had their machine-gunner well covered and protected by snipers - it was almost as if they knew we had run out of RPGs or anything similar. This time it was the German's turn to take the lead, as he jumped out of a window and ran toward the position of the sniper - it was obvious from the angle of the bullet that missed me where he had fired. Seconds after he left an explosion was followed by silence, even the heavy machine-gun halted - it was now eerily quiet.

Taking the opportunity to join Klaus, I ran out of the building through a hole in a blown out wall toward my comrade who was standing only metres away from where the sniper lay dead. We heard shouting as I ran into another building and up some stairs - both of us headed toward the blown out windows on the upper floor of a smashed factory. We were now not too far away from our main target. For the moment we were safe, so we sat down among the rubble and debris watching the flames outside as they continued to consume all in their path. We could feel their heat, it was obvious that this building would also quickly fall victim to the inferno. We recuperated for a minute or so, guzzling down at least half a bottle of water each - it was needed, the coldness giving us both a temporary, extra lease of life. I was becoming drained by the physical and mental activity of war.

The respite didn't serve me well in that respect, I had too much time to think about our situation - my heart was OK for the moment, while my stamina remained good, perhaps the dehydration was taking over. A decision was taken to circumvent the blazing building opposite and instead to go to our left, then forward before turning back to our right.

Suddenly we heard shouts from behind us, my German friend called out and realised that it was our own soldiers - another two Germans and three Croats. I recognised them as they wearily ascended the stairs, their faces streaked with paint and dirt, their uniforms covered in grime. It was not strange, this was war and reality, and we were a right wild bunch. There was genuine relief in our laughter; it was the boys' school, a relief to have such a situation. As comrades we were loyal, dedicated to each other. As a unit we took to each other, working against the odds, against reason and for madness. We on the ground knew the rights and wrongs of any given circumstance or event. It was our blood that was spilt on the soil as we fought for freedom.

After the laughter and trivialities were over we decided that it would be better if their group took out the machine-gun emplacement, while Klaus and I flanked the main factory and covered them from higher-ground. We were told that a main group of HVO, comprising some 20 men, was nearing the factory that lay to our east. There was enough in that main combat group to keep their forces preoccupied and it was this realisation, in addition to the fact that our number had tripled within minutes, which boosted my confidence.

One of our 'new' recruits was a German called Hans. He was a skinny little character with little or no fear. His body and arms were covered in tattoos and he cared little other than that all communists who picked up a gun should be killed - in short he was a little fighting machine. In his hands he held the Draganov sniper rifle taken from the dead Muslim who had fired at me - the butt had a piece of shrapnel stuck into it - no big deal. He joined Klaus and I in a covering role.

On we went through a broken downstairs window, before running across some small spare ground. We took cover, making sure that we hadn't been seen, before moving off again through another broken building and it was only then that we came under serious enemy fire. We threw ourselves into another wrecked building and took cover below a broken upper floor window. This confirmed my initial thoughts regarding the factory. There was something of great strategic value in taking it - it was most probably the Muslim headquarters in Gornji Vakuf. That was why it was so well protected and it was also the reason why the Muslims seemed to have ten times as much ammunition as normal.

The sun was starting to break through now even though the nights were lengthening in the autumn. But we were fighting against a determined type of soldier. Of course the Muslims and Croats should have been on the same side fighting the common Serb enemy, but this was not to be at the time, so we got on with it - every casualty inflicted by one against the other only serving to strengthen Serb chances, as we tore at each others throats, knifing each other in the head and body - giving butchers a bad name.

This was the accepted way of our war, the world didn't seem to care as we inflicted pain on each other - just the other side of Hungary and Slovenia and a boat ride away from Italy. The real victims were not the soldiers but their wives, sisters, infirm uncles and aunts who perished amid the genocide. They were the people soldiers on all sides fought for; for me it was a reason to fight - criminality was in my past, this was the very real present. Some would leave the war-zone mentally or physically disabled, but no one fought on either side in a cowardly way here, this was the real game.

I reasoned that there was no way the three of us were going to get into the factory by ourselves. The rate of fire confirmed my earlier theory that the factory was the command centre - they had plenty of ammunition, but taking it was the reason we were in Special Forces - we had to find a way. Klaus took out a dice and threw for the highest number - the loser would have to fight his way back to the school (our base) and return with the MGL rocket launcher. It was crazy that we had not brought it in the first place, but I think the extra weight was the decisive factor in that earlier decision.

Anyway Klaus lost his little gamble, rolling a three. But he was fit and agile enough to get there and back in no time, while Hans and I covered our front, making sure that none of the enemy broke out in our direction. I took stock of my armoury - 4 grenades, all with 4 second delay fuses which worked best in a street fighting environment, 6 AK47 magazines of 30 bullets each, my killing knife, boot knife, semi automatic pistol and 1 plastic charge (enough to blow up a tank) which I had 'acquired' in Slatina in East Prozor.

The plastic explosive had taken a circuitous route to get here and underlined the complex system of International help all sides received in the war. It was made in the then USSR and had been smuggled in via Libya (thanks Colonel Gaddafi) and had somehow found its way past the blockade of British and American warships patrolling the Adriatic. This was but one of the complex system of arms routes that supplied all sides in Bosnia. One Croatian supply line route came through one of the many small islands off the Dalmatian coast where a runway had been built to accept covert Russian supplies of weapons (remember the Russians were supposed to be the Serbs' main allies).

My personal arsenal was sufficient for the moment, so we waited hoping that they didn't all decide to take Hans and I on with grenades - that would certainly make for a nasty situation, they would be lethal in the close confines of these streets. So for several minutes Hans and I watched, listening for every relevant sound. Then the firing stopped and we could hear shouts coming from the factory. According to Hans's translation they seemed to think that they were now totally surrounded. Perhaps it was a ruse to lull us into a false sense of security. If the factory was that important they would surely have sent for reinforcements by now. Ten minutes went by with only the odd crack of rifle fire to remind us we were at war. By now our reserve soldiers would have advanced to form a new frontline from the buildings we had taken and cleared.

It was light now, Hans and I had been so intent on the enemy that we hadn't realised it was a new day. Hans moved over to one of the windows to peer at the factory. It seemed that we were a lot closer to it now in the daylight than I had realised. It was only 20 metres away, the pale sun glinting off its walls - all was peaceful and quiet, but obviously as this was war that in itself was quite disturbing.

Hans lowered his head and crawled back while I continued to watch the gable end of the factory. There were three long windows on each floor and the roof was secured with sand bags on each corner and at each end window. Hans told me he had seen two heads or possibly three moving about within the building. There was no movement on the roof itself although Hans swore that he could see the tip of an M53 machine-gun (at 1200 round per minute I did not wish to investigate that matter much further) - it was similar to the gun I had used to kill Serbs in Babice during my first action in Bosnia.

Hans moved away and told me to watch the windows. He crawled a few metres away and moved his helmet about in the left corner window - the helmet went flying behind him - a bullet had gone right through it and struck the far wall. Hans sat there laughing to himself, at how clever he had been. But he had given our position away, the Muslims would be in no doubt that we were in this building so close to them.

'Hans, you crazy bastard come over here, they're sure to blast us to smithereens now', I said as he crawled over like a sidewinder snake, still laughing. Then it came - the rattle of death as the machine-gun on the roof started up. At least it proved Hans's theory that there was a gun on the roof - but that was little consolation as we knew we had given our position away, the bullets tearing up the window, spitting concrete, brick and glass into the room.

We raced downstairs, a piece of stone hitting Hans in the head causing both me and him to roll helter-skelter down the stairs - these Germans have a habit of knocking people flying. The fusillade lasted for several minutes at least, and the gunner knew that anyone still alive in the building would have gone downstairs. Within seconds though Hans had flown back upstairs (I liked this guy's thinking) and silenced the gunner - the little German terror had killed the gunman.

The gunner had had to lift himself up to cover the downstairs exit and windows. Hans, quick on the uptake as usual, had thought all this out in a second and ended our brief nightmare. The gunner lay dead on the floor outside the factory. As I ventured back upstairs Klaus returned with the supplies - an MGL launcher and a canvas (belt of grenades),

The Silent Cry

'Quick Klaus, get the fuck here with us now before they have time to get to their senses', I ordered.

He ran up to us as we crouched; shots were coming thick and fast from all three windows, then a Kalashnikov opened up from the roof's other corner. The MGL launcher was already loaded - I took it in my hands and steadied myself - 'Cover me, both of you' I yelled. Hans had already moved up to the left-hand window - but just as he was getting ready to fire there was an explosion from the direction of the earlier Chinese machine-gunner position - then a second blast.

'Fuck You', I shouted as I got up and fired a grenade over and through the middle window on the second floor - I'd picked that one hoping that the explosion would be most effective there. What a sound it made as it went off! Smoke billowed, then there were a few other explosions before the window frame came free and landed outside the factory next to the dead gunner who had fallen from the rooftop.

'Whack', I fired another grenade, hitting the edge of the roof just below the sand bags where another rifleman was hiding - my second shot was not good enough; flipping the lever to bring the third round to the firing chamber (it was a six shot launcher) I shot again at the middle window - a blast then seconds later screams - a direct hit. Launcher down I grabbed my AK and raked fire at the windows - all three of us now blasting the factory, giving those inside as little chance as possible to get their act together. But amazingly they recovered. At that moment the enemy were trying to cover the rifleman on the ground that Hans had shot. He was desperately making for a door near the corner of the building - I shot him just as other bullets ripped into his body.

I looked at Klaus, he had been hit and was lying on his back, a hand to his chest. I crawled over while Hans continued to blast away as if he were engaged in a one-man war. The bullet had gone through Klaus's chest to the right of his left nipple, probably missing his lung I thought 'A mere scratch' I said trying to reassure him, 'you lucky German bastard'.

He mumbled something, cursing me in his own tongue. In truth I didn't have much time for Klaus - he was a thief and a liar. He was fine at times and acceptable in battle; but as a thief I couldn't tolerate him. 'Hang on in there Hans' I told the other German, 'while I take Klaus back a building'. Hans turned around briefly, 'Go, go John, take the horrible bastard away from us', he laughed, enjoying his shoot-out at the OK Corral.

I tended to Klaus - he winced, as I took out my boot knife ready to extract the bullet. I've often offered to do 'on the field' operations, but even dying men seem to turn me down for some reason - after all I'd sat in on enough operations in Tomislavgrad and Mostar to know what to do. Sadly Klaus wouldn't let me gain a little practical experience as he pushed me away shouting over his walrus moustache, 'you Scottish bastard, you will kill me 'legally' and no one will know! You'll be a hero and I will be dead'.

So I simply bandaged him up and dragged him by the legs across the floor as he screamed his annoyance - which meant he wasn't that badly hurt, he pleaded with me not to drag him feet first down the stairs. 'Klaus, you German 'Gruppenfuhrer', I want you alive - to stand trial for War Crimes like stealing my fuckin' chocolate - admit it you Kraut, admit it' - seconds later he was confessing all, to the chocolate and the theft of five tins of my British Army rations.

Then I explained to him that his thievery was the reason I had given the contents of his suitcase away to the refugees from Jajce as they hung around outside the monastery - in his present state he could neither argue nor complain. A building away, I found more of our men. One of them could speak good English and he assured me that Klaus would be looked after. Klaus was a shit at times - he would steal medicines and get well in with the Military Police so that he could plunder vehicles at roadblocks and 'tax' the civilian population. But for now I had to return to Hans - I took two Croatian kids with me, they were young and eager and as it turned out were worth their weight in gold. Right on my heels they were as I ran back, the English speaking Croat was with us and seemed a strong, sturdy type as we made our way back to a man of worth, battling it out solo.

Hans was lying prone now as bullets zinged into our top floor vantage point. I asked the two Croatians to take the downstairs and told them that there was a small room under the stairs in which they could take cover if the machine-gun started up again. Little did I know that a Croatian sniper had manoeuvred himself into position on our building's roof. He was covering the factory roof opposite saving us a lot of problems, later I thanked him profusely.

That was why there was no firing from their rooftop, it later turned out that he had taken out the rifleman who I had shot as he tried to crawl toward the door. The Muslims were firing from every window-space now, they did not shirk at their job of fighting. I kept regretting that we'd had to turn on each other, because they would have made worthy allies.

There was no let-up, but the action seemed to have arrived at a bit of a standoff. We respected one another's ability to kill and so both sides were wary of making a big move - we kept one another at arm's length. Several metres below, to our left as we looked out of the windows in the direction of the British UN base, was our line covering the factory.

The Silent Cry

Hopefully they were under full orders not to fire unless the Muslims broke out in their direction.

By this time it was midday. This had been a long, long operation and still there seemed to be no end in sight, a war of attrition with neither side prepared to risk too much to win it just yet. So as the Croatians kept watch, Hans and I ate some rations. I considered the situation again; we would probably have to wait until nightfall to resolve the situation and take the factory. This was mainly because in the last few hours we had sustained a few fatalities and injuries that made us wary of an all-out attack. To date, the counteroffensive had cost us 17 dead and many more wounded and out of action. For those dead and wounded we had to break through and put the factory out of action - it would be a significant achievement.

What added to our problems in Gornji Vakuf was the fact that we were under Serb pressure on our frontline to the west near Kupres and in other areas. This meant that with a limited number of soldiers and a rising casualty list, sustaining worthwhile attacks on both enemies was proving difficult. Sporadic fighting continued here and there - the odd grenade going off. Messages had been circulated that snipers were at work (and effectively too) most of our dead had come from accurate sniper fire. It was a silly way to lose soldiers - it was always a personal rule that a soldier should not give his life up so easily and carelessly.

Throughout the afternoon we ducked and dived as our enemy made a concerted defensive effort. Our losses were really hitting us now - as Special Forces we were split and really needed our whole unit to work as one. It was true that our ordinary units were determined but being outnumbered five or six to one was a great disadvantage. The Muslims were using many of the weapons we had given them when we were allies - morale was at stake now, it was a must that we made a last ditch effort to oust the Muslims from the factory - only then could we secure the surrounding area.

The only way they could gain extra weapons and ammo was by smuggling it in under the guise of Humanitarian Operations. My views were known on this, as to how we should search every vehicle to the 'bone' so to speak. The French had been caught out in Sarajevo when they used trucks to smuggle 40mm ammo into the city. Whether it was politically approved or not I do not know, there was never confirmation either way. Whatever was taking place, we were suffering heavy casualties for the amount of men allocated to our sector. Our task was to take areas before handing them over to regular units - the problem here was that they had men in numbers to defend the factory.

We could see activity inside the factory following my grenade attack

- if I was in their position I would have sandbagged a couple of metres behind the window and it appeared to me that that was what they were trying to do. It was decided among our group that, as we were holding the building nearest the factory, we should try and get close enough to the building to lay a charge and blow the wall at our end. It was feasible that we could blow it and enter, but I had second thoughts, perhaps it was too ambitious a plan. It was coming into autumn now so the nights were getting longer, yet we still had four or five hours to wait until dark. Finally we agreed that one of our number would fire the MGL launcher into a top and bottom window in quick succession to provide cover for the detonation of .the gable end. Timing would be critical.

Also, I asked that one of our snipers on the roof should keep the factory roof well covered - our lives depended upon the two men deployed on the roof - a Croatian guy went off to arrange that side of things with an old hunter friend of his. A watch was kept while the rest of us dozed off - shattered by our night and day. The bare concrete floor didn't make a great sleeping place - I could smell the piss of the toilets, a reminder of prison cells and beatings - we were in a right hole!

Light shone into the top-floor from holes in the roof and window, illuminating our temporary barracks; old, smashed furniture, broken tables and metal shelves lay in tangles about the place - we were in the shit alright, it had been used as toilets by the Muslims. We had been too busy shooting up the factory to really notice the stink before. In any case I dozed off.

A scream from the factory awoke me from another nightmare - Klaus the thief had been stealing from my dead body, in particular my demon 'super boots'. I rubbed my eyes and asked what was happening - before an answer could be given, we were being raked with AK fire, all of their windows erupting with muzzle-flashes. Our snipers replied immediately, keeping the enemy fire down to a minimum.

As it turned out, our old hunter friend on the roof had shot a Muslim soldier so we couldn't really complain about our sleep being disturbed. Two hours or so had gone by since I had dozed off, I hugged the wall just by the far left window - this protected me better when I fired as I am right-handed. Hans was a metre or so away at the other side of the same window. The German had scrawled 'Kilroy, done a runner' on the wall above him which was quite funny for a German - I congratulated him on his sense of humour and he bowed his head in acknowledgement of his genius. 'Of course, I am showing Germanic superiority by such writing', he said, I had to laugh, even amid the piss and crap he was a 'case' and liked by all of us.

It broke the tension - even the Croatians knew about old 'Kilroy', we laughed so loud that the Muslims began to shoot at us to try and shut us up. They were not happy as it later turned out - they had four dead from the grenades I had fired into the factory and three were also wounded when added to the two riflemen shot dead on the roof and the extra man shot by the old codger on our roof made for quite a predicament.

Odd shots were exchanged but by and large we had reached an impasse. Sleep was beyond us all, well the 'genius' and myself that is. We both knew that it was us who would have to volunteer to go forward and detonate the building. There was no question of heroics with Hans and I - it was all about being friends, comrades-in-arms to be precise. We shared our predicaments, so we waited, talking in hushed voices as we finalised the plans to blow up the factory - we would either demolish it or die in the process. We also knew that if we succeeded and emerged alive we would be given six or seven days leave as a tasty bonus.

I dozed off for a while but was awoken by a tremendous explosion - there were screams and cries as I got up and grabbed the MGL and fired grenade after grenade into every window in sight. Turning round I saw that one Croatian soldier lay dead, literally a mash of flesh and exposed entrails, his head had been blown off - his arm a few yards away from him - he'd taken a direct hit from an RPG antipersonnel rocket. Two other Croatians lay wounded - one fatally - his face mashed open from ear-to-ear, his brain hanging out, yet he was alive as thick blood poured from his mouth. I ran over, a parachute flare from outside lighting up the gruesome sight - there was no way of saving him, so I put him out of his misery shooting him in the head with my .45 pistol.

The remaining Croatian was slumped against a wall - I ripped a British Army field dressing open and put it around his wounded neck, it was a shrapnel wound. Then I saw his right hand, it was missing part of the palm and some fingers - the tip of his thumb hanging by a thread. I never normally balked at the sight of wounded men - it was all part of the game after all - but this kid was different. He was only 17. They say the good die young and I was 43 years old then, more than twice the age of this good kid.

The first two dead Croatians had come as reinforcements while I was asleep, that was why I did not immediately recognise them. The last wounded man had come with me eagerly when I took Klaus back to another building. I regained control. This was all part of war, part and parcel of the political mismanagement that pitted Muslim against Croat. We had been reinforced, ready for the final push and the reinforcements had perished. The others were staring, shocked at the human wreckage. Turning around I shone my torch on the dislocated head as it lay on the floor staring back at me. It was gruesome and eerie, but the others urged me to pick it up. I did so by the hair, wrapping it in an old curtain and laying it beside the remnants of the dead soldier.

By now there were about eight or nine Croatians waiting with us, the shock of the dead men had hit them all. We got the bandaged man up and out, a friend helping him back to the school where we had a medical station - there were no hospitals in Gornji Vakuf. Hans and I crawled about and began covering the bodies with tarpaulin. Everyone was glad of this, as it was hard to concentrate on the imminent attack with dead faces for company. None of the other soldiers wanted to carry the bodies away so we left them there for the moment.

The firing intensified outside - there was to be no let-up now. I looked over the windowsill and saw two Muslims on the roof firing at us. Hans began blasting at them - why wasn't our sniper above killing them? He had a clear shot from there - no angles. Later we found out that he'd copped one through a shoulder - nothing too bad as it turned out but bad enough to allow them to get back to their machine gun emplacement.

Just as suddenly a machine gun opened up on a lower floor as Hans and I took evasive action, flying to the floor. I looked over the sill again and saw a door across from our building open and two men race through it. This was it, the bastards were right on top us. Another RPG rocket hit, just above the window, deafening us once more. Hans and I chucked a grenade each down into the street before running downstairs, to the ground floor.

We had to react so quickly or it would all be over - Christ knows how many of them had emerged from the factory. Our sniper was active again. The machine gun was silent but relentless, AK fire was coming our way. 'Are the bastards dead?' Hans called out, peering from a hole in the wall just below the window - there were no bodies out there.

I tried to convince a scared Croatian guy to go back and have a small mortar fire put down on the factory and spare ground but he resisted. We had to get outside to see where the enemy had gone. I opened the door into a small adjoining room where I had earlier told the Croatians to take cover - 'Oh fuck'; a tanned face confronted me - he was no regular Muslim soldier, but looked more like a Yemeni tribesman.

'Wham', a grenade blew the door down as I had shut it in shock. I knew the Muslim would have had a grenade ready, as that's how I would have done it. Hans pulled me up. I calculated that they would probably try around the back or through the side-room. I stuck my head and gun round the corner of the door and fired my automatic into one Muslim who was just about to climb in.

Hans had disappeared out the back and I could hear shots and a tangle of bodies fighting hand to hand - both Hans and the enemy had knives and were rolling about in the back yard. I ran over and tried to aim a kick at the Muslim's head. He was about the same size as Hans and fought like a man possessed - I finally managed a decent kick at the Bosnian, allowing Hans a split second to plunge his knife into his chest.

This was backstreet fighting Hamburg or Glasgow style - we were fighting from the gutter again, just as we had been taught as kids. Murder and mayhem was all about us now; our machine-guns and mortars opened up, crashing bullets and shells into the end window and doorway of the factory. Some shells fell short exploding mines, as Hans and I returned to the building to protect ourselves from shrapnel.

Then there was a mighty explosion at the gable end of the factory wall - Hans and I ran back to the window where three Croatians were repeatedly firing before ducking down below the line of the window. The end of the factory had been blasted wide open! But the shelling continued - another hit the top right of the factory shaking the ground as it exploded. From the disintegrated roof corner masonry and sand bags were sent flying for some distance - some of it flying through our window - most of it burying the body of the dead gunner who had fallen in the afternoon. 'Let's go! Let's go straight over!' I shouted to Hans.

Our men had thankfully ceased firing, the commander of that brigade certainly read our minds. We pelted toward the opening and eased our way through a five-foot gap in the wall. Inside the factory there were no lights anywhere, everything was pitch black - above us we could hear the enemy running and then a right din came from beyond the far wall. There were two doors - one at each end of the far wall and Hans and I covered one apiece. It was strangely silent - there was no firing from inside the building although our units were continuing to blast away at the upper windows of their base.

Two, three and then more of our soldiers came into the building - it was all too quiet for my liking. One minute they were coming at us hell for leather and nearly succeeding, the next they had gone quiet - it was almost as if they had disappeared. I signalled for the reinforcements to move back from the door on the left, Hans was still covering the right hand door. At this point a local commander appeared and thanked us for taking the factory so swiftly - but I had other things on my mind. I was trying to open the door (which I presumed would be booby-trapped) without causing injury to any of our side now massed in this corner of the factory.

I slowly turned the handle, just enough to open the door a fraction, enough to undo the lock. There could be no mercury switch or ball bearing device. One of our men peered around the corner of the door and was blasted at as he withdrew his head. Now we had to take the building first, to oust them completely and hold out against any possible counter-attacks.

Making sure everyone was back, I picked up three bricks stuck together by plaster and threw them with all my might against the half-open door. The blast came instantly, disintegrating the door and part of the wall with the power of the explosion. They had laid three small mines between the door and a heavy obstacle. My bricks had done the trick and blasted me onto my back, my trigger finger accidentally squeezing a shot into the ceiling sending concrete chips down upon us.

A rearguard of Muslims had been left behind to give it to us good and proper. I cautiously peered around the doorway. Sure enough I was blasted at as I flung myself down behind a pile of boxes. Suddenly a Croatian soldier appeared, unleashing half a magazine or so into the far doorway where our enemy hid behind a wall. Footsteps were heard running away from us as I rose and followed the Croatian in pursuit. Through the corridor, a Kerosene lamp lit the next room but again there was an uneasy silence about it - perhaps they had left in a hurry, or were they lying in wait?

The men to the east and front of the factory were now within its perimeters as we searched the lower floors. A commander was with us. He conversed with the giant who had come up behind me and in turn he barked orders to a soldier to the effect that under no circumstances should the main centre force start firing - the factory seemed to be empty. Hans, it turned out, had taken several of our soldiers upstairs after he had dismantled the booby-trap at the other door. Below the factory we discovered an atomic shelter, a hangover from Tito's regime. There we found food supplies, most tins and boxes had Arabic writing on them, like children our soldiers dived on these much needed supplies and took all they could carry.

I remained at the large protective door - this was a bunker for use in atomic war, for the use of party officials - it was something. There were cases and cases of ammunition, brand new AKs, hand grenades - there was enough to set up my own army. Military papers were also discovered. They had information about the region, places of hidden weapons and explanations about a new code structure. This was a moment of great pride and elation for me - my head and my body tingled as I stood there with pride watching the animated conversations of the soldiers, examining the details of the bunker, the food and the origins of the ammunition. There were shouts from the stairway - it was then that I realised Hans had returned from upstairs.

'Hans you little shit. What are you laughing for?' I called to him as he came into view, a rifle slung over his shoulder. In his hands he held bundles of crisp new Deutschmarks, in his left hand he held 100 DM bills, in the other five hundreds. Hans winked and nodded meaningfully at me. Each man stopped what he was doing and stared at our wealthy German friend as he clutched the bounty. 'You keep, you keep Deutschlander' said the commander, before continuing 'good boys, good boys' as he trooped off to inspect the rest of the building.

I pulled Hans away and took him upstairs to question him as to how he'd found all the money. He didn't explain but the shit gave me an armful of the money - they were the 100DM bills. We both laughed. We had killed and evaded death so many times over the last two days that our laughter might have been regarded as relief. But this was different. We had succeeded in taking out an important military target - the Muslim's base, and we were about to enjoy the spoils for all the death, destruction and hardship we had endured.

The Muslims were full of bottle, no one could question their bravery. But our experience and determination had won through for us, there had been no luck for us with the two enemies that had nearly accounted for both Hans and I - respect had to be given to any of our enemies be they Muslim or Serb. The fact that the Muslims had turned from allies to enemies only made the fighting harder.

THE AFTERMATH

I returned from Gornji Vakuf to be greeted not like a hero, more like the devil. I arrived at Tomislavgrad hospital to be confronted by nurse Milani, a bitch of the highest order. I was trying to discover the whereabouts of a couple of French volunteers who had been injured in Gornji Vakuf, but this woman was having none of it.

My intention had been to visit Dr. Ljubic, a brilliant surgeon with a specialism in saving limbs. He got plenty of practice in our hometown hospital and there were few who could match his ability. But my arrival in the hospital entrance must have alarmed those hanging around. I was battle-weary, armed with an AK rifle, a couple of grenades and a little blood on my arm and forehead. Fresh from the conflict I ran right into nurse Milani, a nun of sorts. That day I had already seen 36 of our men perish in Gornji Vakuf and wasn't in the best of moods when she started in on me mouthing 'out, out, out' as soon as I had set foot in the building.

'You go', she continued as I approached, ' no bombs no guns, go'. It was as if the bigmouth fool wanted me to come off the frontline dressed for a meeting with His Holiness the Pope.

'Got to hell' I replied, once I'd collected myself from her verbal assault. 'Fuck-off, men are dying for the likes of you up there while you sit back here condemning those going through shit on your behalf'.

Immediately Dr Ljubic appeared and tried to calm the whole thing down. He sensed I was getting a little worked up, but I was incensed that a nun should preach at me when I had spent all the last day and night ducking and diving so she could live in peace and continue to pray. I loved the Croatian people but occasionally would run into one of their 'associates' who I could not bear. To me life was simple and relatively straightforward – the doctor was a bit embarrassed, he knew who I was and appreciated me as a volunteer. He also knew that there were so many things I had done but could not talk about, so I kept my mouth shut.

It might have been a hospital but we happened to be in a war-zone. Ljubic calmed me down and introduced me to a few more doctors and nurses some of whom I had met before. Cakes and coffee were passed around, other nurses smiled, there was no preaching from them, just an honest appreciation, I smiled back.

Everyone feared and respected guns there. More than most they had had to deal with the effects of them during the past year or so, so I removed the magazine from my AK to make them feel a little safer. All the ambulancemen carried weapons; AKs, pistols and shotguns – ambulances were prime targets for extremists – we had lost 11 of them in Mostar this way, some of them were Muslim drivers sniped by our own side as they attempted to cross their own frontline.

Every week I would drop off supplies at Tomislavgrad hospital: cigarettes, soap, eggs, tins of fish and much more besides which had been secured from the British UN base or from British soldiers. The doctors and nurses were appreciative of this and the soldiers felt they were doing their bit – there was only so much they could achieve from within the UN.

Sometimes, while waiting for a fresh supply, I would take the opportunity to snatch a photograph, an intelligence map or report. I also kept at our commander to secure clearance so that we could hack into the UN computers as we had with their telephone and other communications – every little bit helped. All sorts of spies and agents were at work in Bosnia - it was a dangerous game for them all and too many times they underestimated the Croatian's ability to weed out the bad egg – if you got away with it once you'd be lucky, few got away with it twice. Back in the tearoom I bid the nurses farewell. I had been offered a lift up to Prozor in an ambulance, from there I could jump on a jeep to the frontline near Kupres where we were holding out against the Serbs, there was little rest for the wicked.

SHELL SHOCK

At this stage of the war the Croat forces were fighting on two fronts. Aside from the Muslim threat in Gornji Vakuf the HVO had to contend with the Serb frontline near Kupres to the West. Forces were stretched as the Bosnian Serbs renewed their assault...

Again and again the shells pounded the ground, exploding on contact - the earth reverberating as debris and fragments of metal whacked out in all directions. Our nerves shelled themselves; the continual onslaught renting the air, threatening a repeat of the many deaths I had witnessed in the year or so I had been in Bosnia. It is hard for a soldier to believe himself invincible at such times, lying upon the ground, wishing to melt into the dirt and soil, hoping that one of the mortars doesn't have your name on it. I barely moved. But amid the chaotic smoke and debris, the torn trees and pitted ground I could see a young soldier. He was a mere 16 years old, blood pouring from a head wound, life seeping from him, but he was alive, in shock, his hands covering his ears.

His features, under the dirt and grime and war, spoke of stark terror, his eyes tried not to look but his brain dared him again - the limbs flying by, men fatally wounded, their horrific wounds inducing him into a trance like state - welcome to hell on earth I thought, this wasn't some well-embroidered Never Never Land, this was reality, a mortal world he couldn't quite believe existed.

The young kid's nose bled, the blood trickling over and down onto his arm, before dripping onto his blackened, bloodstained uniform. This was 'life' at its lowest point, death and destruction a mere heartbeat away. As suddenly as the shelling began it stopped. Then the familiar screams and calls as the death count began. Terrorised gurgles issued forth from our frontline-turned-abattoir - but we were all numb, the explosive rain of shells still falling in our minds and reverberating around our brains. Those who have not seen war and death will find it hard to fathom - the deaths of mothers, sisters, grandfathers and children - why fight? Why war?

Now our young soldier faltered and fell to the ground. Holed, rented and torn, the soil cradled him briefly as the blood flowed upon it from his veins. Hans, my young, wiry, German comrade, got up as we slowly made our way towards him. The little German knelt down slowly so as not to startle the boy, who lay on his side in a foetal position - back to the comfort of the womb - his shock had given him the hope that he hadn't been born, as he instinctively sought protection from any source. Hans cradled the boy, held him firmly yet tenderly as he lay - I couldn't believe that Hans, a killing machine in the harshest circumstances, could display such a fatherly touch toward a kid who was only 6 or 7 years his junior.

My ears slowly cleared from the mortars that had landed so very close to where I had tried to bury myself. I looked again. Medics ran to and through our area, as did the soldiers, searching for their comrades; some conscious, others on their way out as the cries continued around me. 'Hans, I'll get a drip. He's dehydrating fast, the shock taking over... get him fuckin' out of it now' I urged.

I looked again as I headed off for the supplies. Hans was applying a dressing to a head wound that, ideally, needed sutures. But the kid hadn't lost much blood, the biggest threat to his life was shock - a soldier could die of it even if he had no mortal injury. It was a psychological thing that had an effect on the nervous system and heart rate - the brain can't understand and in its confused state forgets to pump blood through to the heart - allied to a slight loss of blood, death can quickly follow.

Ambulances crawled along the track that led to our small clearing in the woods - a number of dead soldiers lay about - I directed the ambulance men to save the stretchers for the wounded. I directed fit soldiers to try and talk to the wounded and seriously wounded telling them that they might yet be saved - they needed to be assured that they were alive, to try and give them a boost as to the fight for life, this process worked most times.

Hustle and bustle took place as the wounded men were manoeuvred into estate cars or jeeps - there was only one military ambulance and one civilian one. Our young man was taken away. I returned to Hans. He was trying to smoke a Camel cigarette and coughing his guts up in the process - I remembered the American navy sailors who used to give me cigs instead of money as a child in Glasgow - Hans coughed up again, the fool should have known better, I laughed out loud at his discomfort as he sat there holding the right side of his chest.

He was trying, it emerged, to calm himself. But the cigs were having a counterproductive effect; smoking makes you dehydrate along with the more obvious effect it has on your lungs. 'Hans you little shit will you never learn that smoking is a weakness of the damned?' I sneered before continuing with 'You are not as the Germans who fought against my father at Monte Casino - they were universal soldiers, you are nothing in comparison'.

'You evil Scottish bastard', he chimed in before coughing again, 'you will pay (cough) in hell'.

The Silent Cry

'Heh, Hans' I said avoiding his swinging fist before handing him a silver flask embossed with a thistle. He didn't understand how much I respected him as a man and a German or the fact that my father, as a young soldier, had respected the German soldiers he fought against. Hans clutched the small flask from my bloody hand and swigged the whisky it contained, downing it in one.

'Black watch Regimental whisky, it will make a man of you', I said knowing full well that Hans was every bit the soldier he thought he was.

'To the Wehrmacht and the Waffen SS I salute them' I shouted, copying his right-armed salute. I had the greatest respect for the guy and his heritage. German soldiers were the most dependable and hardy of our volunteers - it was my tribute to them and him, the best German of the bunch.

Just then one of our T.55 tanks rumbled by. They were battle hardened and tested - they had seen more action than any other type of tank since the end of the Second World War, rumbling through Czechoslovakia, Saigon and now Bosnia. The sight of it gave all of us a boost - to think that such a tank was first manufactured 40 years or so ago and still being updated to meet a nuclear threat. By this time Hans had recovered his composure and was red in the face, his blood pressure had jumped considerably following his consumption of the small flask of whisky. We looked at each other and smiled, then laughed aloud at the madness of war.

Just then Hans started fiddling with a small transistor radio and on came 'Tears on my pillow' by Johnny Nash - it was a soft-soap record but still we got up and started to dance like a pair of prize idiots. By this time the wounded and dead had been carted off to hospital and medical stations nearby and, as we became more foolish in our movements, Croatian soldiers sat gawping at us, shaking their heads in disbelief.

Our intention was to lighten what had been a scary morning. There was darkness in the souls of the soldiers on this frontline but as the song ended seriousness returned to our predicament. Our forces were pounding the enemy, wreaking havoc in revenge for the carnage they had brought to us. We stopped in our tracks, the sound of the radio fading into the background as flames descended on the Serb positions followed by clapping and cheering from the Croatian forces around us - they had never heard such a bombardment, it was the harshest shelling I had heard outside Mostar when we pounded the Muslim lines to a pulp.

Within this sector there was to be no more forward advance by our enemy - we were to hold and harry the Serbs. At the same time talks were being held in Zagreb between Turkish and Croatian diplomats aimed at trying to curtail the incessant fighting between the Muslims and ourselves. Both sides knew that the Serbs loved this war within a war, as evidenced by their reports of it on Serb TV and radio.

Regular units slowly took over our positions with instructions to hold the enemy. Hands were shaken and pleasantries exchanged in Croatian, German and English - then off we went for a few days respite from the fighting and patrolling. We never did find out what happened to the young guy, whether he went back into the fighting; he had been recruited that summer when call-up papers were issued to every 16 to 60 year old in Croatia. Yet despite this war effort we were still out numbered 6 to one by Muslims and Serbs.

By the end of autumn I had left the remainder of the foreign contingent in HVO. Once the Germans and the French had left through injury I returned to my Croat comrades - I trusted them far more than the 'foreigners'. By and large the Germans and French were trustworthy fighters. The few Americans and British fighting for Croatia could also be good in battle but both were a little too friendly with the UN for my liking. The British in particular had mixed with the UN and their conversations would turn to politics and as to how we managed to arm ourselves - a few of the British gave information while pretending to be loyal to the HVO, we knew who they were. Hans returned to Germany and was rumoured to have been arrested for some crime or other and the last I heard he was in prison.

NOVEMBER 1993 - FROSTBITE

That winter I returned to my Croat colleagues up in Babice. I was in charge of training the many raw recruits; the national call-up having included every male aged 16 to 60 and what a way to train in the freezing cold of Babice! The winters in Bosnia were as cruel as our Serb enemy. The freezing hours on guard dragged by at a weary pace, the cold taking the life from limbs, slowing reaction times and distracting one's concentration. These were cruel conditions reminiscent of First World War trench life...

A Croat soldier showed me his fingers. They were quite discoloured, turning to a blue-black at the fingertips. He had an understandably pained expression on his face, his hands were purple and seemed devoid of blood; the guy was useless to himself and a danger to us.

I signalled to another soldier in the bunker and he up and left to find a medic - the nearest doctor would be in Suica, the virtual ghost town in the valley between Babice and the Serb held Malovan Mountains. It was 8.15 am and the doctor typically slept in his car at night behind our lines before making his way down the valley to Suica at first light.

A moment or so later the soldier returned with the news that someone had to bring the frostbitten soldier to the town below - this had happened to me a year before when I was near collapse after five days heavy shelling. Regardless of the snowfall, descending the valley was a precarious business. The track took a circuitous route but it would have to be done - it was our duty to one another. The frostbite, it turned out, had set in the night before while he was on duty - he should have told me of it the moment he realised he couldn't move his fingers, especially as on guard duty you had to have your trigger finger at the ready for any possible attack. Minutes later the position jeep trundled down the track carrying the frostbitten soldier down the tree and bush lined road to Suica.

Cold was an integral part of our lives in Babice at this time. Unremitting, freezing cold conditions had to be tolerated and acclimatised to - survival meant having nimble fingers - even with gloves on in the gun emplacement you would fumble and a nanosecond meant everything in the fixed positions up there.

It was almost impossible to keep warm on duty; you had to stay stock-still, jumping up and down or flapping your arms about wasn't an option, it just made you a target. Temperatures in Babice could reach 43 below zero, but more typically stayed around minus 21 to 23 - wind chill factors increased this nightmarish scenario reaching a point at which oil would freeze and carbide would be needed to operate our weapons. Pain beyond toothache or earache would affect my ears, to the extent that it would bring tears to my eyes. I suffered more than most because of my age and ill health.

Every now and again I would return to the frontline to remind myself of the worst conditions of war - how life was for a regular soldier. Seldom after that winter did I volunteer again, to have to suffer one night up there was intolerable. At least when we were patrolling or generally going about our destructive business in Special Forces our blood was active and we had Gore-Tex clothing and insulated boots to retain a little heat. On the frontline there was little of this; I truly felt for our men up there, they were better men, if not soldiers, than we in Special Forces. The result of the frostbitten soldier's delay in seeking medical help was the loss of the tips of three of his fingers, the rest were saved which meant he could return, eventually, to frontline duty.

Winter continued meanwhile - the wind continued to take the breath from every soldier, a glance at their faces would tell you of their desire to withstand the pain for the next few seconds as they dreamt of the warm summer sun, before they finally gave up to cough and splutter their way through another winter's day in Bosnia.....

JANUARY 1994

Once the Bosnian winter set in the action generally slowed. Time was allowed on both sides to celebrate Christmas while conditions remained harsh enough to prevent large-scale attacks. Even so there were a few on both sides willing to risk all in pursuit of the enemy.

Storms come and go but this one was something else. Winds were well in excess of one hundred kilometres an hour; they ripped through the woods at a rate that tore everything loose. Everyone took cover. In foxholes and gun-emplacements each soldier hid from nature's assault, no one would venture into the open air. Scurries of snow were blown all over the place, pieces of stone whacked at us, one came through the machine-gun slot - at first I thought we were being sniped by the enemy, using a silenced weapon - then laughed with relief as I realised that the 'bullet' was a piece of rock that had smashed into the wall behind us.

It was a day and night to remember. Not one of us wanted to exchange places, to move from gun-emplacement to bunker meant risking a few metres of open ground. But out we went as it was much more preferable to sleep in a bunker just behind the actual frontline than duck for cover behind a few logs. I crashed over the emplacement and was flung against a tree. Barely gripping my AK 47, I was fortunate that I had remembered to fasten my helmet. Most certainly I would have lost my rifle to the winds if I had not kept both hands tightly gripped around it. I fumbled about on the ground, turning my back on the bitter, cold wind - the kind that would take the breath from your lungs.

When I eventually got up I was blown around again as I felt my way forwards tree-by-tree and then down the few steps toward the bunker door; pulling it towards me, I went flying in with some force, crashing over all sorts of equipment - ammunition boxes, ration crates and rifles before coming to rest tangled up with the lot of it. My curses could be heard above the crashing winds - welcome to frontline life in Bosnia-Herzegovina. I threw myself down on an empty bunk. The bunker was full of make-shift beds, it reminded me of an illegal immigrants house I had visited in Shepherds Bush in the early 60's - but the rest and relative tranquillity was more than welcome as the winds howled through the forest a few metres above.

It took a little time to draw myself into a slumber - my mind was preoccupied with the madness of war, a situation I could never quite adjust to in Bosnia; I had seen people go mad already and didn't wish to join the loony bin just yet - fortunately madness was only in the short-term for me. Others were more fortunate, after a few days away from the fighting a soldier's mind would moderate, when seeing and being with their families - if they were still alive.

Throughout the night my sleep was interrupted by the sound of the storm outside accompanied by the cackle of machine-gun fire (shells would be counterproductive in this weather). The Serb enemy would know that all of us would be in bunkers or machine-gun emplacements which, to even a heavy 120mm mortar, meant relative safety. My annoyance at the machine-gun fire lessened after the first few weeks of combat, it became part and parcel of daily life and sleep had to be had regardless of the noise. An insomniac was useless for the concentrated effort that was needed to go on until the day when we could hit back and push the enemy from the ground they had captured in April 1992.

I slept until 6 am. Then it was time for me to struggle out of the bunker and into the blizzard conditions again. I came to appreciate that these were typical winter conditions in the mountains of Bosnia. Winter clothing was in good supply now, unlike the first winter I had spent here when 11 of our men had perished from the cold - literally frozen to death.

That cold, blustery morning the rose-hip tea arrived early which was a blessing as our Lexi-stove had run out of fuel and we couldn't make a fire inside our bunkers. I sat next to a young Croatian guy I had met the night before. He had been a little nervous then and I had reassured him about certain things on the frontline. He seemed a little calmer with me for company once a Croat had translated several points to him. Now he forced a smile, happy to be alive after two watches in action - then again there had been little or no chance of either side attacking us in the middle of this blizzard. Weather-wise it had eased a little by morning, giving us a break of sorts, although the favours offered by the weather failed to brighten the mood, it was still bitterly cold.

Eventually we ate a little breakfast; bread and jam, followed by cheese, sardines and boiled eggs for me. It was the same food every morning, there was little variation in our rations, a monotonous diet typical of trench life. I took my new comrade out to the gun-emplacement, exchanging places with a couple of Croatians who had spent their two hour shift trying to keep warm, they were more than glad to get the hell out of it.

It was still dark. All was crisp, cold and windy - but as we changed over there was a drastic reduction in the wind, which in itself was most welcome. I went through the procedure again. Checking the MG.42 to make sure that it had not frozen up during the night, I let out a short burst of fire into the woods nearby, waking up everyone in the vicinity. The guy beside me jumped at the sound - his nerves far too taut for war.

Just as I had let go a burst of fire, other machine-guns on the frontline erupted into the cold morning air, blasting forward into the dark early winter's morning before we resumed our vigil in utter silence, the sun obstinately refusing to show. Snow continued to fall in thick, large flakes as we watched the area immediately within our field of vision; waiting for an enemy attack. It would be just like the Serbs, I thought, to act out of devilment - it was their way, they enjoyed the audacity of an out of the blue move.

Just as I was considering this a grenade exploded down and to our right - shots streaked the air, cutting through the snow in the semi-darkness. Further shots came at us this time - repeated over and over again. I growled in annoyance; gripping the machine-gun tightly I began to spray the area before me - rip after rip the bullets sped out fifty or so metres into the sparse undergrowth before I set off a mini-flare by hand; it illuminated the area and showed that the snow had been disturbed here and there on the edge of the glade in front of us.

Again and again I fired heavily to the edge of the trees and into what remained of the snow covered vegetation. Suddenly, two snow-camouflaged figures broke for cover, trying to retreat while firing from the hip - in seconds the murderous rate of fire from my machine-gun cut them down. The Croatian to my right shot into the bodies as they fell to the snow; there was a muffle to the shots now being fired - calls and shouts came to us from our own positions as the two dead lay there before us - blood oozing onto the white powder.

I patted the young Croatian on the back. He had been 'blooded' now, had shot two enemy without panic - he looked pleased, inside I knew he was elated. Silence returned to the frontline. There was little or no sense in them maintaining their fire as the trees prevented all but the odd bullet from getting through on target. Time would pass before any attempt could be made to venture out over our minefield and check the dead. Soon enough the bodies would be brought into our encampment and searched before being taken away for burial - unlike the other sides in this war we didn't mutilate the bodies before disposing of them.

A runner came to us as we had failed to hear the radio call - an excited Croatian guy spoke to my friend who was still somewhat stunned as to the speed of events and his part in them. My blood pressure receded with the cold air that stung my ears and lungs. Fear and trepidation had been overcome once more. I will not categorically state that I no longer felt fear - it was still within me, but it is so difficult to explain, a very different fear to that experienced everyday in civilian life.

The runner asked us about the exchange of fire that had taken place and we told him about the dead enemy out in the glade. We in turn were informed that two of our men had been wounded but not seriously;

one had a piece of shrapnel score across his cheek and thud into a log behind him, the other had a piece of metal penetrate into his shoulder and lodge in his collar bone - he was on his way to hospital.

Once satisfied as to our kills, our runner made his way back to the sleeping quarters behind us. There was no particular reason for me being on the frontline. I wasn't ordered there, it was more a matter of keeping in touch with the frontline troops during the winter months and also to give some confidence and comfort to men who had had a bad time up in the hills.

They were not places to be relished, it was far preferable to be in action elsewhere, to be attacking our enemies in warmer conditions rather than sat freezing behind a machine-gun, a sitting duck for a Serb attack. Now, following the kill, mortar shell after mortar shell came at us, some detonating on the tops of trees, others hitting the ground lifting rocks, dirt and snow into the air. This was a relentless shell attack, some crashed a few metres away and deafened me once more. Others started to blow our position apart, scoring direct hits on our bunkers and reminding me of the time I had been trapped in one when a shell hit.

Several minutes passed with the incessant mortar fire. If a shell managed to find me it would all be over in an instant, I reasoned - an end to the cold, the war, everything. Finally the shelling stopped and much activity was to be seen as one of our bunkers had caved in causing a few minor casualties, cuts and bruises but nothing that would cost us a man.

We returned to the cold. In our inactivity the chill held our attention, keeping warm preoccupied our time. Silence descended again as morning fitfully flickered into life. The clouds broke a little, revealing a sun that was quickly submerged by a cold and dismal sky. With the arrival of the sun, the snowfall lessened and my Croatian friend and I saw out our shift until 8 am with no more excitement.

It was at about this time that an old friend appeared within the emplacement - 'Scot!' he shouted out, 'where have you been. As soon as I heard you were here I had to see you, come let's go and get a drink, tell me all that has happened since we last met'. He was a handy guy, but always happy-go-lucky, whereas many Croats could be quite sombre until you got to know them well enough. Old times were discussed as we sat down on the logs near to a campfire - it warmed us a little while a couple of soldiers went out beyond the minefield to return the dead bodies. Some blood was found on a nearby tree suggesting that there may have been a third Serb dead or wounded. Life went on as my comrade and I sat around the fire, recalling a few comrades who were dead and wondering about the whereabouts of those wounded. As always drink was offered but I naturally declined. The one time I had succumbed was in Prozor when I had a few tots of Rakija and 'went off my head'.

The story about the two British girls at the Tomislavgrad UN base feeling up my kilt was retold and the soldiers around roared with laughter. The story had a few exaggerations, but it offered a break from the monotony of frontline winter existence up here in the woods.

Summer was fine, the sun would beat down and there was a fantastic view over the hills from our position. To the left was the abandoned town of Suica and that valley went all the way back to Tomislavgrad, past the steep gorge that our trucks and jeeps had to negotiate without a bridge. Alas, this was winter and our time consuming talk finished I felt tired, a few hours sleep would make all the difference. My blood pressure was low in the cold and it made me more tired than usual.

Three or fours hours later I was awoken by shouts for volunteers - a truck had bogged down a kilometre or so away back down the mountain track; that was halfway between us and our next main position down the line. Declining the invitation I snuggled back down to sleep when I was awoken again by an agitated call from my young Croatian colleague who had been 'blooded' that morning. He was trying to tell me that one of the dead Serbs hadn't been a Serb but in fact a Russian. He tried to convey this by making growling noises, like a bear, while repeating the words Vodka and Moscow several times. Replying in German I told him that I understood him and patted him on the back. He was now even more pleased that he had killed a Russian.

'So,' I thought, 'that is why there was a little adventurous mini-attack'. A Russian or two had been among their number and to them these conditions were ideal, in fact their natural habitat. I went out into the morning, my eyes fixed on the enemy positions looking for a Red Star; I was now a little paranoid as to the possibility of an all out Russian assault on our lines - unlikely, but possible. There was no doubt that Serbs and Russians were 'brothers' and that these Red Army volunteers would be tougher than the average Serb, adding a new dimension to the war and a fresh threat to our frontline existence. I gestured to my young comrade to bring me some lunch - there was no way I could leave him alone to keep watch now that I was preoccupied with this latest development as I stared intently into the distance once again...

7 - THE TIDE TURNS

JANUARY 1994

The inactive, bitter cold existence of the frontline behind me I returned to Special Forces. Unusual amounts of Serb activity in the area around Prozor had alerted HVO command and my unit was ordered in to 'recce' their movements.

We continued our tiresome journey from Tomislavgrad toward the base of the hills.' As usual when we reached the checkpoint under the shadow of the mountains in Southern Bosnia groans could be heard from our number. It was a sign of the trepidation we felt out there, the annoyance covering up the inner fears and anxieties among us. The mountains were a bittersweet sight for this was our battleground, the place where we continued our job as professional killers.

War is a poor substitute for peace but still we enjoyed our work, if we didn't we wouldn't do it. You have to like what you do to survive, to be free of conscience, avoid the screams and nightmares. I believe every human has the ability to kill; the first taste of blood makes you thirst for more and eventually taking a life becomes a perk of the job, a consolation for all the other shit you have to put up with.

It was dark as we approached an enemy camp, a machete stabbing at the head of a guard, then through his neck and shoulder before his head toppled, his body wavering for a moment before it followed its control centre. We had little time to watch the mass of spurting blood before we were onto the next 'job', my Skorpion silencer spitting into another torso, head and heart. The corpse silently lowered to the floor by my comrade, we were now free to enter our adversaries' encampment.

The rats squealed as we stabbed, shot and maimed them - there was the stench that normally accompanies killing, all in violent death becomes putrid, we went on. The enemy knew their turn had arrived - suddenly a metallic thud hit the earth's dust and rocks - a twang a split second before a blood-curdling scream. One of our own had copped it and, as he fell to the floor, my comrade cried out to let me know that it wasn't he who had been hit. No time for confessions or flowers - we carried forth into the night barely stopping for our unfortunate comrade. Memorials and regrets could come later.

A grenade went off and all hell broke loose. Stabbing, chopping: another stain on humanity as we stole more lives in the winter darkness. Bullets hit a tree to my right and I stumbled. I gripped a branch, ran on and then pulled a couple of large splinters from my thumb and forefinger, the blood too salty to taste. Mortar fire came at us with grim predictability as we massacred, committing more atrocities for the pages of UN reports. It was another night, another saga of mayhem and killing as we continued our winter patrol recce.

We finally came to rest. We had escaped the net of Serb forces, taken them by surprise before blowing through their defences and now we waited by a snow-covered field. A shrouded figure came into view. 'Crack', the bullet seared through the winter air hitting the soldier, or was it a civilian?

After a moment's respite the body toppled onto the snow. The blood corrupting the whiteness of the field. A nervous smile flickered on the lips of the killer to my right as the wind whipped up another snow flurry, covering the body with pure whiteness. It seemed like moments, as we watched and waited, but it was more like an hour before they arrived, venturing within 40 metres or so of the corpse. A scurry of snow flew with the bitter winds, we could hear the snarls from 600 metres away. I watched as the wolves circled their prey - they could sense a kill from miles away.

A young soldier lifted his rifle clicking it to automatic - I gently placed a gloved hand under the barrel and lifted it a few inches. I looked deep into his eyes and envied the young soldier's humanity and decency - I didn't care anymore. The wolves began to chew at the frozen corpse. Nature's scavengers finding sustenance in the most recent victim of human conflict as they gnawed at the human carrion.

Sobs could be heard from the corner. The 16-year-old soldier had killed and sadly discovered that the victim was an old woman. I tried to calm him by saying that I had checked with the village and she had been cold and starving and had ventured into the field to look for food or die, as a result his shot had prevented her suffering. Now she was being reclaimed by nature, providing succour for the wolves of Bosnia.

After what consolation I could offer the soldier, I returned selfishly to my own circumstances, remembered the bitter cold and damp freezing my undercarriage, stinging my ears. And, as the command jeep pulled up, I contemplated what I would do before I died. I've always wanted to

The Silent Cry

visit Glasgow before I go, our death averages were up these days, being in the 'Intervention Force' we were sent anywhere at any time. Death was an occupational hazard, colleague after colleague had succumbed to it.

Our commander, Zjelko Glasnovic, was exceptional, a soldier's soldier - he was no nonsense and would take up frontline positions for the cause - he would never send you on a suicide mission unless you begged him and even then he would warn you that you were volunteering. As usual I was foolish enough to volunteer for anything, especially as the winter months were fairly dull. There had been reports of some movement to the west of here, so after a brief rest we changed into 'snow gear' and headed out towards the upheaval.

Our point man was changed every hour as we trudged along the mountain track knowing that there could be no respite for a couple of hours. Our first point man was an Australian, a particularly annoying character who would always moan and complain about Croatians - he was a right pain in the arse at times. Nevertheless after an uneventful hour or so we stopped to exchange codes by radio. We received coordinates and ventured over a ridge deep behind the enemy before circling back towards a fixed position overlooking the crossroads above Kupres, 40 or so kilometres away from our frontline at Suica.

The Serbs had plundered these majestic mountains in July 1992 as the ill-equipped Croatian army retreated to strongholds further south. 8 Serbian tanks had smashed their way down on Kupres while our forces had only 3 anti-tank guns left to counteract the threat at the time. So over 18 months later we were back. We checked out all we saw, although the blanket of snow left us in the dark about a few things, as we reccied their positions for signs of movement and disturbance.

The beautiful perfection of winter was all about; this was the Balkans, a stumbling block for so many foreign powers. Hitler, Mussolini and Stalin - all had succumbed to the infighting of the locals and the harshness of the conditions. By now a blizzard was blowing, we were in the shit but hardly a man flinched as we made our way back toward our frontlines by a shorter route which was not so hazardous because of the weather conditions.

My heart pounded with the strain. I kept telling myself that I would make it. The cold helped me, made my breathing easier - it was about eight or nine degrees below zero as we faltered forwards, staggering towards our own lines. We stopped for a half-hour break in a deserted hut, which offered a little protection from the winds, if not the cold. Within 20 minutes, having eaten our frozen rations, I ordered us to pull out, our limbs were numbing in the bitter cold, 10 minutes more of it and we'd freeze to death.

So I drove our men on, instructing the point man to walk straight

168

ahead. Suddenly he signalled; 'Everyone down', we hit flat in a second, guns trained ahead, there was some sparse vegetation where the point-man lay and I could make out a broken sign.

'Kaa-boom' - he'd tripped a jumping pineapple - a mine that is triggered to jump 8 feet in the air- sending metal chunks down on us.

'Don't move' I screamed at everyone. A yell went up - one man had been wounded - one of our number crawled over to him - we were in a fuckin' minefield.

My nerves screamed at the memories of my previous lapses, but I just had to live with these momentary lapses of fear at that moment of panic. I followed the first guy to the front, sticking to the snow tracks made by the others while our little group tried to calm themselves - only our Aussie friend was shitting himself.

Our point man had been blown to smithereens. The Serbs had planted this little field well and it had reaped a deathly reward. The mines had been recently set - they knew that anyone moving through this ground would use the vegetation as it was the only protection in an otherwise sparse, open space. We raced back to the hut and tried to compose ourselves.

The body of our man lay out there; normally he would have got away with losing a leg or a foot, but as he had been crawling forward it got him in the face and neck - outright death. Without order a man ran back through the snow back toward the body and red slush surrounding it. No shots were fired, just utter silence - this was no time to scream or rebuke - it was time to move as quickly as possible in the direction we had originally intended.

'To hell with the mines' I thought, the choice was simple - freeze to death in enemy territory or attempt a risky return to the warmth of our own lines - my men had already made up their minds. True, there was an element of craziness to it all, particularly as the blast of the mines would have been heard by the Serb forces nearby, but it was really our only option. Whoever had planted the mine had been a real professional, a woodsman not to be underestimated - he had already claimed one of ours, we were damned if we were going to let him claim any more.

Quickly we reached a clearing along a small trail and set up an ambush, deciding to give the Chetniks 20 minutes to come and check on their kill. An arc of fire was hastily arranged. Under no circumstances was anyone to enter it, anyone who did would be regarded as the enemy and be killed - these rules laid, down we waited. Twenty, then thirty minutes passed in the freezing blizzard. My limbs began to numb, the thought of revenge forcing me to stay silent and hope for a kill.

Just as I was beginning to lose hope a noise in the distance foretold of human activity. A huge bearded Chetnik was leading a patrol right into our trap. He was big by any standards; he wasn't wearing winter camouflage, just a JNA uniform. He was followed by four, five, six others - all bedraggled looking soldiers - to me they were vermin, but vermin that could kill you as easily as you them.

On and on their steps crunched the snow, as I readied myself, waking from my temporary hibernation. Suddenly one of our men circled around behind them as they continued to thud toward the clearing, their huge bearded leader spotted the movement and moved swiftly over the snow towards our man. A light machine-gun barked out into the open space, coughing the means of death from beneath its white cloth covered barrel, tearing and killing the lead Serb - bullets ripping into his stomach, chest and face - he was dead a split second before he hit the snow as we turned our attention to the others.

One Serb sprayed automatic at our lead gunner, it hit the magazine on his machine-gun and deflected up through his cheek and into his eye - there was no more sound from our comrade, he was down and out. Immediately three bullets hit the Serb who had responded so gamely - he had been reactive, instinctive, in such a trap and at such a moment he had responded well - he had found himself in a crossfire but had cut one of our number down despite our man being well camouflaged, within seconds he had also been silenced along with his colleagues. The firing ceased upon a screamed order.

Three men maintained their positions as the rest of us darted toward the enemy bodies. The last to get hit, and the only one by me, lay silent but not dead - his eyes met mine, there was no pleading to his look yet he still lived and breathed. A matter of moments passed and after all the years of killing I wondered, for the first time, 'What would my father have done in the same position?'. The Kalashnikov in my hands contained a single shot, so I shot the Serb dead - no prisoners were called for or wanted, I later thought I should have left him out there in the cold to suffer for as long as fate allowed.

At the time I knew that my hatred of the enemy had compelled me to kill. I was not acting with a logic based on survival, but on a lust to destroy as much as possible, to satiate the desire of my twisted brain; comprehension and calculation had little place in my war, they were left for the more sober moments back at base where the losses and gains could be totted up, or new objectives targeted - out here in the winter woods of Bosnia I acted with an animal instinct.

Killing is vastly important to soldiers, it is their perk. For some the perks are raping and plundering, but the rapists and plunderers are usual those too weak to meet the demands of a battlefield. Too weak to kill an equal, they are cowards who find solace in taking their frustration out on the innocent. We rounded up their supplies of ammunition, checking the dead bodies for anything that might be useful - everything counted in such a hostile environment. Meanwhile we covered our own men with snow - there was no will or strength among us to dig into frozen ground - so we moved on.

Our giant Chetnik was found to have a pair of dried human ears in a leather grenade pouch. For what it was worth I kicked the Chetnik's face, booting his skull, making it crunch and fracture - there was no way I was going to let him have a hero's funeral, I made sure he was a mess.

Later the others laughed at how I had gone 'off it' - telling me that the animal was in me. But we had pushed our luck to the extreme and the terrain and winter conditions in Bosnia had brought out the animal in me - I regretted that we hadn't taken the bearded beast of war alive. Again the war didn't lend itself to humanity.

It was time to evacuate our winter playground and, as we trudged back toward our lines, I realised that it was my fault that we'd fucked-up. Our ambush had worked, as planned, but it was clearly against our intended recce mission, which had been merely to survey the enemy's winter movements.

There would be much for me to answer for when I returned; one man dead and gone in the ambush, I was truly at fault there, I should have laid small Pasteta mines to prevent that death, I thought, I had erred again. The death in the minefield could probably be excused as 'one of those things', the snow had been against our point man. But I knew that I would have to explain both deaths to my commander in a verbal statement upon his return from Zagreb - a tricky situation despite the fact that he was a good bloke.

We continued our hasty retreat to safety. It was a tiresome journey over hills and mountains, as we stumbled and faltered, taking turns to enter deep drifts, my temper fraying at the thought of our two dead left in the winter wastes. But not one man blamed me, it was all part of the madness of the winter war in Bosnia, they accepted it. By late afternoon we entered some trees to relax. A little light snow was falling but it would be some time before our tracks would be covered, consequently we couldn't relax properly until then - every near or distant tree looked like a Serb in our tiredness, the woods making us uneasy about our surroundings.

As a result we decided to sleep. A man was placed on point duty and we laid a few booby-traps at the best possible approaches to our enclosure. It was brass monkey weather alright, so in an attempt to ward off a little of the lower wind we heaped together some snow in a circle and tried to get to sleep. Off we wandered, to cold sleep, trying to maintain our basic warmth within our Gore-Tex clothing. Despite these advantages only 'surface' sleep could be had and, as the evening wore on, it was soon my turn to take an hour's watch. A hand shook my ankle lightly - this was our way of signalling that it was one of your own - anything other than that grip in the dark was a sign of danger.

I shook my head clear and made my way to the edge of the circle, my teeth chattering as I concentrated on the shadows and images before my eyes. I donned my facemask, a useful article stolen from a British Army soldier of fifteen years service called Duggie - he was OK as Englishmen were, especially as he once gave me a lift from Tomislavgrad back to Tamworth. He was big, fat and ugly and insisted on playing fascist music tapes all the way home, as if he was trying to brainwash me or something. Our few booby-traps were handy but not enough to make us feel really secure while we slept. Nonetheless the small mines were welcome out here, no good soldier went anywhere without two or three.

Finally, having all taken an hour's watch, we were up and about, forcing our legs into movement as we ate our tasteless, frozen rations before a Croatian led the way forward, this was his territory, the land he had known since childhood. He reckoned that we were only a matter of a few kilometres away from our section-post, but we knew that we would have to traverse all manner of land mines and the dreaded no-mans land to reach safety.

Difficulties always arise on frontlines. The soldiers there are always looking to shoot up anything that moves, a heightened state of awareness brought on by all the freezing nights and loss of sleep, as those on guard seek compensation for the frostbitten toes and pent-up emotion. Onwards we trekked into the snow and sleet, visibility deteriorating as we continued - this was good as it hid us from the immediate view of the enemy lines. My main hope was that our own side were prepared for us at both points of entry to the lines.

The six of us struggled against the elements, those last few kilometres through the Serb lines were hell as we waited for the inevitable bullets to eliminate us. Having survived that side of things without incident we ventured on toward our own lines. A red distress flare shot 80 or so metres into the air, the sound could not be disguised as it blasted up into the dismal grey sky engulfing the region.

Still the snow came down as the flare descended - our lads should now know that we were in the last stretch and nearly home. In any case shells came down as expected from the Serb side, but it was a choice for us - whether it was radio or flare (the radio transmission would have been intercepted in any case) we would have copped for something - the Serbs were no fools.

We ran, exhausted, the remaining distance to our bunkers and machine-gun positions, thankful that none of them opened up on us. Enemy shells continued to land with a precision that came from years of practise, as we tumbled into two separate machine-gun bunkers cleared for our purpose. Yet still there was no laughter (as was usual upon returning safely), our nerves were stretched taut during this final leg, we had been in as much danger here as at any stage during the long trek we had endured. The thought of going down with your own men behind the guns always made my palms sweat a little more.

Welcome faces, slaps and grins eventually greeted us as we waited in the bunker for several minutes while the shelling stopped. On the Serb side there would be rage. Our radio interception unit had picked up reports that two of our men had bitten the dust. Translations were made to me and I grimaced at the memory.

We ran over the slope to the main bunkers and gave a run-down of events to the temporary commander, relating the number we had killed was helpful, our two deaths and the bodies left behind to (probably) be dismembered, not so helpful. One after the other the mortar shells whacked into our encampment - clearly the animals were upset as I pondered again from where that 'Frankenstein' character with the dead ears had come.

REVENGE MISSION

Relations between the Bosnian Croats and the Bosnian government thawed in early 1994. The dismissal of Mate Boban, the separatist leader of the proposed Croatian statelet of Herceg-Bosna, on February 8th, led to talks between Croatia proper and the Bosnian government and an agreement was signed under pressure from the United States in Washington on March 1st.

The agreement outlined a confederation of Swiss-style cantons in those areas in Bosnia dominated by Croats and Muslims before the war. This included Herzegovina (southwest Bosnia) and Central Bosnia. There was also a looser confederation involving Croatia proper. Crucially, however, agreement had yet to be reached with the Bosnian Serbs or the Serb government.

There was a seriousness on the faces of all fourteen men - not one of them spoke openly about the consequences of failure or the chances of success, but the thoughts were there all the same, the familiar doubts creeping in before cold professionalism took over once more.

Orders were given, area maps studied, checked and checked again. The men were briefed; we were Special Forces and we needed to be special for this mission behind Serb lines. Each one of us aware that 'special'

The Silent Cry

meant understanding the price of your own life and the need to preserve that of your comrade.

As a group it was understood that we were about to reach the point of no return. We were a tight knit group; only one man had not trained with the other fourteen, but he was well known and trusted by another three. I made sure that they understood our objectives and the need to take the enemy out swiftly and efficiently.

All men landed safely; weapons checked again, co-ordinates re-checked - no mishaps or breakages - so far so good. Everything about this mission had been 'last minute' so as to maintain secrecy and make best advantage of our best weapon - surprise. By 1994 I had become infamous among my regular unit for the frequency of my disappearances - the other soldiers often wondered where I had disappeared and would enquire curiously on my return to the regular unit. My replies remained vague (principally because any association with the HOS paramilitary group would be frowned upon by my commander) which led them to the common assumption that I was some kind of terrorist, a crazy guy who loved to shoot for the sake of shooting or explode something for the sound and chaos of it.

The reality was that I had become a law unto myself - I was disposed to go when and where I wanted, the commanders trusted me - this mission was an example of such. My second-in-command gathered the men while three others kept watch in a triangular pattern around us. A quick ground briefing took place reminding the squad of our objectives before I ordered them away quietly through a small wood - as usual we were led by a local who knew the terrain well, essential in an area where you literally couldn't see the wood for the trees. We were silent - no sound, not a word as we stealthily made our way through the forest.

There was no luck involved in this operation - we had seen the satellite close-ups - of course the Serbs had moved their trucks a few kilometres into cover but we had accurate information coming in 20 minutes before take-off stating that little else had changed. The 'free-fall' I hated, being not over experienced at jumping, but my nerves managed to hold up and I could hardly admit to my men that I had continued medical problems or that would have been that.

Two men ventured to the edge of the wood as a few long, hard minutes passed - a dryness taking hold of my throat as I waited, determined to remain impassive to my men - I could show no emotion, no weakness, I'd bluffed my fitness as it was but we would be alright provided it didn't 'come on top' before we had hit our two objectives first. We were to lay charges on their vehicles and missile stores so timing was obviously going to be essential to the success of the operation - but for the price of us fourteen men the success of this mission would be a great morale boost for our side - it all depended on the timing.

My precision planning had taken two days study of the satellite photographs and nearby positions and this was very much my own mission - at least, I thought as I waited in the woods, if I die in the course of a successful mission my tactics and planning will have been worthwhile. The enemy had not underestimated our threat either as they'd doubled up on security in the wake of a number of lightning attacks to the north and west of their main positions.

This operation was so different in that it concentrated not on propaganda but on military expertise and speed of response - of course they could and would replace what we destroyed; but success would leave other objectives open as they protected the areas we had recently hit. We continued our patrol, avoiding a few lit houses and within 30 minutes we were close to our first objective.

This was going to be the trickiest part of the operation. We would have to delay timers on the charges for long enough so that we could reach our second objective before being discovered - I'd set them all myself and to make absolutely sure I'd used double-timers and detonators - there was absolutely no margin for error. I stopped to double-check every gun, grenade and charge carried by the men and myself. They and I knew that our lives and the lives of the civilians in surrounding villages depended on the success of the operation, we had to show the Serbs how much of a force we had really become. We had not brought our own ammunition, save for that which was already loaded - but we were told that there was plenty of it on the ground and in truth there was more there than I'd imagined, the Serbs were well equipped alright, they had planned and horded ammunition for years - there was no spontaneity to this lot.

It was my honour to lead this group - whether by luck or otherwise I had proven myself down country on a number of occasions and been fortunate that independent soldiers had seen my controlled madness - I knew, however, that failure here would mean death or an early exit from the war in self-disgrace. But defeat never entered my head; I counted on those around me and had a confidence in them coming from our common struggle. I was the only foreigner here; volunteers, I had decided by 1994, were usually gung-ho and full of bullshit, the Croats on the other hand were dedicated to building themselves a future - that was the difference.

Time was still on our side as I placed two men just ahead of me; one as point man, the other just 10 metres behind him. I kept close to this guy, just 5 metres to his rear and right - we all knew each other, knew instinctively each other's movements and sign language. The air was warm for the time of year as we pushed on - our snipers to the rear supplemented by other personnel with night-vision.

I tried to control my blood pressure. I had taken the precaution of taking three tablets before take-off, but moving quickly had caught up with me and now we were almost upon the ORKAN missile launcher - objective one. The order had been to lay charges and withdraw immediately, avoiding contact if and when possible, a certain stress had been placed on the latter. I swapped positions with the guide (our point man) - the advantage of this patrol was that we were all of a certain level of skill and experience. We knew each other's jobs well enough to take over from one another in the event of a mishap. I now moved into position to silently dispose of the two guards on duty outside the compound.

I took one out and the second the same way - my knife smashing hard and deep into the guards' throats and up inside the skull; I laid him down quietly and, before my partner could reach the third, I already had him, my knife entering his throat. He had been lying down which made the job a little harder, but I swiftly nutted him to make sure before removing my knife with a sideways flick motion that left blood on his jacket.

I nearly fucked-up though as my comrade looked at me shaking his head; my quick movement had slightly alerted him but the devil was on our side this time and we had successfully killed them against orders - thankfully they were clean kills. The others were all trained to 'neck' them if possible so that they wouldn't scream before they were killed, as nowadays most alert enemy had ammo jackets that disallowed a frontal attack. I had therefore issued instructions to target the neck - it was the quietest, swiftest method.

I quickly laid a main charge to effect a blast that would blow their main re-supply to the truck. We had to delay the charge so as to reach the next target several kilometres away before this one went off. We removed the bodies but we were sure that within the next 30 minutes or so someone would come and check and find the guards missing - as usual the Serbs had been drinking so that was in our favour but it only took one alert enemy to spill the beans. A few booby traps were laid on the perimeter of the objective as a way of delaying them finding our charges, which we had also booby-trapped, to go off if discovered. Our hearts were racing by now. We had a five minute check on all weapons before continuing - this was a particularly welcome rest for me. I regained my composure.

Onwards and up a steep hill; I took to the rear to cover any of my breathing problems - it would be wrong to let them see their group commander breathing hard. I could excuse it by saying my third kill had got me in the ribs, but I made up for this shortcoming by taking up the rear which everybody always hated. Meanwhile the other soldiers ribbed me about being too old, I was just about to curse them when a series of huge explosions ripped from our rear. We flung ourselves to the floor, then another explosion and another - the sky was lit up. I had never seen anything like it before in my life as a dozen 253mm warheads exploded at the same time.

The ground was shaking and though I was pleased at the destruction we had caused we were still miles away from the next target. Nevertheless looking around I checked the looks on the other soldier's faces; grimy with soot and camouflage cream I could make out their eyes shining brightly, their broken teeth glinting in the light. If they were happy, I was happy. If I died now I'd know that I'd done the job, 'fuck the UN', I thought, 'this is our war'.

I looked around. Flames and smoke were trailing into the air - it was as if a mini atomic bomb had gone off, but we were already on our way to objective two. Trekking on I stole myself for a while. The second objective would now be a nightmare - they would be on tenterhooks alright. As we approached the second target, machine-gun fire was being sprayed everywhere - they didn't have a fix on us yet but were desperately trying to hit something, anything.

I gave a clear order to wait, to allow the enemy to expend a little nervous energy, a period of quiet would reduce their fear and, as a result, their awareness. They might have heard by now of the guards taken out at target one and would be aware that they would be next, but when and where we would strike remained a mystery to them and, to be honest, it remained a mystery to me.

Some Serbs were shooting into the air which meant that they were most probably drunk or had misinformation that the last attack had been an air strike. It would be hell for us now. I looked at their young faces; they betrayed no emotion but I could read their minds; they would die with me if I led them into hell. I weakened momentarily - I could do this last piece on my own, I thought. If I could just get through the barrage of fire while they were being distracted...

There was a small village within our objective and there were civilians, probably intentionally placed by our enemy, as a cover or human shield. To me only the young are innocent in war and this was no time to wonder as to the possibilities or eventualities. It was a case of go on and destroy all within your path, anything that moved you killed, coldly and professionally - emotion was for our untrained enemy.

We had our orders, we were to take out target two and anyone standing in the way of this would be sacrificed for that goal. I wanted to take out three of the bastards up ahead but night-sight or snipers could not be used as we did not want to give them a second to warn those in the village below a few 100 metres away, to take out three at once was nevertheless a possibility. So four of our group set off toward the underbrush (vegetation that should have been cleared by the Serbs in their defensive position). The Serbs were reasonably well camouflaged, but they did not have a solid concrete bunker to hide in, only ones made of earth.

Throughout, while we waited, shots were being fired from all around the village - I felt regret that I'd let the four soldiers volunteer to go up ahead, but it was their right and they had already proved themselves capable. A shot was fired from their position...fuck it... we waited as any shots from us would merely reveal our position - our two snipers, however, moved swiftly into place. I took up the night glasses handed to me by the youngest in the patrol. I could see that our men had reached right up to their position. They needed no encouragement as they viewed at close quarters those who had murdered their families, friends and countrymen over the past four years.

Throughout the Bosnian War the reserves of strength and determination exhibited by the Croat army were consistently underestimated - the UN at one point estimated that it would take a force of over 100,000 UN troops and four years' conflict to remove the Bosnian Serbs. But the end of the conflict was expedited by a considerably smaller force of Croats and Bosnians within a few days. The period at the end of the war was a proud moment for Croats and Bosnians as they managed to complete a job at which the UN had previously failed - namely protecting their own while defeating the Bosnian-Serb enemy.

Back to the ground and, as I later discovered, the first soldier to force entry into the camp was shot in the throat and died a little later, but the others surprised the three guards and disposed of them quickly. The single shot which took out that young guy was painful for me - he took the bullet instead of me, I thought, his young life wasted while my worthless existence continued. He had handed me his crucifix before he had gone on this mission, when I remembered this I searched for it in vain, it must have come loose from me during the chaos.

I allowed myself little time to think of the consequences of this young guy's death as we continued onward, rushing through the darkness. I fired another shot and another body slumped to the floor as we headed toward the village by the base. At this time I thought we still hadn't been compromised but then I noticed an old woman and her husband in a nearby house. The old lady had sent her man up the hill to alert the mad-dogs guarding the missile launcher at the base - it was all going wrong after such a smooth start.

I can tell you that there is little or no honour in war. The bullets that ripped into the 'defenceless' old man as he tried to climb the hill and give away our position illustrated that. Down he tumbled - no bones about it in my eyes, he was the dog that barked, a death mitigated by our circumstances. One of our number took the wounded soldier to a position where we could re-group if things went pear-shaped, as we continued to kill anything and everything in the village.

Then, just as it seemed that the chaos had reached a peak, a T-72 tank appeared, spitting bullets and shells in all directions. We had no OSA anti-tank grenades to protect us, the .50 calibre bullets whacking into everything in sight. I was deafened now (as well as half-blinded) by the close explosion of shells as masonry and plaster descended on us from a nearby house - but the explosion seemed to make me stronger, the proximity of danger awakening my senses. Then one of the more inventive of our men laid a charge on the turret of the tank, giving both of us five seconds to duck for cover.

Looking round, a huge explosion lifted the turret from the tank and, as my comrade and I were temporarily shaken by the explosion, I wondered whether I had been hit or not, through all the confusion I couldn't tell. I thudded back to earth landing on my already damaged kidneys, taking more air from my pneumonic lungs - pain searing through my legs, 'fuck' I thought, 'I've really copped one this time'.

I tried to get up, stumbled and then re-erected myself. I told myself to be steel-like, immovable, unshakeable. My comrades had seen me take one and believed I was dead, but I couldn't take it in as I continued forward, racing for their missile dump - I had to carry on for the sake of the mission, it was an automatic response.

Suddenly a face appeared before me and before I could consider a response I had been hit in the side, as I tottered trying to regain my balance. I fired again and again as chaos claimed another piece of this war, mortars were being directed at us now, the hard ground reverberating with shells, shaking everyone for miles around. The bunker was just ahead down some steps, 10 metres below ground protected by an armour plated door which had been blown apart. I took a swig from my water bottle as I waited.

The serious business had begun. Three of our soldiers emerged carrying the other as I watched. I forgot about my metabolic and psychological state and was going into some kind of shock; my left eye was bleeding and blinded, the other one seemed to have a mind of its own as it zoomed in and out at random. Up they came - a sight for very sore eyes - as we quickly shot our way toward temporary safety, taking cover in a house at the end of the village while I took a headcount - we had lost two of our men.

There was a truck a little further on. I was assured by my second that it was immovable and charged. I handed my command over to him, as I was jabbed with a Morphine Syrette and half carried in a daze, not knowing whether I had been hit or not. I looked around me. We were three kilometres from objective 2 and I was holding back for our dead comrade. I could hardly face one soldier as he carried his brother's corpse; I quickly shut his dead brother's eyes and laid him to rest, trying to hold back the tears.

At this time my head and eye ached and I thought that I might have to order my men to leave me behind. I didn't have the heart to tell one of our men to bury his brother, I blamed myself for his death, assured that that bullet was meant for me. We took cover in a clearing of bushes and trees and quickly refreshed ourselves.

Shells came on top of us again, shaking the ground. I shook and trembled, my heart was real, it pained. Three quick explosions later and I felt sick, my blood pressure was up and I wondered why? - I demanded that the others leave me and pulled a pin from a grenade threatening them as if they were my enemies.

'Leave me Igor,' I pleaded, 'you stupid bastards, leave me' I shouted.

My comrades were shocked by my madness as Igor turned to me with a stern face and said, 'Soldier! I give you a direct order - you will come with us or you will be court-martialled. We will drag you by the feet if you don't come - what do you think of that?' I struggled to answer this last threat - but continued 'you shits are the worst soldiers I have ever come across' to say this hurt me deeply, but what could I do - time was not on their side and I would only slow them down, I was an obstacle to the success of the mission now, and as I have previously stated the mission was vital.

Their objective was a few kilometres away near the river and I feigned, threatening to booby-trap myself, I thought I was dying. In those moments I realised why I must go on. These soldiers were like brothers to me. Against this though I screamed at them to let me die; we had been through hell and high water together, had been in the thick of it all night. I told them that I wasn't interested in their cause and told them to fuck off to the river. They just stood there a little shocked, shaking their heads. Pointing my gun at them I gestured that they get a move on as I got up and made my way in a trance like state toward the village, I was performing robotically now, trying to take control of things beyond my control.

I went back to the village, soon it would be light and there would be no chance of escape. The village was burning, the fires crackling as bullets went off here and there, what a spectacle. I could feel the heat as I approached. Soldiers were lying dead here and there, some moaning and crying in the death throes as I fired at them, single sure-shot fire to put them out of their misery. In the distance I heard shouts, then the roar of trucks and tanks.

I looked down at an enemy officer, his eye bleeding like mine, staring up at me pleadingly. His legs had gone, but I knew how much enmity and hate he had perpetrated on the area over the past three years, recognised his thirst for destruction even in the last moments of his life. He pleaded for water. All around was the general stench of death and burning rubber - the bodies melting and mummifying as the odd grenade and bullet exploded sparked by fire. I recognised the guy. He was a Bosnian working for Serb Special Forces, not Arkan's mob but another's. He had been around when Almira was murdered and up in Slatina when Ante was killed and now he was before me.

This was fate. The reality of a long hoped for revenge within my vision, I booted his already mashed up legs - there was no sound, only a grimace - a look of hatred coming from his eyes. I shot him through the face. There was little time for anything else, as the sound of tank engines grew closer, drowning out all other noise and before I realised what was happening some of my men were dragging me away - they had returned from the other end of the village and despite my tirade of abuse were trying to bandage my head and make me ready for the helicopter home.

I could barely walk. The forces within me trying to make it easier for them to help me, I lost the will to speak; I was dehydrated, my lips parched as on and on we went. We were trying to reach a river to the northeast - darkness had descended and this helped us in our escape as we sought cover on the long journey to safety. We took to the country, avoiding roads and villages - the journey seemed to take an eternity, but my recollections of it remain vague, as I concentrated on the pain which seemed to be shooting all the way through my body.

It was a nightmare end to the operation. My head was spinning, I felt sick, then drained as the shock slowly took over. What I do remember is that we were due to rendezvous with a helicopter on the Sava River. We reached a point and waited, I was falling into unconsciousness and by the time the helicopter arrived I was all but out of it.

I came to in a small makeshift military hospital and looking around everything seemed so secret. I was told I was fine and that it didn't matter where I was and that I should rest. I wrote a letter to my children and managed to get it to a guy in the Red Cross building on the mountain overlooking Zagreb. My mental state was more affected by the operation than any slight wound I might have received on my body. I bear the scars on my neck to this day, but the mental scars worry me more, the images keep me awake at night and take me back to the chaos and murder in the village.

The Silent Cry
FLIGHT FROM SREBRENICA

The war between the Croats and Muslims apparently at an end, John MacPhee and Special Forces moved into central Bosnia in a clear-up operation. The purpose: to recce ahead of frontline areas and establish control. But not all Muslims and all Croats could tolerate the newly formed 'Federation'...

A tank blazed. Soldiers emerged from the burning carcass, each of them on fire. Yet only one of their number was screaming - not for help but out of pain and horror. Then shocked silence descended on him. Each one of those men we killed as swiftly as our AKs would allow us, there was no desire to see their agony prolonged any longer.

Yes, at times we did scream in rage at burning men alive, but in reality we never meant it; unless of course we knew beyond a shadow of a doubt that they had done such to one of our own. Cloth and flesh burned still. The three of us looked at one other and shook our heads - our eyes showing the pity we felt for the dead enemy. Despite the fact that they were Serbian we knew that this was no way to die as they had fought us as soldiers - we had respect for that.

Life and death would go on, for eternity perhaps; we would possibly die ourselves, perhaps before too long - but we had to draw a line some of the time as to respecting life. We were soldiers who fought a politician's war, who sheltered them from the harsh reality of the worst excesses of conflict. What could they really expect from us under the most adverse circumstances in a war they had helped stoke up?

This war was one of International responsibility, as much as it was the fault of exiled Serbs. Much of the hatred was inflamed at the end of the Second World War when matters were concluded too swiftly and with little thought. The formation of Yugoslavia suited the allies, freezing the countries here in aspic - this was, in fact, a continuation of the infighting that had taken place throughout these lands during the Second World War and which consequently remained unresolved.

Now we watched the immediate aftermath of men's deaths - our adversaries were no more than human beings. They were once children but the end result is always the same - we die, are buried and nature consumes us once more. My only hope during the war was that of every soldier - that I did not die alone, on a mountain path, helpless with no one there to record my final moments. I turned and walked wearily with my comrades, the sound of ammunition receding as we walked away from the burning scene. We were patrolling in Kiseljak in Central Bosnia, not far from Sarajevo.

I tried to remember why we were fighting again. It was often difficult in such a long conflict to remember from day to day, incident to incident why I was there. As a foreigner I may eventually be forgotten, as a doctor on the island of Corfu once told me. But deep within my heart I knew I would always find some small place within the hearts of the Croatian people. They were a proud and loving race - one not quick to forget their enemies or friends.

The three of us walked on toward a ridge, the wind whistling across our faces. In the distance, a few kilometres away, we could make out a village and to its left a few hundred metres away was a whitewashed church and steeple, a small graveyard sloping up toward it. I took out my binoculars. There appeared to be no one around, nor were there any of the stranded domestic animals typical of an abandoned Bosnian village.

The three of us walked on a little. We didn't care that we were few in number. We always preferred to break from our main forces. We kept in radio contact and knew that there was back up available if need be, but out here we could work independently, reccying the areas and reporting back. We knew the military circumstances of every area and, although things can change quickly in war, we kept ourselves to ourselves, making sure that we took advantage of every bit of cover - boulders, trees or bushes.

The sky was bright blue, streaked by the vapour of a jet - almost certainly a UN plane as civilian air-traffic was banned over Bosnia and Croatia. It would be foolish for anyone to fly over here as even at a great height it was far too dangerous. My mind came away from the peacefulness of the heavens and returned to earth - away in the distance the boom of artillery could be heard, resounding back on us as we advanced, reminding us of the Muslim forces in the area.

Suddenly a tree full of birds fluttered into the air to our right, immediately Zjelko put his palm down, but there was no need - we had stopped and had already lowered ourselves. My eyes peered out ahead toward the village about three-quarters of a kilometre ahead of us. Igor stayed put, lying down, fixing his RPG with an antipersonnel warhead. Zjelko moved to the right in a circular fashion - I the same to the left.

Carefully, we watched the birds flutter above their nests. It was spring and the birds were nesting; they had young and would not fly away without good reason. We reasoned that there must be human life in the woods, possibly soldiers who had been moving carefully towards us until the birds took off. This was the reason I felt a presence, the birds flew directly at us, a portent of human movement aimed in our direction. I also thought that there must be a number of them to have scared the birds that easily. Keeping track of each other we closed down our prey - the birds above became frantic as we neared their nests and the enemy.

The Silent Cry

Closing the gap, we tried to avoid the nests if we could, it was then that we heard cries of 'don't shoot, don't shoot'. Several scruffily clad civilians, including three youngish children, stood up fully to our view. We remained crouched so as not to give anyone a target in the event that it might be a trap; using the civilians as bait - it was a typical Serb trick, but something that could happen in any war.

A few hand signals were made between Zjelko and I as we rose, our AKs at hip level, on automatic. We carefully screened each sadly attired individual - Zjelko ordered the old man and the woman to move slowly apart and to keep their hands held high above their heads, which they did. Igor remained prone, watching for any sudden movement. Quick conversation took place between Zjelko and the old man who then turned around and shouted - four more figures emerged as ordered.

The ones who had just emerged were teenagers and probably thought we would kill them as, in recent months, the Muslims had made a habit of killing anyone over the age of 12. There was no way we would kill children unless they picked up a gun and looked likely to fire at us - this was a circumstance that very rarely happened. Once it was more or less established that we were not going to kill the younger boys everyone eased off - the tension receding from the situation a little.

There was a little nervous laughter - it seemed that they had come through from Srebrenica and were petrified but thought they would be better chancing it with Croat soldiers rather than Serbians, their luck had held on this occasion and they were alive. For the first time in weeks I smiled; I felt human again, especially after the deaths of the Serb tank crew I had just witnessed. The real mystery was how the Serb tank had got there; this was disputed territory between the Muslims and ourselves.

All of our number made our way cautiously toward the village. It was deserted. Those who had lived here had left long ago, some buildings had been 'fired', others looked lived-in, as if the occupants had only just left. Tinned UNHCR rations were discovered indicating that someone had left in a hurry. We were sure there was no life at all in the village, not even an animal, but it was better to be safe than sorry.

We brought the refugees into the most habitable house in the village with all the tins of food and told them not to light a fire, create any smoke or go near any of the windows under any circumstances. But they didn't need telling - they were just happy to have survived their long ordeal. It was good to see them eat. Igor, as big and brutal as he seemed, showed his human side as he gathered up clothes from the other houses and brought them over for the refugees. It mattered not that they were Muslim - to all of us they were innocents of war - people with every right to live and breathe.

184

At such times even I, who had become hardened to the ruthless ways of this war, was humbled by these people, seeing the looks and smiles of appreciation upon their weathered, tired faces. In the early days of the war I had felt for the ordinary Muslim people, doing all I could to help them. Every day I would go to the Albanian cafe just down from the Tomislavgrad hotel; the small cafe bar was situated up some steps in an alleyway.

Tension had come about as Muslims and Croats began to skirmish with each other and gradually some Croats resented me going to the cafe at that time, as a result I went less and less; eventually the proprietor, his wife and children moved back to Albania where I have since unsuccessfully tried to contact them. It was a shame because basically the Muslims and ourselves were fighting the same fight, for the same rights.

Igor tried repeatedly to contact our frontline on the radio but to no avail. This left us in a quandary - in all reality we should gather up the refugees and backtrack toward our original position. Now that everyone had eaten and bolstered their hopes at survival the refugees began to look somewhat confident that we could lead them to freedom; hence our concern at trying to get through to Command, to procure a truck so that they could be taken back swiftly and safely.

Matters were too quiet for comfort down here. There were a number of Muslim units who would still not come to terms with us despite the recent political agreements and our refugees related that they had seen or heard little activity and, in the main, walked only at night fearing that daytime patrols might shoot them on sight. They were relatively safe for now, but at a moment's notice we might have to abandon them - that would be cause for guilt enough, leaving them in the lurch once more.

A number of hours had gone by since our encounter with the unfortunate civilians - it was late afternoon turning into early evening. Spring days would soon turn into early summer but for now we really had to move these people with us. No way would I feel safe staying in this village; it was a cruel trick of this war to leave houses empty, offering tempting accommodation before returning at night to torch the house, killing whoever occupied it.

Radio contact had been made but no truck was immediately available. Northwest of here there had been considerable fighting and we were consequently on our own for the moment. It was decided to take out a working tractor and small trailer and let the refugees get on it with some food and blankets. The tractor had been well looked after and recently used it appeared. Few traces of whomever lived in the village remained - Muslim or Croat - safe to say that the house in which we stayed, the sole house in the village unaffected by fire or damage, was Serbian.

We swiftly loaded our human cargo and were off trundling along a track as best we could, trying to keep off the roads. This was all madness but it was life, it is what makes life interesting, escorting a tractor full of refugees in the semi-darkness down an alien road. All of us, young and old, laughed at ourselves - we'd reported back our point observations and informed Command a point at which we could establish ourselves and hold with relative ease.

A couple of kilometres away we camped down for the night. Our own frontline position wasn't too far away but Igor, Zjelko and I decided that we should keep forward of it as the enemy were sure to come back and fire the village that evening. When they returned they would also plant mines further down the road hoping to blow our tanks to kingdom come the next day. To guard against this we had mined a few points in the village ourselves and set a few grenade booby-traps so that even if they just came back for a peek they would cop something.

Darkness fell, protecting us from general view. It was welcome for me, if not the others. At times it did fill me with fear but I really welcomed it - I have lived most of my life in darkness, in prison cells or on the run and feel comfortable in the cloak of night. Most soldiers I knew, on the other hand, hated nighttime, although they were quick to use it to wreak murder and mayhem on the opposition. Just as darkness descended an explosion came from the direction of the village - a grenade, I was sure, from one of the booby-traps. Hopefully we had killed one or more of the enemy; suddenly two further explosions followed - these were the two plastic antipersonnel mines. Our experience had most probably terminated more lives in Bosnia, but it was they who had intended to torch civilians while they slept.

All hell swiftly broke loose - shots were fired, both single and automatic, the explosions had angered the enemy, they were firing at anything. From our vantage point we could just about see what was occurring back there. We had been extremely wise to leave the village otherwise our deaths would have been a near certainty - common sense earned from this hard war had triumphed once again. The refugees awoke from their slumbers, huddled in fear and expectancy that any shooting by their 'side' might lead to their death. Their fears were unjustified on this occasion as we were more likely to retreat rather than face-off against any large numbers. The night continued in expectant silence, as the enemy sought out more victims within the vicinity. Beyond us there would be the rush of medics, assuming they had some available, the enemy had paid for a bloodthirsty intent which we had reversed on them.

Igor tried to calm the refugees, assuring them that they were in no danger and that whoever was out there, in the dark of night, had unfortunately run into a forgotten minefield. However such assurances failed to calm them down. They continually murmured - the oldest woman moaned aloud and had to be shouted at to shut her up. As a result our nerves started to fray - we needed none of this, we had to listen for every little sound, to differentiate between each and specify and log the surrounding area to work out if danger was imminent.

Silence slowly returned. As security we placed our last two mines strategically upon two possible approaches to our 'camp' about fifty or sixty metres away. We were hidden from view and had scattered branches and leaves about as an early warning system - if we heard a twig break then we would know someone was out there and open fire. In turns we sought a little sleep - in those hours I am sure all three of us were too nervous to shut our eyes.

We were shattered and needed to stand down our straining nerves; to uphold the right to live. A squealing could be heard, it broke the silence and heightened our fears - perhaps an owl had copped a prey, I wondered, and was wickedly carrying it away for supper as we lay there in a kind of stunned silence. Death was all around us; one simple mistake and it would be over. I say simple mistake, but a mistake that led to our deaths would not be simple, it would merely be final.

Finally I awoke to a chilly spring morning, my body damp and stiff. The sun rose, diminishing the darkness as the quarter moon dipped below the tree line. I had tried to sleep but found it virtually impossible. I closed my eyes, my nerves shredded, hoping for a lull in the fighting and an opportunity to return our charges to some 'safe haven'. Creatures scurried about the landscape now; a scorpion lay in wait for an unsuspecting prey, a creature of great purpose and deadliness it had many enemies and so many times I could not bring myself to crunch the insect with my boot as I could with human beings.

Would I ever rid myself of my cold, callous ways? I had honed myself, these years in Bosnia, to disregard my feelings and have no mercy. Could I return to 'civilised society'? I was shaken from my weary thinking by the old man. 'Voda', the man cried. He said 'voda' as if he were making a statement of his rights that I should give him my water bottle.

I was a soldier, I was going to survive, even if this man died, I thought. He had run most of his course and would figure late on in my reckoning for water. Evolution was for those who carried on regardless of others I reasoned. The old man's face, wizened but with clear-cut eyes, stared at me. They searched out to understand me, fathom my reasoning, my distance, my coldness. Then I lifted his left hand, what was left of it, as his eyes seemed to say, 'I understand you. The water is for those who kill to survive'. His eyes were intelligent alright, with a hint of aggressiveness that I hadn't spotted before. He had killed in the past I thought.

Lowering his left hand he lifted his right to show five medals, they were from the Second World War - he had been a Partisan. I looked at him with greater respect. I undid the cap on my water bottle and handed it to him as he slowly put back his medals into the pocket of his tattered black jacket. The withered and gnarled hand - his good hand - reached out and touched mine as he gently took the water bottle from me - it was the elixir of life to him in those moments.

'Dobra, dobra' he spoke quietly as if to a shadow.

Igor broke the quietness explaining to me that this old Muslim guy was a real soldier, not just like us but a patriot to that which we all aspired - freedom.

As the old guy went to hand me back the water bottle I gestured for him to keep it and told him I had another he couldn't see (in fact I didn't have another but it was the only way I could convey my respect to him). Then we stretched our legs as the mist lifted and the sun began to shine upon us, offering satisfactory warmth.

Radio contact was made and the good news came through that matters north had gone well and the truck would be with us within the hour - we were told to sit tight. I then reluctantly handed out my chocolate bars (I always had plenty in reserve). The old man laughed at me after my good friend Igor related that I was one of the most generous Scotsmen that ever lived.

Our refugees laughed at this, life went on and I felt I was becoming more human everyday as the wind whisked across my skin confirming that I had taken on a positive side to my nature. The truck eventually picked us up an hour late and took us to the relative safety of Kiseljak. The refugees were taken off our hands and there were some complaints when they were discovered to be Muslims, our comrades thought it strange that we should help the enemy. I replied by saying they were refugees and our responsibility, regardless of race, was to hand them over to their own frontlines and that would be that - they understood, I think.

TRAVNIK - AUTUMN 1994

I approached the small, white cottage with some trepidation. There were bits and pieces in the yard, the odd rusty shovel and pail, the windows were dirty (some broken) and there was some wood chopped and stacked by the wall but, unusually in this area, there was no sign of shell or bullet damage. A tap dripped water onto a stone slab in the yard next to the door; it had been painted green sometime ago and, like the house itself, had clearly seen better days. The pain had peeled to reveal grey, tarnished wood beneath, the door was ajar.

I pushed the barrel of my AK against it and withdrew thinking that someone might have spotted it if they were waiting in the hallway. There was no sound so I continued. It swung open and I entered, a dry, stale smell accompanying me into the house. The house smelt as if it hadn't been lived in for sometime. There was an odour of decay and an absence of the usual smells of life - cooking, sweat, paraffin or oil - while a heavy dust hung like a cloak about everything in the hallway.

I was on my own, looking for evidence of military activity, trying to assess whether the house had been used as a temporary barracks by the Serbs. The door fully opened, I waited for sometime expecting a grenade or some booby-trap device to go off - we were still in a war zone, so the chances of the Serbs laying tripwires remained high.

Silence, the eerie quiet of desertion, accompanied the smell of 'death au naturelle'. It was aged and un-violent, a rare civilised moment in a land of barbarism. The sun shone through the hallway, reflecting off the myriad dust particles floating there, I waited again, certain of a presence. Whoever owned the dilapidated house was certainly not at home, I decided and, advancing firmly toward the 'living room', I saw an old woman slumped in a chair, her head lolling onto a once well-scrubbed table. Her skin was dry, parched and wrinkled. Her eyes and mouth closed, a hint of a smile appearing on her face as I moved forward. Perhaps, I considered, it was the knowledge that this old bird had survived two World Wars that made her smile.

Certainly a better existence awaited her in the next life, her house was sparse, a one room cottage lit solely by the glare of the autumn sun streaming over its owner's corpse. I went over to the curtain, checked outside again and then turned my attention to what remained in the house. There was a large rickety bed covered by a patchwork quilt that looked as old as the woman.

How old was she? How long had she been dead? Her face had turned almost yellow, her wizened hands clasped in her lap, her hair a steel grey colour and tied back beneath the typical black headdress worn by the old country people of the Balkans. A glint of light reflected from some rosary beads and silver crucifix necklace on the stone floor. I scooped them up, the floor looked well scrubbed save for the accumulated dust since the passing of the old woman.

The Silent Cry

I stared at the crucifix. Who had died for whom? These past years had seen the people carved in Christ's image degrade themselves to the extent that one of our soldiers had been crucified by Muslims up in Slatina. But I was still amazed that this woman, living in Central Bosnia where some of the fiercest fighting had taken place for the past two and a half years, had died such a natural and dignified death.

She looked mummified, shrunken by her many years, her skin tarnished by the summer sun and now discoloured by death. She was certainly one of the few to die in such a peaceful fashion in the Balkans during that time. The house also remained untouched - unlooted by Serbs, Muslims or Croats - in the middle of this most vicious and bloody war some form of sanity and respect had been shown, a rare sign that perhaps normality could return to Bosnia. I awoke from these thoughts and placed the cross over the clasped hands of the dead woman. She had had enough of life, I thought, but somehow in her death she had out-shadowed this gruesome conflict and given me a moment's relief from the insanity raging all around.

I left the house and closed the heavy front door with a feeling that her death had taught me something about inner-peace but I couldn't exactly tell where I would find it. After months and months of constant fear and a battle for survival the serene existence of this woman, her body and house untouched, made me realise that perhaps I would like to die like her, silently and free of conscience. I trod along the path and away, someone would come soon and find her and bury her. It was possible that some of her family were alive and would return. Many old men and women in Bosnia would not flee with their families, preferring instead to stay and die in their homes, it was another aspect of the Balkan psyche I could, yet could not, understand.

8 - THE FINAL CUT

FEBRUARY 1995
A MEETING NEAR SREBRENICA

A meeting took place within a small dilapidated building that appeared to be more of a cattle shed than someone's home. The roof was leaking, while the walls offered no protection from the cold, biting winds outside. I had been waiting for five hours in this stinking place and still nothing.

I asked my translator to check again and he duly poked his head out of the door before I pulled him back, a woman was approaching our hut. Boy was she dour-faced. A knock on the door and she came in. I struggled to recognise her but she was vaguely familiar - then I saw that it was Ksenjia, a friend of mine who was a psychologist. Both of us stood staring at one another for a while, then we hugged before I sharply brought us back to the purpose of my long vigil.

'Right Ksenjia, let's sort this out', I knew that Ksenjia was somehow attracted to me. She was aware that I had spent the last three years stalking Bosnia and for some reason she wanted to heal my bitter life, but I remained as spiky as ever.

'You know the set-up woman', I said with as near a smile as my miserable face could allow. 'Look, we need to know all the relevant factors as to SAS movements and their intentions as far as your sector can know. Savvy woman.'

'Yes, of course Sir' she bit back. I ignored the sarcastic 'sir' this was one woman who was not to be trifled with, she had an intelligence that frightened me. The preliminaries done with we got down to the business of war. 'So you're absolutely certain that they are no threat and are not up to any subterfuge other than to monitor Serbian gun and Tank emplacements?' I finished. The Serbs, by 1995, had resorted to the old Iraqi trick of burying their tanks and covering them with foil just below the surface - this way they wouldn't be picked up by radar or satellite. But there had been much interest within Croat intelligence as to the real intentions of the British relative to Croatia and Bosnia.

As is little known within England, the British military were behind the handing over of Croat military units to Tito's communists at the end of the Second World War. This justified a certain amount of bitterness within Croat ranks, particularly in the intelligentsia, about the real aims of the British action. But what mattered now was that we needed to be sure about their intentions in 1995 not 1945 and Ksenjia had provided enough intelligence so far to suggest that her reports were accurate.

'Right Ksenjia, is there anything else that we need to know about General Rose and his little contingent of SAS?'

'No John, we have accumulated all that is relevant and necessary for you to know - unless of course you are interested in the kind of boots they are wearing.' This was a veiled reference to my liking for Demon boots. To me they were a must in war but my 'designer' footwear had come in for some criticism when an intellectual complained that while I strode about the war in Italian designer wear most peasants were grateful to receive their next meal.

Certain computer and audio files were handed to me in a hermetically sealed ration pack. I had seen literally hundreds of these used in Bosnia - they were an easy way to seal up roofs during the damp, cold winters up there, where 'eagles' don't dare.

Ksenjia went to put her arms around me as she left, but I wouldn't allow it - this stupid one-sided love affair was a drag, she could go back to her offices in Zagreb and dream about another fucked-up mercenary that she could rehabilitate as far as I was concerned. Tears came to her eyes as I told her I wasn't long for this world and that I could only ever love Jaka - the girl soldier who had bewitched me since my early days in Bosnia. She cried, but she knew that I could only ever really understand the mentality of a soldier, especially as Jaka had been wounded and captured in defence of her freedom. Her family had a long history of sacrifice, her grandfather having been handed over by the British at the end of the Second World War.

I flashed the Maglite in my hand five times, signalling to those outside to expect us to come out. The girl before me turned as I called to her - a beam of delight lighting up her face as she expectantly anticipated that my ugly mug would kiss her and display my true feelings. Instead I offered her a jar of Nescafe. In response to this she tried to slap my face and I caught her hand, placing the jar of coffee in it before bundling her out of the door. My signal from the cloth covered window should have been seen by at least two of our men standing out there, freezing their balls off.

Out into the night and its cold, bitter rain I trudged. The Croat soldiers watching me as I descended the hill, waiting for a bullet to strike me perhaps as I made may way wearily down the few hundred metres to the wood where two guards waited. We were behind enemy lines, not far from the infamous UN enclave of Srebrenica that at the time was surrounded by Serbs. By now the two men accompanying me had reached the edge of the hilly woods and as I approached them the smaller of the two piped up, 'Scot, all OK? Nehma Problema?'

'Da. Ok, ok', I replied short and factually.

The same small guy seemed to be some sort of 'prize-fighter' and a soldier to be reckoned with. The guy I'd left behind at the hut told me that this fellow was a commander from Mostar, informing me of the honour attached to his visit; but for the life of me I couldn't place the guy there, despite the many times that I had travelled to and from Mostar Intelligence Headquarters. But I could see that he was the type of stocky character that taught you to love or loath him but not to play games with him, unless you had him with your sights trained on his back.

The other character I vaguely remembered from a time when he had been wounded at Mostar Hospital, when the hospital grounds were shelled. Yes, it was he - he'd refused to be treated as there were several civilians within the emergency rooms and an actual operation going on in the theatre where an old man had lost an arm to some shrapnel.

Now we had to get a move on, back through the mountains and forests and eventually through the Serb lines surrounding the enclave of Srebrenica. This was definitely enemy territory to me; we were on the other side of Bosnia from our typical stomping ground. It would be a long journey back, first on foot until we hit our nearest frontline and then back by jeep to Mostar.

Conditions seemed harsher to me on this side of Bosnia and I slowly began to understand the Serb mentality. The Ottoman Empire had bred a stiffness and harshness in the Serbs as a result of these lands being on the edge of Europe, the clash of Western and Eastern cultures created pressures that proved impossible to stem. In this way the Serbs lived within history, tied by its bounds and, although I never accepted their desire to rip their neighbours to shreds, I came to understand it. After all there was hell on all sides - the Serbians undoubtedly topped the atrocity league but the Muslims had done their share of the dirty work, in the main to gain revenge on the Serbo-Chetniks who had learnt, as stated, from the original Ottoman invaders.

And the Croatians? It may well be thought that I am covering for them but what would such an account achieve? I will not bludgeon the events I witnessed there; all I can say is that there were aspects of the war that I loved and those that I hated. In all war-zones all sides can be termed guilty of this crime or that, no matter that that side might be fighting for a just and right cause. Regardless, we are all guilty by the fact that we allowed a war such as this to take place at all. But I will admit that some Croatians went too far at times.

There were rumours about individual acts of ruthlessness but as far as I understand it 'ethnic cleansing' and the like was never sanctioned by either the government or the army. Tomislavgrad Command was strict beyond belief and within our sector there were few problems with the Muslims for the year or so that we fought them. As proof of this the few Muslims in the area eventually fought alongside us at the conclusion of the war.

Not far from Tomislavgrad lay a Serbian village. They were never shot-up or killed, and they remained there throughout the war - perhaps they were not happy but they never starved. At all times Army Command, in particular our own commander Zjelko Glasnovic, protected them if ever there were a rumour that they were in danger. Our enemies also received the same hospital treatment as that accorded Croatians - I often helped out at the hospital myself during my spare time, obtaining medical and food supplies for them where and when I could find them. As a result the doctors and nurses would ask my permission to use the supplies I had acquired on non-Croats.

By my reckoning the Croatians were too soft in war. Alright, they asked me for that permission because they knew my stance with regard to the enemy, but still I told them it was up to them how they used their resources. Our Special Unit were never overshadowed when it came to death and destruction. We more than likely killed more enemy in three and a half years in Bosnia than the SAS managed in fifty. That is not an overstatement, I know within an approximation how many I killed and others far outstripped me.

As far as War Crimes are concerned things are a little grey. For instance, if an unarmed civilian tried to inform an enemy soldier of your position they became, in my mind, targets and I killed them. There was no rigmarole or scruples attached to this act; I left that up to the lounge lizards and armchair generals in the UN.

Only when you hold the dead bodies of your lover and her child in your arms and you experience real loss can you truly understand the war. As you have already read it was my misfortune to suffer that deep loss out there and I felt the effect of war more directly as a result. That kind of suffering and degradation was not supposed to be seen in a civilised world. The conditions of this war were unacceptable to all parties except the Chetniks (ultra nationalist Serbs).

From the start of the war the terms of engagement were set by the Federal Yugoslav Government under the auspices of the Serb majority. Inside this warped mind of mine I can find no excuses for the killing in which I took part but rather than condemn me for every act I might be ashamed of, think first of how you might have reacted in such a situation. For this reason I feel it hard to make personal verdicts on the German nation as a whole. My forefathers died fighting Germany but my understanding has come a long way since those childhood days when my Grandmother forbade us to utter the word 'German'. As a result it is not forgiveness which I request but a little understanding of the pressures under which I was operating, death and hatred being the order of the day.

Back on the road my thoughts returned to the physical exhaustion of trekking toward our lines. Then it was a long journey by jeep to Mostar and when I finally arrived in the divided city I made for Intelligence Headquarters to hand over the package to an officer I had met sometime before. At that time he had asked me about General Rose and the British presence in Bosnia and I gave a personal view about their intentions. I was often asked questions by officers at Intelligence; sometimes they would ask to test my loyalty, at other times they wanted my feelings and perceptions on certain matters.

A debriefing took place and I was asked whether I trusted Ksenjia. I replied simply that she had delivered the goods asked of her and that she remained within an enclave surrounded by Serbians, not a situation that any of us would enjoy - as a result the basic evidence spoke for itself. The Croat Intelligence service had made great strides by 1995. War is the mother of invention and I had to respect them for the way they adapted to the demands of Mostar and Bosnia as a whole. It might take years before they reached a really high standard; there were few experienced personnel as prior to the war the Serbs had dominated and controlled all Yugoslav intelligence.

I answered the questions put to me in the debriefing sharply. I may have seemed a little defensive but I meant no offence, and I believe none was taken, but I still felt the eyes of the office workers upon me as I left. But my standing in Intelligence remained high for something I had done a little earlier in the war.

Back in 1993 a friend in Zagreb had phoned and asked if I could visit their offices to see if any assistance was available for the hospitals at Livno, Tomislavgrad and Rumboci. The Rumboci hospital was particularly vital as it was positioned not far from the frontline and acted as a 'stopgap' en route to other better equipped facilities down the road, without this many of our men would have died unnecessarily. As a result of this request I had gone to the UN's offices in Zagreb and was discussing the matter with an official who then explained that he would go and find a Dutch colonel who knew more about the situation.

In the meantime he left me alone with a satellite map covering the whole of Bosnia. My nerves shook a little as I realised the possibility of stealing it from under their noses. Quickly I took the opportunity and was folding the map as it came off the wall, trying to make it as small as possible to fit under my camouflage jacket. What a racket it made, all I wanted to do now was get out of the office before they realised their loss.

'See you' I shouted to the official, 'thanks for all your help' and I disappeared downstairs and out of the car park before they knew it. There were shouts from the top floor office window where I'd nicked the map but no danger; I'd already disappeared into the Croatian capital.

A little later I sat down with the map at a cafe and saw that it accurately plotted the positions of the forces on all sides and by that afternoon I had delivered the map to the offices of our Communications and Intelligence for Bosna-Herceg. Upon showing the map and its marked positions, a tremendous smile came over the face of the intelligence officer. 'Scot', he said with a little astonishment, 'I know now why you are named 'Super Scot''.

'Well Sir, of course you have a definite point as to my nickname.'

'Scot, no one told me that you were so modest. What do you want from us? Anything just name it!' he continued.

For a moment I kept him guessing, and then sheepishly replied, 'Is it possible that you could fix me up with your beautiful Miss Croatia?'

The fall of Srebrenica was one of the blackest moments in the Bosnian War. Serb forces invaded on July 11 1995 (while a Dutch UN corps of 32 soldiers looked on) separated the male inhabitants and sent them to their deaths. The remaining women, children, old, infirm and sick were sent to Tuzla airport to the north. Neither the UN nor Nato seemed capable of preventing this action, which led to the discovery of 4 mass graves in Serbia holding an estimated 3,000 bodies.

Despite the announcement of a 'Federation' between Muslims and Croats the conclusion of the Bosnian War was still regarded as some way off by Western leaders. UN estimates claimed that a fighting force of several hundred thousand troops supported by 'Special Forces' from every Nato power would be required to remove Bosnian Serbs from captured territories in Bosnia and Croatia before peace could be contemplated.

These territories included the Krajina region, an area on the Croat side to the west of the Bosnian-Croatian border and Western and Eastern Slavonia in the north of Croatia. The Krajina Serbs had done much to aggravate the tense situation in Croatia at the start of the war in 1991 and, along with Serb controlled Western Slavonia, represented an army of occupation in Croatia proper. In Bosnia itself the alliance between Croat and Muslim meant a lull in the fighting as the newly formed alliance prepared itself for a final assault on the Serbs in the following months.

MAY 1995 - WESTERN SLAVONIA

This was it, the final offensive. Tensions had been rising in Western Slavonia following the shooting of a Serb civilian at a petrol station and Serb paramilitaries had responded by opening fire on a number of Croat vehicles passing along the newly opened UN highway in the region. This was the final reason needed by the Croat forces to bring the war to a conclusion nearly 4 years after the initial Serb attack on Croatia.

The genocidal mentality of Serbian paramilitaries had forced the Croatian government's hand at last as HV (regular Croatian units) moved in; thousands of troops arranging themselves on the border near Gradiska over the river from Bosnia as UN troops were finally brushed aside. Western and Nato powers were taken by surprise on that occasion, the swiftness of events showing the Serbs not to be the invincible force everyone believed them to be. Numerous HV tanks rumbled into enemy territory before Croat army units gained a grip capturing thousands of Bosnian-Serb soldiers as they vainly attempted to escape the net.

The underdogs were now not the Croats, as they had been for so long since 1991, but the Bosnian Serb paramilitaries who had enthusiastically cleansed the area, causing havoc, death and destruction in equal measure. As a result the Bosnian Serbs swiftly realised the futility of their fight and the fragility of their brotherhood with rump Yugoslavia - their party was coming to a swift conclusion as the Croats reclaimed their land.

Days prior to this offensive I had been in Slavonski Brod on the border of Bosnia and Croatia, an area that had been persistently shelled since early 1991. Travelling there from Bosnia meant catching a ferry over the river as the only bridge had long since disappeared. The HVO held enclave had been torn to shreds by the war, along the highways the evidence of explosions and destruction was all about - buildings gutted, remnants of armour-plated vehicles lay rusting along the highway and as the jeep sped toward the town we became wary of a possible attack. There was something-big stirring. But as we entered the outskirts of Slavonski Brod not one house or shop we passed looked to have been hit, each building was left strangely unscathed.

The Silent Cry

I had been reading a heroic account of Marshal Tito's exploits in the Second World War. It was obviously a propaganda book and made the 'father of Yugoslavia' out to be perfect but his exploits had stirred something in me, it made me think of how I might have reacted in certain situations. Ironically I was now on my way to eliminate Tito's descendants from Western Slavonia. The Croats, for their part, had suffered greatly under Tito after the war; even Croat members of the communist Partisans had been executed in revenge for the role of the fascist Ustashe. This was how my mind wandered as the jeep made its way toward the town before we slammed to a halt outside a sandbagged military police station.

Soldiers milled about and talked in a relaxed fashion, but there was an undeniable excitement in the air; we were going forward, the offensive was working; it was all over for the Serbs. The confidence gleaned from imminent victory transmitted itself to the people of Bosnia and Croatia, morale was rising by the day, and everyone seemed to be smiling.

I was put up for the night in a local house. Two of the family's sons were out on the frontline somewhere - their daughter, a lovely looking 18 year old (they all are in Croatia), together with the mother and father put on a great spread and made me feel right at home, even to the extent of pandering to my vegetarian needs. I had quickly polished off a bowl of home-made vegetable soup when another was placed in front of me and I remembered a conversation I once had with a professor in Zagreb who told me to take my time with my food or else the hosts would just keep it coming - it was a sign of respect to a foreign volunteer soldier.

Talk went on for hours after the meal, as I told them about Scotland, my native Glasgow and my other travels in Bosnia and Croatia. I entertained them in my own fashion telling them of a few of my exploits and they laughed at me. Perhaps, I thought, I am a clown - clowns are said to be the saddest people in the world. There were several reasons for my sadness within Bosnia. I had seen and experienced so much during my years there - hell and death, friends wounded and killed, the plight of the refugees of all sides some of whom I had known before they became homeless.

I remembered the tears I had shed and those who had died within my arms, most especially the girl I had loved and her child; taken from me, bitterly and horrendously taken. These memories forever changed my spirit and served to fuel a hatred that continues to burn like the charred remains of their bodies I held in that wood. Within days our tanks battered their way into Serb territory, the enemy surrendered without bloodshed and it was the HVO's role to round up prisoners.

The abject Serb surrender left a few questions unanswered. Some of the 'prisoners' were not as they first appeared - they might have worn neatly pressed and washed civilian clothes but their faces told of combat. The captured Serbs all claimed to be innocent, claimed to have been mere witnesses to the past 4 years killing.

But the guilt could be seen within their faces, most especially the look in their eyes. They might have accepted surrender as an easy way out of Croatia but their eyes told of four years of power-crazed slaughter, they took no prisoners then and I saw no reason to take any now. The Chetniks did not want to fight now that the odds were stacked against them, to me that made them cowards - at least if they had lost an honourable fight they might have earned a little respect from the Croat forces.

Later that day I entertained the family again, but this time I was in a reflective mood. I played Pink Floyd's 'Dark Side of the Moon', a tape I had used to annoy the Serbs on the frontline before; I used to play it at full volume down in Babice and within minutes they would start shelling us, I always thought that it kept them on their toes. As a result people often claimed I came from the Dark Side of the Moon. I would always reply that I came from Mars; if they thought I was crazy then they would quickly realise that I knew I was not a full shilling myself - the war in Bosnia had merely confirmed this feeling.

Then I played a bit of Bob Dylan's 'Masters of War'. 'You that build the guns, You that build the death planes, You that build the big bombs, You that hide behind desks'. Tears were in the eyes of all four of us, the song was so relevant to both the family and myself and, as I looked at them, I could see they were hoping for the safe return of their sons.

'John', the mother finally spoke, 'you are a son of Croatia'.

I was a little choked but replied 'and you, your family, the whole of Croatia are the children of freedom.' I felt a tear coming on as I continued, 'my grandfather died for freedom, my father shed his blood just over the Adriatic from Croatia - I know now that they did not persevere in vain'. At this the mother and daughter kissed me and I shook hands with the father as he said, 'Live for the future Scot', words that are easier to say than to do. Emotionally charged I left the house with the family waving to me - it was a summer's day, a bright blue sky, light wind and a clear, hot summer sun. A flowery perfume floated over the whole area, it was the scent of freedom, I thought - all I ever wanted to know during my 4 years in Bosnia was that I was fighting for a cause, not money, not land, but freedom.

To the left and right I glanced at the scene - I breathed in the summer air, the warmth of life was all around me - the streets, the hills and valleys, all around me felt marvellous, I think I even smiled. Days passed over our heads like the clouds and the war; we rounded up too many prisoners and the media flared again with claim and counterclaim.

President Tudjman, a man I had initially disliked, grew in stature - he had ordered us to remove our Ace of Spades badges midway through the conflict because the Croatian people did not appreciate the association with fascism - he was a nationalist but no fascist and most importantly, he was victorious. Reports continued in the following weeks about the human cost of the Croatian offensive. 200 Serbs were killed in Medak in the Krajina region and accusations were made of a brutal confrontation - some press even claimed that we had killed prisoners when in fact these 200 Krajina Serbs had fought to the last, for a cause and a belief that was now utterly routed.

By July 1995 Srebrenica and Zepa were hit hard and fast by the Serbs while General Rose, his SAS and the UN in general could do nothing. Serbs slaughtered several thousand Bosnian Muslims in Srebrenica while Dutch UN officers, limited by their 'terms of engagement', looked on - many of the Muslims killed each other rather than succumb to the Serbs, it was a tragedy and another disgrace for the UN. I know I would have fought the Serbs in such a position, their deaths would have been honourable and understandable.

Newspaper reporters slowly changed their attitude as the HV and HVO merged - smashing their way into Serb strongholds, returning the land to its rightful owners. The aura of victory was palpable in Croatia. Emotions ran high everywhere, after 4 years on the back foot the doctors, nurses and hospital workers sensed these emotions more than most, they had had the most gruesome of tasks, patching up men, women and children, and I loved them all.

In those months I loved humanity, to the extent that I even became semi-law abiding and promised myself that I would only steal from the UN or UNHCR, they remained targets in my eyes especially as they insisted on turning up in Zagreb with brand new equipment and fresh tea and coffee. The final assault on the Bihac Pocket confirmed Serb ruthlessness. The Yugoslav General Mladic turning his forces on the Croat backed Muslims there, after such a long, hard war it was a cruel twist in the tail for those civilians.

KNIN - AUGUST 1995

A formidable array of Serb weaponry and troops had occupied the Krajina region of Croatia since 1991. There were an estimated 400 Serb tanks, supported by 40,000 tried and tested troops from the JNA and Serb paramilitaries and the general feeling remained that they were all but immovable.

The Krajina Serbs had declared their own autonomous province back in 1991 when the conflict started in Croatia. And although attention had since turned to matters in Bosnia, the question of the Serb presence in both Western Slavonia and the Krajina had still to be resolved. The UN and Nato had tried to demilitarise both zones with little success. The HV (regular Croatian Army) had been successful in containing Serb elements in both areas but doubts remained as to whether they could be evicted from their area of occupation.

By August 1995 the successes in Western Slavonia and within Bosnia in the Bihac pocket had shown that the Bosnian and Croatian armies represented a serious threat to Serb forces. Moreover the lack of support the Serbs had received from Belgrade during these operations led many to question the true level of resistance among the Krajina Serbs. All along the frontline the HV continued to strike, as regular units smashed their way into Serb held Krajina. Years of army training against the worst excesses of Serb paramilitary tactics began to reap their reward as fresh confidence led the Croatians to victory after victory. The HVO attacked from the Bosnian side while the regular HV units rained in on the Krajina Serbs from Croatian territory. Between the two the enemy were trapped, beaten by superior numbers and forced deeper into Bosnia.

Within 48 hours since the orders were given to 'up and out, lock and load', tanks, trucks and supply lines had advanced so effectively and wreaked havoc on the region so swiftly that the name of the operation 'OLUJA' meaning storm, could be said to have been an understatement. The swiftness of the battle reminded me of the 6-Day War fought by Israel against its Arab enemies. I had been in the area in 1967 a few weeks before the start of that assault and experts had claimed then that victory would be hard fought and time consuming. They were wrong then and they were wrong now.

In the surrounding areas there was a feeling of elation as the Croat army advanced. They, like us, had supposed that a long, hard fought battle would have to be undertaken to remove the Krajina Serbs. We had expected success certainly, but the swiftness of our advance was a bonus and added to the euphoric atmosphere. The Croats were backed in their

The Silent Cry

efforts by the US government, they had helped train and arm certain elements (although they wisely stayed out of any direct action so as to appease the Russians) but it was the experience of 4 years' hard graft that contributed most to the victories.

The swiftness of victory inevitably led to complaints from some quarters that we were ethnically cleansing the region (a bit rich when you consider the plight of the Krajinan and Slavonian Croats in 1991). President Tudjman offered assurances to the world's press (who by this time were having a field day - no danger and plenty of easy stories to report) that the Krajina Serbs could stay and have their human rights guaranteed if they accepted Croatian sovereignty over the region.

But the tide had turned so swiftly that most had already made up their minds. The Serbs left in droves heading for Bosnia, Serbia or anywhere that would take them. In turn we bombarded the Serb frontlines. This made a change, throughout my stay in Bosnia we had always had to suffer from lack of munitions. Now the tables had turned, there were few losses on either side as stores of arms were discovered which beggared belief.

Most of the glory of this campaign reflected on President Tudjman. I had had my doubts about him for sometime, but you cannot argue with the way he concluded the war. He turned opportunity into victory within months and rightly received the plaudits for his success. I attended a government press conference some days after the successful campaign in Bihac. There I met an eye specialist from Texas who wanted to build a clinic in Sarajevo to tend the war wounded. He was a down to earth, likeable character.

He asked me if I could help an American reporter get into Bihac and after speaking to my friend in the ministry she told all present that a bus would be available to escort the western media through the fighting to the city (the HV were still 'mopping-up' pockets of resistance, lone snipers and the like). The main road through into Bosnia was littered with knocked-out tanks and armoured vehicles; trucks were set ablaze and it was a 'press-glory' situation.

Forgive my cynicism but I saw none of this enthusiasm for frontline reporting when we were fighting in Central Bosnia. At that time the Croatians had been the bad guys, portrayed as the forces of evil with foreign volunteers like myself who were described by members of the UNHCR as 'butcher-type soldiers'. Now, at the end of the war, everyone wanted a piece of the action, conveniently forgetting the several hundred thousand lives the war had accounted for.

Croat refugees returned to their homes to find them burnt to the ground in most cases. Hundreds of thousands made the journey back to

Northern Dalmatia and Krajina to find only blackened remains where once there were personal belongings, the area will take years to recover. Yet despite the victory the British still found time to complain. They remained suspicious of the Croat government for some reason, when in fact both the Bosnians and ourselves had merely performed a duty that was beyond the capability of the British Army, namely protecting our own while recovering territory that was, by rights, non-Serb.

Of course attention has recently returned following the crisis in Kosovo. That is a much smaller territory but showed once more the reluctance of the UN and Western governments to send in proper ground troops - it remains an impossibility to secure total military victory without some loss of life, a reality Western liberals refuse to accept.

9 - A WAR WITHOUT END

KOSOVO - SEPTEMBER 1998

Kosovo had been the making of Slobodan Milosevic in 1990. On that occasion Kosovan Serbs had complained about discrimination against them by their Muslim neighbours and Milosevic had pledged to protect the Serb prescence in the province 'to the last man'. But later, while Serbian attentions turned to Bosnia and Croatia, the Kosovan cause was put on the back-burner and it wasn't until the end of those conflicts that a re-focusing of the Serbian War machine on Muslim dominated Kosovo could take place.

Later, when Nato planes took the unusual step of bombing sovereign Serbian soil, I had mixed emotions. I understood the plight of the Kosovans, understood more than most the worst excesses of the Serbian war machine and knew that the unconfirmed reports of atrocities in Kosovo were more than likely accurate on past Serb performances. But I also knew Serb people. In reality they were, by and large, a decent people. I remembered the Serb woman who had given me food in Jajce at the start of my travels in Bosnia and the fate of those Serbians in Vukovar who helped their Croat neighbours. As a consequence I knew that there would be casualties among their number who were just as innocent as the Kosovans.

For months my thoughts were troubled as once more news reports told of a fresh crisis just a few years after the conclusion of the Bosnian War. On a personal level my health had deteriorated following the conclusion of the Bosnian conflict. I reflected on the charmed life I had led in Bosnia; the occasions I escaped bullets that I knew were meant for me but which fate had allowed to take a comrade.

Physical illness, in the form of a series of hospital stays, kept me out of the brief Albanian civil war. Meanwhile the UN, eager to step in decisively this time, propped-up the ailing Marxist government and within months of the start of it it was all over - money, the root cause of the problems in the first place, was a problem the West was easily capable of solving.

So I never got to Albania on that occasion. But the development that most interested me was the formation of the KLA (Kosovo Liberation Army). News of civilian killings and 'ethnic cleansing' in Kosovo began to trickle through in a gruesome rerun of those perpetrated against Croats and Muslims a few years earlier. Memories flooded back, the nightmares began again and there were no doctors I could speak to. Most of them didn't believe in post-traumatic stress disorder and the only ones who would listen were army medics or Harley Street's finest - both of which were unavailable to me. So I decided upon my own 'therapy' and in September 1998 I made preparations to visit the Balkans again.

I contacted the Albanian who used to run the cafe in Tomislavgrad. He had since moved to Tirana and I wrote him a letter recalling the time my late friend Ante and I had fled Montenegro following the bungled attempt to capture Colonel Sljivancanin. Writing that letter brought back mixed emotions. Ante and I had defied everyone by successfully escaping rump Yugoslavia that night. Then, when we had set sail down the coast, we had run out of fuel and ended up floating down the Adriatic before we landed in Albania, then a Marxist state.

There was always the threat, wherever you were in the Balkans, that capture would mean months of torture in camps such as Omaska, Manjaca or Glina. The ITN film of the skeletal Croat and Muslim prisoners were a painful reminder to me, the old anxieties and fears returning to fuel my long held loathing of the Serbs. For weeks I wrestled with the prospect of returning to the Balkans once more. I didn't want to chance my arm with fate again but I decided that it was the only way to conquer my fears. So by the summer of 1998 I had decided to pick up a gun once more and meet up with the KLA.

Getting into a war zone isn't easy. I had to take a circuitous route from Zagreb. First I made my way to Pula military air base on the Dalmatian coast and from there I caught an Autobus to Rijeka - the Croatian seaport and ferry terminal. After speaking to an old friend of mine I managed to get myself aboard a ship bound for Albania via Split. Nothing untoward happened on the journey, I was wearing civilian clothing and kept myself to myself although I did manage to have a laugh with some Albanian truck drivers. They were a great bunch of guys, hearts of gold with personalities to match.

The trucks they drove were antique and I joked with them about what would happen to their gold teeth if they came where I was going. They couldn't do enough for me - they gave up a cabin for me to sleep in,

The Silent Cry

I couldn't refuse, as it would have been seen as an affront to these people. It was their way of showing how they felt about humanity, they were poor, the poorest people in Europe, but for all that they showed me the finest hospitality.

That uneventful boat trip down the Croatian coast also brought memories flooding back as I looked at the many islands dotted down the coast. On we sailed, past Zadar until we reached my favourite city of Split. Sun up and a fresh breeze blowing, I rose from my cabin and took in the freshness of the morning, gulping down the ozone, stretching myself as my eyes scanned the shore as Split came into view.

There it was, the city fresh and inviting (the only city in the world I can say that about) bringing forth an inner excitement and butterflies in the stomach. As we docked I was in the city's awe, and before I knew it I was on the dockside down from the bus terminal. There was the usual hustle and bustle in Split harbour, people coming and going and a drunk with an arm missing, probably from the war, singing away in the morning. It took me back to Glasgow's Plantation docks where I grew up, but the sheer life and sunshine of this place was utterly different - the drunken guy was the sole reminder of the war.

Down onto the wharf, I caught the eye of several people as they scanned my shaven head and harsh features. So I smiled at them disarmingly, 'Dobra Jutro' I called to all who would listen, 'dobra' as I pointed to the sun and a beautiful Croatian girl. The women of Split are remarkable creatures. Always clean and well attired they seem to have a natural pride and always, without exception, they smile. It is a unique aspect of Split and I lived to see and be in the company of such women - I decided that it was all part of my therapy.

Army rucksack over my shoulder and into town, stopping only to rejoice in the city - 'Life is wonderful,' I shouted, 'it is beautiful as are the girls of Split', as my eyes took in a number of ladies in an open-air cafe bar. They looked my way and laughed - I had no kilt or sporran on so they laughed at my words, or me - probably the latter. Approaching them they giggled before a red-haired girl said, 'Englesi, you are?'

'Ah' my hand went to my heart 'you kill me - I am Scottish - Scottish' I said in return, dropping my rucksack to the ground at an adjoining table.

'Sorry, sorry' the redhead returned in an exaggerated manner.

'You have wounded my heart, my soul,' I continued piling on the melodrama, 'I will never be the same again, hurt by such a beautiful girl'. I made out I was fatally wounded but when no one seemed to be coming to my aid I righted myself and introduced myself as, 'John B, at your service'.

They asked me who I was and of course I told them the truth, 'I am a pirate who has travelled'

'Sailed' interrupted one of the girls.

'Sailed, thousands of leagues to be with you, fighting off the marauding British and American navies while wrestling with sharks in the Adriatic.'

'But Scotsman, there are no sharks in the Adriatic' said one of them, her eyes smiling at me, making me lose my composure for a second.

'I hereby renounce my being Pirate - I will work as a goat-herd as long as your gold spun hair is near to me and your eyes shine like that forever.' All five of them burst out laughing - they always liked a joke the girls in Split, making a fool of yourself was a sure-fire way of ingratiating yourself with them.

'For you', I spoke to the youngest, 'I will pay a thousand camels and a large pack of Scott's Porridge Oats to your parents'. I had hit my clown form again, it was in such moments that I found myself, life became worth it, all the years of hardship and imprisonment rolled away when I made those girls laugh.

'You are no pirate Scot' said one of them as I left, 'you are our soldier'. I replied that I didn't deserve their company and I would marry them all given the chance and with that I left them to it.

I had a few hours before the boat was due to leave again but eventually we got underway once more. Passing Montenegro I closed my mind to the past but as we arrived in Albania I remembered Ante and I drifting toward the shore, fearing we were falling into a Serbian trap. Notification had been given to my contacts in Albania that I would be arriving on one of two vessels bound for the coast that day - to show my eagerness I arrived on the first. A small Yugo car was parked near the dockside and I shook my head at the two men who met me before I got in the Serb-made vehicle and drove off.

Albania is an extremely poor country - I could sense the poverty there. I realised then that it was little wonder that there had been a civil war but some semblance of normality had returned since that short conflict and the ordinary people continued to smile. On we drove through the countryside, making our way to Tirana where I would stay the night at some apartment or other - it didn't really matter where I stayed as long as I made contact with the KLA soon.

I had yet to decide whether I would risk life and limb for their cause. Some friends of mine from Germany were also considering joining and they would take my word as to whether to join or not - the KLA needed us more than we needed them. The main problem was that we would be fighting on the Muslim side. In Bosnia I had killed many of the relatives I would be fighting for while Muslims had similarly killed Croatian civilians and soldiers - so it was all a little sensitive.

We finally arrived in Tirana and I was still fresh and in a positive frame of mind, willing to take matters as I found them. Sleep that night was hard to come by - the room I was given was spotless but for hours I lay restless, eager to get to Kosovo, my thoughts swimming with old memories and fresh fears.

Morning finally dawned with the sound of traffic beneath my window. The view from the apartment window revealed a large Soviet influence over Tirana - my few hours' sleep had slightly refreshed my mind and I was soon summoned by the lady of the house for breakfast. Then my contact came to the door, showing me the bathroom, a fresh towel and a bar of soap. It reminded me of prison soap and smelled even worse - but I wasn't about to complain as I might in a British house, I accepted that this was a poor country and had come to terms with such.

Having washed and eaten we were soon on our way. I was shown into a Volvo estate car and we began our journey north through the countryside, climbing hills until we reached the border region. The people looked poorer and poorer the further we ventured toward Kosovo. We stopped briefly at a cafe bar to talk seriously about the latest developments in the region and the organisation of the newly formed KLA - their problems and weaponry requirements. I gave the guy some contact numbers and my name as an introduction, I knew that whether I stayed or not they could obtain all they wanted if they had the money - I knew that the Kosovan cause had many supporters in the United States and the rest of Europe.

We continued our ascent of the hills. Once more I was being driven in a crazy manner around steep bends, one wheel hanging over sheer drops and by the time we stopped later that night we had crossed the border into Kosovo and picked up AKs and ammunition. I felt better at this as it unnerved me to be unarmed in a war-zone. We were met at a KLA base camp by a handful of eager soldiers. I was given a warm welcome before my contact left me to stay at a nearby village on his way back to Tirana.

It was cold in the hills, a light mist hanging over the whole area as we made our way forward. The terrain was rocky, with trees here and there, and within half an hour we had reached a loose position and I was shown to a small bunker by the commander. Out like a light with my gun at the ready I was awakened just after six by a squat character who must have come in just after I had dozed off. He had an ear and two front teeth missing, this told me enough.

208

'Serbi,' he said and repeated, 'Serbi' pointing to his absent teeth and mutilated ear, he laughed then smiled again. 'Come, come' he gestured to me leaving the bunker, crouching as he went outside. His finger signed for me to follow him and he made an eating gesture, 'Iz good Albani food'.

So out I went, rubbing my eyes as the sun hit them, this was the life I thought. This guy was a real character, I liked him at face value, he had undoubtedly suffered greatly in the past but like his people he was a survivor. Over to the edge of the tree line I followed him. I was offered a bucket of ice-cold water to wash in, half a loaf of bread, jam and fish paste for breakfast and some disgusting tasting coffee to drink.

'You are ready soon Scot? We can move out and take you to see what is what over the hills. Perhaps we can even kill Serb?' spoke my newfound friend.

'No worries, I'll get my pack as we shall be a few days'

'Ok, no worry Scot' he smiled back.

It was then, as he walked over to a group of soldiers waiting to depart, that I spotted a tall, slim character in uniform staring at me. His eyes betrayed his real feelings and I sensed that he knew all about my HVO connections and the actions we were accused of. I stared back, not wishing to back down, and thought that he was most probably a Bosnian Muslim - I didn't know it for sure but sensed it - I also knew that I would have to kill him first.

As a result of my 'staring contest' with this guy I hadn't noticed the approach of the commander until he stood right beside me. He realised the animosity and tension growing between us. He spoke to the Bosnian in Albanian and by the tone of his voice I could tell he was telling him to back off.

Then he turned to me. 'Ok Scot, he is bitter. He was up in Ahmici and all his family were killed so he hates all HVO, even foreigners. He knows who you are, many Muslims do - you are killing in Ahmici I don't believe'.

'No commander', I replied, 'only soldiers have I killed. Ahmici was all but over when I arrived. Whatever happened there Croatian men, women and children died also in that village and surrounding areas.'

'No problem for you here - the Albanian cafe owner in Tomislavgrad and his family speak well of you. You helped Bosnian refugees - you also gave chocolate and food to a Serbian village near Tomislavgrad'. To say I was amazed was an understatement as the guy went on, 'How do I know? You wonder, eh Scotsman?'

We walked toward the main group of men. They were ready to trek into the unknown. I stopped and could sense something in the commander, a likeness...

The Silent Cry

'You know the cafe owner who sold up and came to Tirana?' I said, still puzzled as to the guy's in-depth knowledge of my activities.

He smiled and laughed as my words ended. 'You were good friends with my uncle, John. You loved the girl who was my cousin. Then she and the baby were killed. I know it all but didn't want to remind you - now it is done - I trust you, we all do, everyone knows.' I was a little stunned as I was handed my rucksack and a fresh canteen of water and without more ado we were off.

Within a few miles I realised I was badly out of shape, my lungs started to burn from the pace and my heart struggled to take the strain - 'hell, I've done it again' I thought, 'put myself in a dangerous situation while my physical shape is still in the gutter'.

Ahead of us one of the Kosovans was on the hill above, on point duty checking ahead, signalling to another up ahead, ever watchful for VJ (Serb forces). It was tough to keep up but I managed it, nothing would stop me doing otherwise. After about three kilometres and two hours trekking we thankfully came to a small gully - three men went to the top, the rest of us resting by a stream, splashing our faces with the cool water.

We laughed and broke out bars of chocolate. I gave the commander a Mars Bar from my rucksack which he readily accepted (I had a giant size one for myself) and while the other soldiers approached the commander asking for a taste of the famed Mars Bar, I quickly scoffed mine down. Then I put several questions to the group about the weaponry they needed and the possibility of smuggling in arms. Their greatest need appeared to be explosives, and anti-aircraft arms and missiles. The latter were desperately needed to threaten Serb tanks and helicopters.

Their morale was strong but perhaps not as strong as they claimed. They said they needed mines, more especially as the KLA was made up of largely inexperienced villagers who had volunteered to fight rather than sit and wait for the Serbs to take them. They needed to get behind Serb lines and cause havoc, I thought. If they could put a doubt in Serb minds by damaging their trucks and tanks then they might be able to wear their enemy down, this might work, particularly in a low-intensity conflict like Kosovo.

Question time over we continued our climb up the gully. A few us slipped to the great amusement of the others until we reached the top of the hill. Each soldier scanned the region from our position overlooking the valley. Smoke was billowing into the sky from the houses dotted about below. I looked through my binoculars and could make out a large group of military trucks and tanks heading east away from the burning village of Dakovica and, as the KLA soldiers watched, a low muttering took place between them.

I could see the rage in their eyes - they were helpless and frustrated. They knew it would be absolute suicide to try and fight such strength in numbers without anti-tank weapons. Even a well-planned, well-positioned ambush would be bound to fail. They desperately needed explosives to stand a chance. I could see the willingness in their eyes but it needed more than resolve to have any success against a Serb enemy with 7 years' experience of war behind it.

The Serbs were no fools. They could be beaten in small sorties and ambushes - just as the Croats managed in Vukovar in 1991 when their inexperienced and ill-equipped forces took out over 300 Yugoslav tanks. But the Kosovans were at a greater disadvantage as they had even fewer experienced soldiers. Their experience had to be gleaned haphazardly in the field.

After witnessing the latest Serb action we continued our journey toward a larger group of KLA over the valley and up into the mountains and woods. This position offered great cover and limited access to Serb tanks. Below, about half a kilometre away, stood a group of three destroyed houses situated next to a barn - these buildings would offer cover as we made our way across the open valley to join up with the larger Kosovan force on the next hill.

Down we went, jogging into a light run, our momentum increasing as we tried to find cover behind boulders, I removed the safety catch from my AK. It didn't take so long before we had half run, half trotted to the burnt buildings. The roofs had completely gone along with most of the walls. Some old and smashed ammunition boxes lay about along with the usual spent cartridges. Someone had holed up here weeks ago, I thought, the buildings had been destroyed some months previously. The building was made of stone - there was no evidence of human remains.

The commander approached me. He was an intelligent guy and recognised, by my looks, as to my thoughts. 'John,' he began, 'the people here were ours; they were taken away - the whole family, three generations. Two daughters were lucky, they are students in America; the others I believe are dead.' There was a finality in his voice. He turned away - glanced up and down the valley then turned back to me and explained about his culture, his people, his hopes and dreams.

Our squad continued to recce the area all afternoon. The Serbs had pushed the KLA so far back and were in Kosovo in such superior numbers that we were on constant alert. Later that night we returned to base. Getting back through the lines from Serb-held territory and finally to Albania's northern border I began to relax as the possibility of treading on a mine or tripping a booby-trap receded.

The Silent Cry

There was a great disappointment on the faces of my new comrades when I hesitated about joining the Kosovan cause. I didn't want to commit myself, or the people I represented, until I had discussed the matter further with them but I also had a few reservations. The glaring eyes of the Bosnian Muslim volunteer had reminded me of the danger of us joining the cause. I knew that my German colleagues would face a similar reception if they came down here. They, like me, had had little time for the Bosnian Army during the war and the thought of fighting alongside those who had caused such carnage among Croat civilians gave me more than pause for thought.

Pleas were made to me as to staying and offering my expertise to the situation. They knew of my considerable experience in dealing with the Serbs and their tactics. They also knew that the Croats had effectively defeated the Serbs and they wanted to know their secrets. But there were a number of other factors to consider. UN involvement in Kosovo had increased in the autumn of 1998 in response to an increase in the Serbian onslaught on the region. This led me on to the feeling that if the UN wanted to get involved then fine, let them do their job. They would undoubtedly crack down on the amount of volunteers joining the KLA and their presence also guaranteed the KLA a little extra support. But I still had mixed feelings about leaving them in the lurch.

I had the greatest respect for the commander - he was a man of fortitude and character, someone that I could trust with my life - the essential quality in a commanding officer. So I was honest with him and told him that I was doubtful that I could bring myself to stay in Kosovo while there were elements from Bosnia. In particular it was reported to me that a former rape counsellor from Mostar, a Muslim, who had been abusing children there in 1993, was at work in Kosovo under the guise of the KLA. I had been told about this guy's 'work' in Mostar and had tracked him down with little success. I wanted to kill the bastard and thought, in the end, that if he were an example of the type of character associated with the KLA then I wanted no part of it. Nevertheless, I informed the commander about certain weapons, explosives and training that might be available to him if he wanted it arranged. Sometimes these could even come free of charge depending on how the arms were secured.

I told the commander that I could arrange these matters with few problems. The guy smiled and reiterated his preference to have the Germans and I train on the job, 'it will give us great confidence', he continued, 'for the soldiers to know that we are being trained by the side which beat the Serbs between 1992 and 1995'. Many hours were spent trying to persuade me when we got back to Tirana. I told them that I'd give the idea some serious thought but would have to think about the

Bosnians and the psychologist - they were the main obstacles.

The commander said he would 'take care of' all these objections. I replied that it was a matter of my word against the psychologist's and he was a fellow Muslim to the commander. Even though he said that that would not come into it, he knew that I really wasn't going to join up. I spent a couple of days in Tirana looking up old friends and discussing 'specialist materials' for supply to the KLA. I promised the commander that I would try and recruit some people for him and would give them his contact number in London and Tirana.

These people touched my heart. They certainly needed more help than Croatia had when I had joined their cause. I knew that the human cost to the Kosovans could be as great as that during my stay in Bosnia between 1992 and 1995.

A WAR IN THE MIND

The complete and utter desolation I felt after the conclusion of the Bosnian War went beyond anything I had known before. There were so many hours when what ordinary people would understand as flashbacks would eat into my mind. These were thoughts and images that were hard to avoid and impossible to erase.

At night reality would give way to an exaggeration of images; a child dying in my arms as I carried her into a room full of people, the stares of them all, their eyes empty and apparently devoid of life. Time after time my voice screamed in silence - the Silent Cry - a noise without sound, space or time. They brought home to me the sharpest of hidden memories, but there was no tiredness about me during these flashbacks, my thoughts and memories forceful and direct before finally fading away.

An image would come into my head, make an impression and then leave. You could call it a definite moving memory, horrific images of varying degrees of severity as my experiences in Bosnia revisited me once more. Just as suddenly and vividly the sky above Bosnia's mountains and valleys would appear; sun-drenched forests and roads would be there with the summer heat shimmering upon them.

I remember the old and weathered women bent double, working in the fields, hardened to the heat - everything in those moments appeared to stand still. Explosions would shake my mind, I even remember being angry with the UN and Western governments in the middle of my dream for doing everything to the make the conflict worse.

Such experiences were unique and had a quality of the absolute of war about them. Peace would jump before my tearful eyes on the horizon;

but always just the other side of the hills lay men, women and children - dead and torn to pieces, bleeding the rivers red.

On occasion I would remember the times when I was free for a while - sitting on top of a rocky outcrop, the wind blowing in my face, experiencing the joys of life. But within days I would be plunged into more torment and conflict - wanting to get the hell out of Bosnia again, wanting to live and survive yet also wanting to end it all in the quickest way possible. There appeared to be no contradiction to these thoughts in my mind.

Fragments of memory still fly, like shrapnel. Some of them real, others from newspaper and TV reports. But I always return to my direct experience; the dying child's last breath unleashing still more memories - I only wish that the death of that girl had been a dream, it might have made the whole thing more bearable. The girl's death reminded me of my father's demise in 1976 - these were the typical nightmares that accompanied my nightly battle for sleep.

In terms of war Bosnia was hell on earth. The UN gave the world the impression that some sort of civilised enterprise was going on when in all reality the UN in the horror of war were an abomination, allowing the killing to continue despite their presence. The wreckage of tanks, trucks and armoured cars could be seen - the bitter feelings manifesting themselves upon grim faces returning from recent battle. The lined civilian faces speaking silently of loss and death.

Civilians, as in any war, could be seen - dead. Their meagre belongings and bodies strewn here and there about the roads that pointed to the turn of the conflict and eventually to the end of the war. Toward the end we in HVO battered our way along mountain highways, through forest tracks and hillside paths. Our victories becoming swift and decisive with the aid of Croatia proper and none of this came too soon for the innocents who had long since lost their souls to the daily threat of terror which reigned over the break-up of Yugoslavia between 1991 and 1995. Sitting up there on the hill overlooking the lakes of Rama I can still see the road which turns through the hillsides, packed with vehicles. The Ant Road I called it, shock-full of vehicles as they wound to and from the frontline on all sides, as explosions continued all around.

APPENDIX

In May 1998 John MacPhee was accused, by the Glasgow Sunday Mail, of being a War Criminal. Under the headline 'Monster' the tabloid demonised the Scottish volunteer and accused him of having a 'grisly role' in the Bosnian War. We have reprinted the story here, after the full tale of his role in the war has been told, to see if you agree with the paper's assertion that this is a book that should never be published. A photograph of the front-page and inside story can be found in that section.

MONSTER

HE'S KILLED DOZENS OF INNOCENT WOMEN AND HE CALLS HIMSELF SUPERSCOT... WHO WILL BRING HIM TO JUSTICE

This evil mercenary has the blood of dozens of innocent women on his hands...

John MacPhee also butchered unarmed men in the bloody Bosnian War. Now the Sunday Mail can reveal that he has written a detailed account of his grisly role.

He is touting it around publishers to cash in on his terrible deeds.

They may instead be used to bring him to justice...

Last night, defence Secretary George Robertson pledged to present our dossier to war crimes investigators in The Hague.

Foreign Secretary Robin Cook also promised to examine the confessions.

Lifelong criminal MacPhee spent three years fighting for an ultra-violent wing of the Croatian army.

He boasts: 'I did my job killing all who came before me. Enemy after enemy we killed. I never looked for a uniform'.

The Silent Cry

Colonel 'Bosnian' Bob Stewart branded MacPhee 'scum'.
UN worker Larry Hollingsworth said: 'The people he associated with were cowboys. They were butcher type soldiers'.

And the story continues:

BLOOD LUST

SCOTS WAR CRIMINAL IS THE BRUTAL BEAST OF BOSNIA

He's the evil beast of Bosnia... the Scots mercenary with the blood of innocents on his hands.
Convicted criminal John MacPhee has admitted slaughtering unarmed men and women during the hellish Bosnian War.
As part of a ruthless unit of the Croatian army John MacPhee took part in atrocities which will shock the world.
Now the evil Scot's killings are to be reported to the War Crimes Tribunal in The Hague.
In an exclusive interview with the Sunday Mail, twisted MacPhee boasted of three years' fighting for the Croatian army.
The 47 year-old revealed : 'I did my job, killing all who came before me'.
Last night, MacPhee and his band of Croat killers were slammed for their part in the bloody conflict.

CRIMES

Retired British Army officer Colonel Bob Stewart, who became Britain's most famous soldier in Bosnia, said 'these men were scum.'
'I will report what he's saying to the war crimes trials in The Hague'.
'As he's admitted killing unarmed civilians I'm sure the Bosnian government would also like to see him. The massacres were so horrendous it makes your blood run cold'.
Glasgow-born MacPhee, 47, has spent most of his life in prisons in England.
He has a long history of violence, firearms offences and drug-running.
And he has links with underworld gangs in Glasgow and Manchester.
Despite having no military background in 1991 he travelled to the war-torn region to fight for Croatia.
MacPhee has written a detailed account of his mercenary role.
The sick Scot is touting his manuscript around publishers in a bid to cash-in on his terrible deeds.
Last night UN official for refugees in Bosnia Peter Kessler, said: 'This

book should never be published'.

In the manuscript MacPhee admits to cold-blooded murder.

The damning evidence could lead to him being arrested and forced to appear at the ongoing United Nations War Crimes trials.

The Sunday Mail had a look at the manuscript – without paying.

MacPhee tells how a fellow soldier accidentally shot a harmless, old man.

He then boasts: 'enemy after enemy we killed, I never looked for a uniform.'

He also claims to have killed a woman and a girl of about 16 in a remote farmhouse.

Of the older victim he says: 'The fact she was a woman gave me no second thoughts'.

'She died like a dog as I shot her'.

He murdered the teenager as she lay in bed by 'crunching my boot into her neck, forcing it to break'.

He adds darkly: 'Stories will fly about as to me being a killer without conscience.

'Even some Croatian intellectuals classed me as the 'bad side of the war'.'

MacPhee attempts to justify his many atrocities saying the reason was to win.

But he admits revenge was taken if they found out the enemy were killing civilians.

In another harrowing incident, the shaven headed giant admits 'accidentally' shooting innocent people.

He tells of storming a building and killing what he thought were enemy soldiers.

He adds: 'Then I saw the civilian clothes but it was too late as I had been squeezing the trigger of my gun'.

'The bullets tore into the remaining wounded. I caught the sound of their moans'.

'War gives more victims than justifiable targets – that is a fact that no one will argue with'.

Aid workers, British Army officers and United Nations staff were all aware of MacPhee's activities.

One aid leader said: 'MacPhee was associated with a very violent wing of the Croatian army'.

'They were commanded by a Canadian Croat and contained a number of German, American and British mercenaries'.

'The fact he admits to killing unarmed civilians is very disturbing and should be fully investigated by the War Crimes Tribunal'.

UN official Larry Hollingsworth said: 'The people he associated with were cowboys.

The Silent Cry

'Most Western mercenaries gravitated towards the Croatian side. And they were good, butcher-type soldiers'.

MacPhee was even accused of making death-threats towards Kessler – which his bosses took seriously.

It's thought they stemmed in part from a notorious incident MacPhee was linked with in 1993.

Then, Croat soldiers allegedly rounded-up and killed Moslem refugees at a stadium in Mostar.

MacPhee's hate-filled tirade continues: 'My name flew back and forward. A rumour went about that I organised the exodus of the stadium.'

'It was all UN propaganda. Kessler, I had words with him a few times. He was a racist against Croatians'.

A source close to American Kessler, now based with the UN in Africa, said:

'Anyone who knows Peter would know that this is pure poison.'

'How can he be racist against Croatians? He's married to one.'

News that MacPhee was trying to publish his archive of atrocities shocked many involved in the war.

A UN spokesman said: 'This is something our War Crimes Tribunal would like to investigate further.'

BOSNIA 1997

Reproduced courtesy of the Library of the University of Texas
www.lib.utexas.edu Copyright CIA 1997